First-Time Authors

**64 Children's Writers'
First Published Pieces—
with Authors' and
Editors' Commentaries**

Writer's Institute
Publications

Editor
Pamela Glass Kelly

Contributing Editors
Cheryl de la Guéronnière
Barbara Cole

Researcher
Maureen Garry

Design and Production
Joanna Horvath

Production Assistant
Susan Capone

www.WritersBookstore.com
Email: Services@WritersBookstore.com
www.InstituteChildrensLit.com

International Standard Book Number 978-1-889715-60-5
10 9 8 7 6 5 4 3

Printed and bound in Canada

Contents

Nonfiction

For Teen Readers

Fiction

Nonfiction

About This Collection

"No lottery winner has jumped around and shouted as much as I did that day. I called everyone I knew. My dream of being a published children's writer came true when I opened the acceptance letter from ON THE LINE. That letter and a copy of my first paycheck as a professional writer hang on the wall behind my computer today."
—Danielle S. Hammelef, Author

Welcome to *First-Time Authors*, a collection of stories and articles that shows how 64 writers became published authors. We've collected their work, published in 40 different children's magazines, so you can read for yourself just what makes a successful adventure story, fantasy, how-to, profile, or inspirational piece. We've gathered comments from the editors who published these submissions. And we've interviewed the writers themselves, to find out where they got their ideas, what kinds of research and revision they did, and how they were able to zero in on just the right market.

An Invitation

Whether you're a recreational reader or a writer-in-training, we invite you to read these selections for enjoyment and to study them as examples of successful fiction and nonfiction. We invite you to get inside editors' heads and look at writers' works from the publishing point of view. And best of all, this collection is an invitation to imagine *yourself* as one of these writers, tearing open an envelope to discover the thrill of an acceptance. We hope the experiences in this book will provide inspiration for you!

The Writers' Stories

Reading the story *behind* a story or article is as useful to a writer as reading the piece itself. Here, you'll read about the authors' original ideas, the challenges they faced in writing and revising, and the steps they took to find markets for their manuscripts. These first-time authors represent a broad spectrum of backgrounds—writers who practice their craft while parenting, teaching, ranching, fire-fighting, and traveling. You'll follow each selection's path to publication, and learn that often, the pieces were first presented as course assignments, read to writers' groups, or submitted as contest entries. Yet each found its way to a magazine for young readers. That process—that journey—is the focus of this anthology.

The Editors' Perspectives

"Talk about a first impression! Karen's first sentence, 'On Wednesday afternoon we were rushing down the highway after a coat! "Hurry, Mom!" I yelled,' is a great example of a real attention-grabber. How could I or any reader not be compelled to read on to find out why they were chasing a coat down the road? She gets our attention and interest, and then tells the story of how the protagonist got to this point. Karen did everything right—hooked us with a great opening, created an imperfect protagonist who works to solve the mess she's in, followed the rules of good story structure, and targeted her market. Her story was a winner!" —Susan Reith Swan, Assistant Editor, STORY FRIENDS

The editors' stories offer a view from the inside as editors reveal the specific reasons why they chose these selections for their magazines. You'll learn what first caught their attention:

"Helen wrote an appealing query letter. It was cheerful and upbeat, and from the title she had chosen—'Ghosts in the Night'—I immediately knew she had an excellent grasp of what would appeal to kids." —Lisa Rao, Editor, DOLPHIN LOG

Why an editor chose a specific piece:

"I needed a story about a boy that would be appropriate for spring, and this story fit the bill. The boys

seemed real—I could hear real junior high boys saying the words."—Mary Clemens Meyer, Editor, ON THE LINE

You'll also get valuable insight into how each editor approaches a submission package:

"I always get a little suspicious when I get a nonfiction package that's thin. I enjoy receiving really thick packages, full of copies of research, a juicy article, a detailed bibliography, and a short, crisp, thoughtful letter of introduction."—Carolyn Yoder, Senior Editor, HIGHLIGHTS FOR CHILDREN

How the Contents Are Organized

This anthology is organized into three main age groups. Each age-level section is further divided into fiction and nonfiction sections. Each story or article selection is followed by its readership span and its word count—both are guides to the intended readership age.

Youngest Reader Section targets ages 3 to 7, who like to listen to stories read aloud long before they can read themselves. The section continues through the primary grades, when children learn to read for fun and information.

Intermediate Section contains stories and articles for children who are approximately 8 to 12 years old—an audience for whom reading is often a recreational activity but also a way to satisfy their curiosity about the larger world. The greatest number of magazines for children are published for this age group, and this fact is reflected in the length of the section—almost half of this book.

Teen Reader Section comprises stories and articles that address the concerns of a wide range of adolescents. While the teen years begin at age 13, some 11- and 12-year-olds enjoy reading young adult magazines, just as some older teenagers are mature enough to move into the adult category.

You'll notice variation in reading level and subject matter within each section as well as some overlapping between sections. Many children's publications are designed to appeal to a range of readership ages, abilities, and interests. *Highlights for Children*, for example, is published for ages 2 through 12, which means you'll see it represented here in both the Youngest and Intermediate sections.

Quick Reference Features

At the end of the anthology, you'll find three indexes: an alphabetical list of titles, an alphabetical list of authors, and a list of the magazines in which the stories and articles originally appeared. You'll find a wide range of publications represented, including general interest magazines, *Boys' Quest*, *U*S* Kids*, and *Cricket*, special interest magazines, *Odyssey*, *ChemMatters*, *Young Rider*, and *Dream Girl: The Arts Magazine for Girls*, along with magazines used in school and religious curricula.

The Spirit of Writing

We hope this collection will kindle your own excitement about writing for children. Editors set high standards, and writers can meet these standards through study, practice, and persistence.

Now it's time for you to find your place among the writers who share their thoughts and dreams with young readers.

The Editors

"No one could have been more surprised than I was when I stumbled into my darkened house one evening, saw the answering machine light blinking, and heard, 'Hello, this is Shannon Lowry from BOYS' LIFE MAGAZINE, and we're interested in purchasing your story.' A writer never forgets something like that."
—Justin Stanchfield, Author

Gabriella's Whisper

By Janice Graham • Art by Dominic Catalano

At the puppet show, Gabriella Elephant sat up in her seat as tall as she could. But Mrs. Hippo's petunia hat blocked the stage.

"I CAN'T SEE!" Gabriella trumpeted.

Mrs. Hippo swivelled around, grunted at Gabriella, and tossed her nose into the air.

"Where is your *whisper*, Gabriella?" asked her father in a voice that sounded like leaves in the wind.

Gabriella looked for her whisper but she couldn't find it.

The next day in preschool, Gabriella sat on the floor with her class at storytime. "I'M THIRSTY!" she blasted to her friend Humphrey Giraffe.

"Where is your *whisper*, Gabriella?" Humphrey asked in a voice that sounded like rain on the roof.

Mrs. Rhino, the teacher, looked up from her book. She squinted her eyes and pointed her horn straight at Gabriella.

Where could my whisper be? thought Gabriella.
She looked in her pockets, but all she found were peanut shells.

At home, Gabriella clomped behind her mother into the baby's room. "CAN I HOLD THE BABY?" she bellowed.

"Where is your *whisper*, Gabriella?" asked Mrs. Elephant in a voice that sounded like a teapot before it whistles.

Not again! Gabriella stamped her foot and thundered, "I'VE LOOKED EVERYWHERE FOR MY WHISPER AND I CAN'T FIND IT!"

Mrs. Elephant motioned for Gabriella to sit in the big, soft rocking chair. Then she took the baby out of his crib and put him in Gabriella's lap.

"*Listen*," said Mrs. Elephant.

Gabriella held the baby close and listened. What she heard was as hushed as leaves in the wind. It was as quiet as rain on the roof. It was as still as a teapot before it whistles.

Gabriella wanted to trumpet. She wanted to blast and bellow and thunder. But she didn't. Instead she said, "I love you, baby," in a voice as soft as a baby's breath.

From the Author

While raising each of my naturally noisy offspring, it always struck me that being quiet, and more specifically, whispering, is a learned skill. Anyone who spends time with little ones knows that they have a difficult time understanding when and why we need to lower our voices. Confident that shushing preschoolers is a universal problem, I decided a story might be a helpful way to introduce this social courtesy.

I had written several stories targeting this age group, but hadn't had any success getting them published. So, I wasn't surprised when my first version of this one, in which the main character was a child, was turned down by one magazine, then another. Feeling I had a good idea that just needed reworking, I stepped out of my comfort zone and rewrote it in a genre I had never tried but had loved as a child: fantasy.

By portraying my protagonist as a talking elephant with the fitting name of Gabriella, my previously lackluster story finally began to develop color and shape. With input from my writers' group, I implemented lively verbs, repeated situations, and the "rule of three," then edited and revised my story down to a brief 350 painstakingly chosen words.

After submitting my reworked story to a fiction contest and two picture book publishers with no success, I looked for a magazine that accepted anthropomorphic stories specifically for small children. From a writers' publication, I learned that *Turtle* was looking for nap-time read-alouds. I thought my story fit the bill and included this selling point in my cover letter. The editor, Terry Harshman, liked it and kept it on hold for more than a year and a half.

From conception to publication, this story grew old enough to go to kindergarten! Like Gabriella, I trumpeted my delight when I finally received my first read-aloud story for preschoolers, delightfully illustrated, in the mail.

I have seven children and five grandchildren who keep me supplied with story ideas. Though I am currently finishing ghostwriting a book for a celebrity, I continue writing for children and hope to do more fantasy. Since "Gabriella's Whisper," I have had stories published in *Highlights for Children*, *The Friend*, *Hopscotch*, *Story Friends*, *Boys' Quest*, *Short Short Stories for Reading Aloud* (the Education Center), and *Spider*. I am a recipient of the Society of Children's Book Writers and Illustrators Magazine Merit Honor Award for nonfiction, and also had the opportunity to serve as a judge for the same award.

—Janice Graham

From the Editor

When I first read "Gabriella's Whisper," there was no hesitation. I knew I wanted to publish this superbly written short story. Very poetic.

I thought it would be perfect for *Turtle*, because I knew preschoolers would have no trouble relating to Gabriella. Sometimes it's hard to know when to speak quietly.

The ending is simple, yet so touching, when Gabriella holds her baby brother. A perfectly satisfying little story. The only thing I had to do was cut the length just a bit to fit spacial requirements.

—Terry Webb Harshman, Editor, *Turtle*

Turtle
2–5 years
300 words

Runaway Rosie

By Shellie Ripple
Art by Deborah Garber

Jeremiah sat on his bed and gazed through the aquarium glass at Rosie, his pet tarantula. Rosie had been a gift from his mother for his seventh birthday two weeks ago. Jeremiah knew that his mother wasn't a huge fan of creepy, crawly creatures, but he had somehow convinced her that a spider was the perfect pet after reading a library book about Chilean rose tarantulas. The book said these tarantulas weren't poisonous and that they could, and should, be handled regularly. The only problem was that Jeremiah hadn't yet found the nerve to hold Rosie.

It's not that I'm afraid of her, Jeremiah thought. He watched the spider slowly climb up the side of the aquarium and tried to imagine her eight tiny feet brushing along his arm. Well, maybe just a little afraid, he decided as he shuddered slightly.

It wasn't the spider's appearance that bothered Jeremiah. Actually, he thought Rosie was rather beautiful. She was a light, pinkish-brown color, and her body and long legs were covered with short, fine, soft-looking hairs. Longer, bristle-like hairs curved downward between the two antennae on her head. Jeremiah knew that Rosie had eight small eyes, but he couldn't tell exactly where they were.

Jeremiah admired Rosie's climbing skill as she reached the top of the glass

> Even with eight eyes on the top and front of its body, a tarantula's sight is limited. It hunts by touch.

tank. He was quickly reminded of how clumsy tarantulas could be as she lost her balance and tumbled to the soft bedding below. Jeremiah held his breath. The book said that a fall from a high place could be deadly for a tarantula. Rosie had only fallen a short distance, but Jeremiah was still relieved when his pet righted herself and once again began to climb.

There was a gentle knock on his bedroom door, and his mother came in.

"Any luck yet?" she asked.

Jeremiah's mother had noticed that he hadn't taken Rosie out of her aquarium.

> Tarantulas should be handled regularly and carefully so that owner and pet can get used to each other. This helps if the tarantula escapes, or when it's time to clean the cage.

"Not yet, Mom," he answered.

"You'll do it when you're ready," his mother said reassuringly as she tousled his curly red hair. "I need to run next door for a minute. Could you listen for the phone?"

> Even spiders that do not spin webs make silk. This thread is sometimes called a "lifeline" because the spider can use it to escape from its enemies.

"Sure, Mom," he said as she left.

Jeremiah trained his eyes on Rosie again. I'm just going to have to do it, he decided. He slowly lifted the lid from the aquarium and placed it on the floor. His heart was beating wildly, but he kept his hand steady as he inched it toward his pet.

I've almost got her, Jeremiah thought. But the movement startled the spider and she skittered sideways, shooting a fine strand of silk behind her. Jeremiah quickly jerked his hand back. More frightened than Rosie, it took

him a minute to realize that the phone was ringing.

Jeremiah sprinted to the phone and took a message for his mom. Then he thought, I'm going to hold Rosie this time no matter what. But when he reached his room, he realized that he had left the lid off the aquarium. Rosie was nowhere to be seen.

"Rosie! Where are you?" cried Jeremiah in a panic. She could be anywhere, he thought. How am I ever going to find her?

Then something caught his eye. Rosie was halfway up his bedroom wall! It only took a moment for Jeremiah to decide what to do. "I have to rescue you before you fall," he said aloud.

Jeremiah calmly stepped onto his bed. He didn't tremble this time as he reached for Rosie. He remembered how the book said to pick up a tarantula. Holding his breath, he slowly cupped his hands over the spider. Rosie froze and drew her eight legs tight against her body. Jeremiah paused a moment and slowly exhaled. OK, he thought, she's not going to fall. Just relax.

Next, he gently scooped Rosie from the wall with his fingers. I'm doing it, he thought. I'm really holding her!

Carrying his pet, he climbed from his bed and sat on the floor. As he opened his hands, Rosie tried to dart away while again releasing a silk thread

> Tarantulas sold as pets rarely bite if they are handled properly. If they do, their bite is not poisonous to humans, though some people may have an allergic reaction.

behind her. Fascinated, Jeremiah let her scramble from one hand to the other as she tried to escape.

"It's all right, girl," Jeremiah whispered. Gradually, Rosie calmed down and came to rest in his left hand. He was surprised at the sturdiness of her body. He had imagined she would feel more squishy. Her feet had sticky pads on them, and he understood how she was able to climb up the glass side of her tank.

Jeremiah heard his mother open the front door as he carefully stroked Rosie's furry abdomen.

"There's a phone message on the note pad, Mom," he called as she came to his room.

"Jeremiah! You did it! You're holding her," his mom exclaimed.

He smiled proudly. "Yeah! I sure am, Mom! Isn't she neat?"

"She's neat all right," his mom replied. "But I hope she doesn't ever escape from her tank."

Jeremiah blushed, but kept smiling. "I'll be careful, Mom."

He sat with Rosie for a while, getting used to her as she got used to him. Then he placed her gently back in her tank, put the lid on tightly, and ran outside to catch a cricket for her dinner.

From the Author

The idea for "Runaway Rosie" came about after my seven-year-old son asked for a pet tarantula. He was afraid to hold her at first and, I admit, I did have the thought, "What if she escapes?"

Before I knew it, I had the three-part plot worked out in my mind. I named the spider Rosie because she is a Rosehair tarantula. The actual story line came first, but the facts were easy to fill in because I had read a book about tarantulas before we brought ours home. I also found a wealth of information on the Internet.

This story was my second course assignment with the Institute of Children's Literature. My instructor suggested some small revisions and encouraged me to submit it. I chose *Click* magazine according to subject matter, age group, and word length. Upon acceptance, *Click*'s editor asked me to write several sidebars to accompany the illustrations and suggested only minor changes to the story. I was very pleased with the finished manuscript.

—Shellie Ripple

From the Editor

Click is a science and discovery magazine for children ages three to seven. The focus is nonfiction and almost all articles are commissioned. However, "Runaway Rosie" fit well the slot we have in each issue for an 800- to 1,000-word story that, in fictional form, presents content relevant to the issue's theme. In this case, the theme was pets, and "Runaway Rosie" gave an example of caring responsibly for a pet, as well as accurate and interesting information about an unusual pet, a tarantula.

"Runaway Rosie" is pitched emotionally at the right level for *Click*. It stars a child in a believable and dramatic situation who solves a significant problem through his own initiative. Jeremiah is active in learning more about his spider. And anyone—child or adult—can identify with his fear of holding a tarantula.

There's an honesty about "Runaway Rosie" that is very appealing. For example, Jeremiah tells himself at first that he isn't afraid of Rosie, but then admits that he might be a little afraid. It's endearing, and a bit unexpected that he thinks Rosie is beautiful. Like Jeremiah, we feel our view of tarantulas changing. And there's a life-and-death issue: If Rosie falls, she can die.

Jeremiah has real responsibility.

Jeremiah's mother is portrayed in an attractive way for *Click*, supportive and reassuring, but not all-knowing or intrusive. The story's problem and its solution come through Jeremiah. Jeremiah's awakening to Rosie's charms, as he holds her and realizes she feels different from what he expected, is very pleasant and affirming. And at the end there's a nice in-joke with the reader when Mom says she hopes Rosie never escapes, and Jeremiah blushes and promises to be careful. Jeremiah doesn't lie, but he keeps what happened to himself. Rosie is his responsibility. After overcoming his fear in order to save her, he is able to play with her while each is getting used to the other, like new friends. Rosie, after all, has to get used to Jeremiah, too.

—Lonnie Plecha, Editor, *Click*

Click
3–7 years
875 words

Squeaks in the Floorboard

By Cynthia Bryning Johnson

Illustrated by Valeri Gorbachev

"I didn't know someone lived here."

Tyler was ready for a good-night kiss. Mom walked into his room and stepped on a noisy wooden floorboard.

SQUEAK, SQUEAK!

"What's that?" asked Tyler.

"Oh, just squeaks in the floorboard," said Mom. "Don't worry, I can get rid of squeaks."

"Oh no," said Squeaks, the little gray mouse who lived under the wooden floor. "They know I'm here, and they plan to get rid of me!" He packed up his small red suitcase. "I'll have to move."

In the morning, Tyler finished his breakfast. He went to the sink to rinse out his cereal bowl. He turned on the faucet.

RUMBLE, RUMBLE!

"What's that?" asked Tyler.

"Oh, just rumbles in the water pipes," said Tyler's big sister.

"Oh no," said Squeaks, who had found a cozy home under the kitchen sink. "I didn't know that someone already lived here. Now, I'll have to move."

That night it was very windy. The wind whooshed down the chimney, rattling the metal vent.

RATTLE, RATTLE!

"What's that?" asked Tyler.

"Oh, just rattles in the chimney," said Dad.

"Oh no," said Squeaks, who had just snuggled into a corner of the big fireplace. "Someone lives here, too! I'll have to find another place to live." He packed up his small red suitcase. "But where can I go?"

Tyler got ready for bed. He was ready for a good-night kiss.

Mom walked into his room. She carefully stepped over the squeaky floorboard.

Tyler looked sad.

"What's wrong?" asked Mom.

"I like squeaks in the floorboard," said Tyler.

"Oh, I can fix that," said Squeaks as he unpacked his small red suitcase.

"I can fix that," said Mom. She walked back across the noisy wooden floorboard.

SQUEAK, SQUEAK!

Tyler smiled.

So did Squeaks.

From the Author

The idea for "Squeaks in the Floorboard" originated from my son, Tyler, an inquisitive child who asked a lot of questions, and always needed an answer. Also, he and my daughter, who is mentioned in the story, but not by name, both love animals. So, in creating this story, I tried to picture a small animal that could be in any home, and that any small child could relate to. A mouse living under a noisy wooden floorboard seemed to be the perfect solution.

Our family has had many different pets throughout the years, and I think of them as young children. So in writing "Squeaks," I tried to imagine how a small, brave child would feel about facing the scary dilemma of having to relocate his home, again and again. My challenge was trying to make my story a little frightening for Squeaks, without being too scary for a young child. Since I have always enjoyed animals,

writing from the viewpoint of how I *think* a mouse would feel came naturally.

I tried to use simple words. My writing partner and I read my story out loud to each other over and over again. Then we would critique the story line and discuss what words needed to be cut out. This was a very helpful process for me.

For such a short story I was amazed at how many revisions were requested. I revised "Squeaks" approximately three different times. Although I thought I was using very simple words, they weren't simple enough, and so I revised and revised. But *Highlights* Editor Marileta Robinson was very encouraging and helpful throughout the revision process, and I feel that I learned so much from her.

—Cynthia Bryning Johnson

From the Editor

When Cynthia sent this story to us, it was close, but needed a bit more work to be the little gem it is. A short story for very young readers is like a poem or a picture book—rhythm is important, and no words can be wasted.

There are several elements of child appeal here—the fun of having the story take place on two levels, literally and figuratively, the play on words, and the play with sounds.

The mouse is really the main character, and

the story ends on a satisfying note of homecoming and acceptance.

—Marileta Robinson, Editor,
Highlights for Children

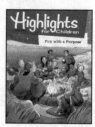

Highlights for Children
2–12 years
275 words

Broccoli Berkeley

By Paula K. Obering

"Well, Erica, how do you feel about our big news?" Dad asked.

Erica stared at her shoes. How did they think she felt? "It's fine. Can I go now?" she asked.

"Sure, honey. I know it's a bit of a shock, but everything will be okay." Her parents sat there smiling as she stood up and left the room.

Wonderful, thought Erica, *just terrific! Our lives will never be the same!* For Erica's whole life it had always been just the three of them. Ten whole years! Now they were going to have a baby? A baby! A screaming, crying, demanding addition to the Berkeley family. What could be worse?

The next day, Erica found out what could be worse.

"Erica, I have to talk to you about something," her mom said. "Because the baby is due in April, we'll have to postpone our spring-break trip to California. It wouldn't be wise to travel so close to the time the baby will be born."

Great, thought Erica. Not only was this little stranger invading her life, it was wrecking it! No Disneyland, no beach, no vacation. What could be worse?

The next week, Erica found out what could be worse.

"Erica, I have news for you," her dad said. "We found out that the baby

is a boy! Isn't that wonderful? You're going to have a brother!"

Terrific, thought Erica. *Just what I need, a dirty, bratty, bug-catching little brother. What could be worse?*

A month later, Erica found out what could be worse.

"Erica, we have to talk to you about something," said Mom.

"Since there are only two bedrooms upstairs, we'd like to make the office downstairs into a bedroom for you. You'll have a bigger room, and the baby can be close to us."

Super, thought Erica. *How am I supposed to tell my mom and dad that sleeping downstairs seems scary? Now because of the baby I'm supposed to act older, more mature, even brave? What could be worse?*

Amazingly enough, the next day things got better!

"Erica, your father and I would like you to choose the baby's name." Her mother handed Erica a book. "I bought a book about names to give you some help. Have fun!"

Wonderful, thought Erica. A chance for revenge! She would choose an awful name for the creepy little invader!

Erica began flipping through the book. It listed thousands of names and what each meant. There were so many possibilities!

First, she looked up her own name. Wow! *Erica* means "ever-powerful." That's just about how she felt. Now, to choose a name for the little brat.

What about Elmer or Egbert? No, those wouldn't do, *Elmer* means "excellent," and *Egbert* means "bright." After hours of studying the book, Erica had the most brilliant idea of all. It didn't matter what the name

mention a good night's sleep! What could be better?

A few hours later, Erica found out what could be better. A nurse gently shook her awake.

"Are you Erica Berkeley?" the nurse asked. "Your parents would like you to come meet your new little brother."

As Erica walked into the hospital room, she saw him. A little, wriggling

Illustration by Kathryn Mitter

meant, as long as it *sounded* perfectly awful! She would name the baby Brock, with the middle name of Lee. Brock Lee Berkeley! He would be teased every day of his life. What could be better?

Late one night, her father woke her up. "Honey, come on, it's time to go to the hospital."

As Erica curled up on the waiting room sofa, she wondered whether her parents would really let her name the baby. As she dozed off, she smiled. Erica was about to get revenge for losing her room and her vacation, not to

bundle tucked in her mother's arms.

"Erica, meet your little brother," her dad said.

He looked so tiny and helpless. Like someone who could really use a big sister. Erica bent over to touch his tiny fist, and suddenly revenge didn't seem very important.

"His name is Brian David," she whispered. "*Brian* means strong, and *David* means loved. I think he will be both strong and loved."

"Brian David Berkeley," said her mom. "Perfect. What could be better?"

From the Author

This story was written as an assignment for my Institute of Children's Literature course. I was studying dialogue at the time, learning about the importance of dialogue for drawing in young readers. The topic, the age of the main character, and my experience working with children all helped to set the tone, and develop the dialogue.

When I was in high school and college, I worked with a church youth group. One of the adult leaders was expecting a baby, and we spent many months trying to come up with the craziest possible name. "Broccoli Berkeley" was at the top of the list.

I did not follow a formal plan or outline. Because "Broccoli Berkeley" was an assignment, the idea, which had been on my mind for years, fed into the perfect exercise to hone the skills I was learning. The added benefit was that it was publishable.

The biggest challenge in meeting magazine word limits is to find the right amount of description (knowing that there will be a limited opportunity for illustrations), without weighing the piece down too much.

The story was revised five or six times. Some revision decisions were based on recommendations from my instructor. Later, after the course was over, I also shared the story with my critique group, and received a few minor suggestions from them. In making revision decisions, I try to evaluate what feels right for the story, what my word limits are (if it's a magazine piece), and the mechanical basics of writing.

I had had positive responses to this story from two other magazines prior to *Pockets*'s acceptance. One of the magazines eventually rejected it. The other offered me a contract, but then went out of business before my story was published. I felt a mixture of excitement and relief after hearing from *Pockets*. I was thrilled to have my story accepted.

I had studied *Pockets*'s theme list, and one of the topics dealt with "big changes." I felt that my story was a perfect match for this theme.

I belong to two different online critique groups, each made up of writers who encourage each other through the ups and downs of writing. I also belong to several online writers' groups, where the topic of writing is discussed daily, keeping me in tune with my fellow writers and the writing market.

—Paula K. Obering

From the Editor

This story was a great fit with the issue's Easter theme, "New Life." The movement in the story from "what could be worse?" to "what could be better?" captured the essence of the theme.

Erica, the first-person narrator, is a wonderfully human little girl—resentful, scared, funny, loving. Although this was quite a short story, Erica is well-developed as a character. The reader really gets a sense of her personality. The story required very little editing.

—Lynn Gilliam, Editor, *Pockets*

Pockets
4–11 years
695 words

No Play for Andrew

By Eileen
Rosenbloom

Nothing could be more fun than building sand castles. Especially on a sticky, summer afternoon. At least, that's what Andrew thought as he watched Patty dig her bare feet into the grainy powder in her sandbox while she shaped wet sand into castles. Surely Patty didn't want to play alone.

"Patty," Andrew called, "can I play in your sandbox?"

Patty looked up and wrinkled her nose. "I don't play with boys. I don't like boys."

"Have you ever played with a boy?" Andrew asked.

Patty rolled her eyes. "Of course not."

"Then how do you know you don't like boys?" asked Andrew.

"Because," said Patty. "Girls know these things."

Andrew's gaze fell. "I'm a sunk ship," he muttered. Andrew stared at the hole in the right knee of his blue jeans. He was already dressed in play clothes. Momma wouldn't mind if he got dirty. If only he could convince Patty to play with him.

Then Andrew had an idea. "If you'll play with me, I'll give you anything you want."

Patty's dark eyes widened. "Anything? Hmmm . . ."

Andrew bit his bottom lip while he waited for Patty's request.

Finally she said, "Bring me something sweet and yummy."

Andrew beamed. "You've got it." He waved goodbye and dashed down the street to his house. This was Andrew's lucky day because Momma had baked chocolate cupcakes for his sister's birthday party. She'd never notice if some were missing.

Arriving home, Andrew crept through the kitchen door. Cupcakes sat out to cool on the table. Breathing in the sweet smell of chocolate, he knew Patty would play with him now. As Andrew reached his hands towards the cupcakes, he was startled to see his sister enter the kitchen.

"What are you doing?" she shouted.

"What's going on?" Momma called from another room.

In a panic, Andrew snatched two cupcakes and darted out the door. "I'm a sunk ship," he thought. "Maybe Momma will understand."

Andrew arrived at Patty's house where she waited in the sandbox. Her face lit up as she spotted the cupcakes. "I spy something yummy."

Andrew beamed. "One for each of us."

Patty grabbed both cupcakes. She ate them, bite after bite, until not a crumb was left. Smacking her lips, she licked the chocolate icing that smeared her mouth until not a trace remained.

"Now can I play with you?" Andrew asked.

Patty's eyes grew big. "Are you crazy? I told you I don't play with boys."

"But," Andrew stammered, "you said if I brought you something sweet and yummy, you'd play with me."

"Yes," she said, "but I don't see anything sweet or yummy. Now go home!"

Andrew hung his head and dragged himself toward home. Patty had tricked him. She may have had a sandbox, but she didn't have good manners.

When Andrew arrived home, Momma was standing in the doorway of the kitchen. Her arms were folded. Her eyes glared. "Andrew," she said, "is there something you'd like to say?"

Andrew looked into her eyes. "I'm a sunk ship."

From the Author

"No Play for Andrew" is a rewrite of my first assignment for the Institute of Children's Literature's course—the one based on the picture of the rabbit stealing the pie. After completing the course, I revisited the story and thought it might be publishable with some revision.

The first thing I did was turn the bunny characters into humans, making the story acceptable to those publications that ruled out anthropomorphic characters. I also changed the pie into cupcakes so it wouldn't scream "Institute assignment" to those familiar with the course, although every story based on that illustration had to be as original and different as its student writers.

Originally the story weighed in at 700 words, which was too long for kids ages three to eight. I noted a lot of redundancy and trimmed the word count to 500 words without losing any of its voice or content. In fact, the story was much better. Long sentences were split into two and other sentences rephrased, making it more appropriate for its young audience. A final tweaking and I mailed it to two magazines. Both sent form rejections.

I e-mailed it to *Wee Ones* e-zine. The next day I received a response from Editor Jennifer Reed notifying me that "No Play for Andrew" would appear in an upcoming issue of *Wee Ones*. I screamed, soaring from my chair, possibly defying the laws of gravity. Nothing like that first sale.

During the course of that year, I had seven additional sales to magazines. While my goal is to write books, I began by writing short stories for magazines. I felt it would give me credibility if I could establish a track record of magazine credits before submitting book manuscripts. I work full-time as a legal assistant and have two teenage children, so I've become an expert in time-stealing for the worthy cause of writing.

The most important thing I've learned is to enjoy the journey. Seeing your story in print and having your work validated with a paycheck is a wonderful feeling, but it's fleeting. It hardly happens every day. The joy is in the writing.

—Eileen Rosenbloom

From the Editor

When I first read "No Play for Andrew," I was relieved to receive a story with real kids as the characters. Eileen's characters exemplified little kids in a realistic manner. It was a well-written piece and needed little editorial work.

Her story filled the needs of *Wee Ones* in a couple of ways. We receive many "animal" stories, but this was a real situation with real people, something I felt children could relate to. It stayed within the allotted word limit; and because we weren't working with many illustrators at the time, I felt I could find some good art to go with it.

—Jennifer B. Reed, Editor, *Wee Ones*

Wee Ones
3–8 years
500 words

My Best Friend Is a Juniper Tree

By Judith Lee Nilsson

This summer I am old enough to visit Grandma and Grandpa. They live way out on the tribal lands. We ride in Grandpa's blue pickup truck. The road is very bumpy! There is a long trail of dust behind the truck.

Grandma and Grandpa have sheep, horses, and an old dog that limps. The old dog that limps does not want me to play with the sheep. The horses are too wild for me. So I tell Grandpa, "I don't have any friends to play with."

Grandpa says, "I will show you a fine friend." Grandpa always wears brown leather cowboy boots. I have new boots. Mine are black. I walk behind Grandpa, stepping in his foot-prints. We walk past the corral and up a little low hill.

Grandpa stops by a tree and says, "This is a juniper tree. It can be your friend."

I say, "Watch me climb the tree, Grandpa! I'm a good climber." First I step onto a branch that is as low as my knees. Then I put both hands on the next higher branch and pull myself up. Step, pull. Step, pull. When I look back at Grandpa, I am already way above his head.

"A good climber always goes slowly and carefully," Grandpa says.

Every day I climb the juniper tree. It has bark that comes off in long, loose strips. Some branches are smooth. Some branches are shaggy. It's fun to wrap my knees around a branch and hang upside down. Things look better this way.

If I sit very still, sometimes a tree lizard will come out and sit on the tree trunk. I whisper, "Hi, Mr. Lizard." Once I almost touched him!

I find a special place high up in the juniper tree. The branches open up into a little window. Through it I can look way across the tan-colored hills. I can look up and see hawks circling in the blue sky. I can see Grandma working in the garden. I can see Grandpa fixing the corral. But they can't see me.

When the puffy white clouds float overhead, I pretend the juniper tree is a ship sailing along in the sky.

"Hey, Grandpa! This is my boat! I'm the captain!"

Grandpa takes off his cowboy hat and waves it at me. I take off my cowboy hat and wave it at Grandpa.

One afternoon while I am playing in the tree, I hear soft thunder rumbling far away. Way off in the distance I can see lightning flashing in the clouds over the sacred mountains. I watch the thunderstorm roll in. The wind blows my hair straight back, and I can smell the wet dirt. A raven on a fence post ruffles his feathers and calls out, "HA! HA!" I see Grandpa's black horses running very fast along the ridge. Then I hear the first big BANG! of thunder.

"Climb down!" Grandma is calling out to me. "Climb down and run to the house!" I climb carefully to the ground. Grandma watches how fast I run to the house—as fast as Grandpa's black horses!

One evening after supper I walk out to the juniper tree. The sun is going down. My shadow looks like I'm a giant. The shadow of the juniper tree stretches to the edge of the canyon.

I climb slowly and carefully, the way Grandpa likes me to. The sunset is so red, it almost looks like the sky is on fire! I hear the evening birds calling and looking for their supper. The tree lizard is not there. Out in the hills, I hear a coyote howl, "Hoooo, hooooo!"

From another hill, a coyote answers,

"Ah-wooo, ah-woooo!"

Best of all, I hear some coyote pups. They do not know how to howl so they just say, "Yip! Yip! Yip-yip-yip!" I wish I could see them.

Some big branches make a cozy seat. I lean back my head and see the first stars looking down at me.

All at once I hear Grandpa say, "You must wake up and come to bed in the house. You fell asleep between the strong branches!"

I say, "Grandpa, I didn't know you climbed trees, too!"

He says, "I always climbed up this tree when I was a boy." He helps me down from the tree and carries me to the house. The old dog that limps follows us. The lights are on in the house. There is Grandma in the doorway. I can hear the crickets singing.

I yawn and look back at the tree. It looks sleepy, too.

I say, "Grandpa, my best friend is a juniper tree."

From the Author

Originally I had great hopes for this story as a picture book, but I finally realized that book publishers must be looking for someone with publishing credits. I recalled how much I enjoyed children's magazines when I was young, so it seemed natural to turn to this venue. *Ladybug* was the first children's magazine I contacted.

I thought about what kind of story my nephews would like. Also, I wanted to take my readers from an ordinary topic, climbing trees, into an extraordinary, but realistic setting—the Navajo people and tribal lands. Those people and landscapes have played recurring and unforgettable episodes in my life.

I used first-person point of view because I felt the little girl was telling the story to herself since she had no kids around her. And it was a way to help her remember all the things she wanted to tell her parents or friends when she finally got back home. I used present tense to convey the breathlessness and immediacy that children use when they describe something exciting.

I took photos of juniper trees so that my story would not be a generic description of a tree. I tried not to stereotype Native Americans, and the ethnicity is not specifically mentioned in my story. My biggest challenge was to write a successful conclusion for the story.

I rewrote the story in my head for a long time, keeping in mind that this story would be read aloud to children. The story was too lengthy for *Ladybug*, so I cut descriptions not vital to the plot or characters. When I read the story aloud to myself, I could immediately hear many places that needed revision. I worked on this story off and on for several years, so it went through about 20 drafts.

Young children can have great moments of joy. If you have writer's block, picture those kids staring at you and asking, "And then what happened? And then what happened?"

I teach English language classes part-time at a factory in Reynosa, Tamaulipas, Mexico. I am also working on a master's degree in English as a Second Language at the University of Texas-Pan American.

—Judith Lee Nilsson

From the Editor

On first reading the manuscript for "My Best Friend Is a Juniper Tree," we considered asking the author for a rewrite. We were charmed with the vivid, sensory descriptions of the natural setting. We found the storm scene particularly evocative. We enjoyed the gentle relationship between the child and her grandparents. Our reservations concerned the lack of plot: a little girl visits her grandparents and spends her summer in a tree. At almost 800 words, the text was very long for its content.

After discussion, we decided to publish the quiet, low-key vignette with minimal editing. The author's cover letter convinced us of the authenticity of her depiction, and we assigned the illustrations to an artist who does careful research and had illustrated Native American stories for us in the past.

The story succeeds in sharing the universal appeal of creative play, love of nature, and the small moments of joy or wonder that enrich life.

—Paula Morrow, Executive Editor,
Ladybug and *Babybug*

Ladybug
2–6 years
770 words

Jamila Did Not Want a Bat in Her House

By Phyllis Ring
Illustrated by Kathryn Mitter

Jamila did not really mind the bat. It was where the bat *was* that bothered Jamila. The bat was inside Jamila's house.

It flew so fast that it made her dizzy just trying to watch it. *Zip, Zip*, it flew, in the shape of an "8."

Her parents would wait for the bat to stop flying, then both of them would run very quickly to catch it. A whole day had passed, and they were still trying. When the bat stopped flying, it would slip inside the tiniest places where they couldn't see it anymore. They only knew it was still in the house by the sounds it made from behind the walls.

"The bat's back!" yelled her brother when it came out again the second morning.

Jamila ran to her bedroom. "Oh, please, God," Jamila prayed, "make this bat go away."

She didn't play in the living room now or go to the kitchen to make a snack. She didn't go down the long, long hallway to brush her teeth unless her mother or father or brother was there. Then she ran very fast.

Jamila was scared, but she didn't say so. She knew that if she did her brother would tease her.

At the bus stop the next morning, Jamila told everyone about the bat while they watched for the school bus.

"Bats are so *ugly*!" her friend Marcy said.

"Bats can get stuck in your *hair*!" Aaron said.

"Here it comes," someone said. Jamila jumped, her heart pounding hard. It was only the bus.

Oh! Jamila did *not* want a bat in her house! Why didn't God make this bat go away?

At dinner that night, when the sun had just set and bats should be flying up in the sky, the bat came back out and flew around the living room. Her father got the wastebasket. Her mother shut the doors in the hallway.

Then Jamila saw it, just before it slipped inside another skinny place. The bat's little face looked just like a mouse. Its wings were all droopy, as if they were tired. *It's scared*, she knew then, *just like I am*. Though maybe she wasn't as scared anymore.

"How will we catch it?" Jamila's mother asked.

"We've *got* to keep trying," Jamila's father said.

"Does it think it's our pet?" Jamila's brother asked.

In bed that night, while she looked at the stars, Jamila thought about the bat that wasn't out flying under the moon like it should be because it was inside Jamila's house.

"God, please help set it free," Jamila prayed. "We can't seem to do it all by ourselves."

The next night, her brother started his homework. Her father stirred a pot of spaghetti. Her mother went out to get the newspaper, and the bat flew right out in front of Jamila.

They all worked together—her brother, her father, her mother, and Jamila. Because she didn't run and hide in her room this time, she was close to the wastebasket.

Jamila picked it up, and the bat swooped down and perched on a curtain. It looked very small with its wings folded up.

Jamila's brother closed off all the doors. Her mother got a towel. Her father, watching, said, "Careful, Jamila . . ."

The basket in Jamila's hands

went over the bat, then her mother wrapped the towel around the basket.

"*Well done*, Jamila!" her father said.

"Yippee!" said her brother as he opened the door.

They all hurried outside to set the captive free.

"Good-bye, little bat," Jamila waved toward the sky.

They all sat down and ate their spaghetti. Then her father scooped ice cream. They all talked about how they had finally caught the bat.

"We had to be patient," Jamila's mother said.

"We had to keep trying," Jamila's father said.

"We all had to help," Jamila's brother said.

Jamila spooned up her Mocha Fudge slowly and said, "We had to care enough about the bat to be brave."

From the Author

My family's Victorian house has regularly been visited by bats over the years. Many times, our family faced what the story's main character and her family did, and some of the life lessons Jamila learned about the power of having faith and working together were ones we learned, too.

Jamila was fashioned after a girl I know who worked really hard to overcome one of her biggest fears. But almost from the story's inception, the characters, as they should, took on a very distinct life of their own. I think that's because I focused on the essence of the story itself, rather than on trying to draw too much from real life, and because the story itself is an amalgam of several influences.

I didn't write this story with a religious market in mind, although a focus on spiritual attributes and values was definitely my intent. In addition to writing to the targeted audience (ages four to eight), I wanted the story's spiritual message to be woven in as naturally as its other descriptive details or plot points. I also wanted to write a story that could be visualized clearly, because I knew there could only be a few illustrations, and I wanted young readers to be able to feel enough action and emotion to be able to see it too.

As it was originally written, this story read like the text for a children's picture book for younger readers. Thus, it had a rhythmic style, more like free-verse poetry. The main dialogue consisted of little trios of statements from Jamila's family and friends, which, almost like a chorus, served to reinforce related ideas. I also used dialogue-style statements for Jamila's thoughts about God's help or her prayer process. I used the small smatterings of dialogue to break up the text with things that I particularly wanted to emphasize.

This was a story that seemed to nearly "write itself" after I had lived with it for about five years or more. Revisions were necessary to polish it, of course, but the main challenge was in persevering to find a home for it.

I write mainly for adults, and this, my first story for children, has a very special place in my heart. Plus, I really appreciate the quality and spirit of *Pockets*, and the beautiful way it features content.

I write on issues related to family, health, and spirituality. I recently spent four months in China teaching English to kindergarten students. I'm currently at work on a book for parents about gender equality in families.

—Phyllis Ring

From the Editor

This story was included in an issue on "Caring for God's Creation." It was a "Wendell Story," intended for the younger end of our readership. Both for the issue and for the magazine's purpose, which is to help children see God work in their everyday lives, this story was a good fit.

Jamila responds to the bat the way most people, children or adults, would. She's afraid, and she does everything she can to avoid the bat. She hopes God will make it go away, but when she finally sees the bat close-up, she sees that the bat is scared, too. She prays for God to help them "set it free." It's wonderful that Jamila is able to be a key player in the bat's "rescue." This story has a nice rhythm that works well for young children, particularly as it is read aloud to them.

—Lynn Gilliam, Editor, *Pockets*

Pockets
4–11 years
650 words

Just a Little Whistle

By Katy Doran
Illustrated by Joanna Horvath

Jason was about the only person he knew who couldn't whistle.

Dad whistled really loud to call Jason to come inside from playing. He heard Dad all over the neighborhood.

Mom whistled for Wags to come. Sometimes she whistled a tune, too. The paperboy's whistle told Jason's family their newspaper was on the front steps.

The mailman whistled when he walked to Jason's front door with the mail. Jason's sister, Sarah, whistled, and so did Tommy, his best friend.

Riding to church in the car, Jason wondered if he would ever learn to whistle.

During the worship service, Jason heard Reverend Gray say something very interesting. He talked about God answering prayer. "God knows your every need," said Reverend Gray.

Jason knew that God knows everything. But there were so many things for God to take care of—hungry children, sick people, war, and stuff like that. If he asked, would God help him learn to whistle?

When Reverend Gray said, "Let us pray," Jason closed his eyes and bowed his head.

"God, it's me, Jason, and I have a need. Could you please help me learn to whistle?" he whispered.

Jason practiced every day, all week long. Sometimes he practiced so hard he made himself dizzy.

He made sure his tongue stayed out of the way. He made sure his cheeks didn't pooch out. He puckered his lips just so, but all he got was a little whoosh. No matter how hard Jason tried, a whistle didn't happen.

"Just keep trying," Mom said with a smile.

"You'll get the hang of it one of these days," Dad said.

Jason wasn't so sure. But he remembered what Reverend Gray said: "God knows your every need." And Jason prayed and he practiced. At every mealtime grace and before he said, "Amen," at bedtime prayers, Jason whispered, "Please, God, help me learn to whistle."

The next Sunday, Jason tried his best pucker and blow in the car going to church, but there was still no whistle. During worship service, Jason sat at the end of the pew on the aisle where he could see everything.

Watching the people greet each other as they took their seats, he heard a familiar whistle. Tommy grinned from where he sat with his mom and dad way across the church. Tommy waggled his fingers on top of his head at Jason. Jason waggled back.

Mrs. Milton reached over and patted Jason's shoulder. A tiny little lady with white hair and twinkly eyes, she had a wide space between her two front teeth.

"Good morning, Jason." Her voice made a little whistling sound between her teeth when she said his name. She winked and sat down behind him.

During Reverend Gray's sermon, Jason watched Mr. Winston across the aisle. His eyes were closed and his head drooped. His glasses slid to the end of his nose. He gave a whistling sigh just before his chin bumped his bow tie. Up jerked Mr. Winston's head. He pushed his glasses up his nose and began all over again.

Little Toby Adams wriggled in his mom's arms in front of Jason, bobbled his head, and drooled a big smile. Toby finally fell asleep on his mom's shoulder, blowing tiny little whistles in his sleep.

Jason frowned and squirmed. Whistles were everywhere.

When Reverend Gray began the closing prayer, Jason sighed. He'd prayed and practiced all week and nothing had happened. He hoped God was listening when he whispered "Please, God . . ."

Eyes closed, Jason lifted his chin. He puckered his lips and sucked his cheeks. He made sure his tongue was out of the way. He took a deep, deep breath and . . .

Out of Jason's puckered lips came a loud, clear, perfectly perfect whistle!

Jason opened his eyes and blinked. Reverend Gray stopped praying. Toby woke up and grinned. Mr. Winston snorted awake. Mrs. Milton tapped his shoulder and winked. Tommy laughed "Ha!" from way across the room.

"Jason," Mom said, "not in church!"

Jason looked at all the people smiling at him. He looked at Mom and grinned. He still heard that long, clear whistle soaring through the air.

When it was Jason's turn to shake Reverend Gray's hand after the service, Jason smiled and said, "You were right, Reverend. God does know our every need!"

And Jason whistled all the way home.

From the Author

A joke about a little boy who whistles out loud in church! The moment I heard it, I had instant recall of my kids trying to whistle—such a complicated maneuver for those little mouths and tongues. There had to be a story behind the punch line.

Learning to whistle is no small thing to a child. Why shouldn't this important event in a child's life be called to God's attention? At the same time, Jason didn't sit back and expect God to grant the ability instantly—he asked God to help him *learn* to whistle.

The original draft went quickly, but the story went through several revisions, paring down excessive narrative, inserting Jason's week of practice, relying on critique partners to confirm the voice and style I was aiming to achieve. I'll be honest—I first envisioned this story as a picture book and submitted it to those markets that publish religion-based books for children. Each editor's rejection was positive about the story's content, but each one suggested it was more appropriate for the inspirational magazine market.

The story's acceptance to *Story Friends* was provisional on its being cut by more than 200 words, requiring one final and probably most difficult rewrite. The result of that final revision has prompted me to focus on "writing spare." Adding is much easier than cutting!

POV (point of view) is one of the elements of writing with which I struggle. If my character can't see it, hear it, or feel it, it doesn't happen. I found myself experiencing everything from inside Jason's head, but told the story using third person. Typical of children, he is so focused on his problem, everything around him is a reminder.

The church setting obviously originated with the joke, but having grown up in a small, community church, I was able to imagi atmosphere and how a young child copes with behaving during a worship service. Limiting the number of scenes holds the reader's attention, but there must be enough to give some variety. No fewer than three, no more than five, seem to be the magic numbers for youngsters.

Creating realistic dialogue can be difficult. People speak in fragments, for one thing. Our grammar is more relaxed and we abbreviate words. Writing with that much realism, especially for children, is choppy and confusing. There must be a balance of how real conversation sounds and how it is read.

Story Friends is a quality magazine in the inspirational market for children and seemed to be a logical place to submit. It was a particular pleasure for me to know that its 6,000 subscribing families had children reading my story!

Some of my ideas emerge from my own childhood memories, but many are more current. I'm a careful listener to accounts by friends and acquaintances of touching or amusing incidents involving their children and grandchildren. I observe kids interacting with each other (at the mall, in parks, and playgrounds) and then allow my imagination to take over. Newspaper articles spark ideas; i.e., a current project is based on a news account about an eight-year-old who missed her school bus and attempted to drive her uncle's car to school. That one simply begs to become a story!

My advice is to read, read, and read—the successful books and stories published for the age range in which you are writing, and the "how-to" books written by successful authors. There are reasons for their success and that expertise will benefit beginning writers.

—Katy Doran

From the Editor

First impressions are important. I receive many submissions that aren't in proper manuscript format or that don't follow my guidelines. Katy's approach was professional in every way, giving her an automatic advantage.

The story contained most of the elements that I look for in a story: a likeable child protagonist, a problem common to many children, the child acting in believable ways to solve his or her dilemma, and the promotion of the values important to our publication without being preachy.

Katy combined these elements into this well-developed story. It was obvious that she had spent a lot of time rewriting and revising in order to produce a piece that really was ready for publication.

Many writers think that writing for a Christian publication means including prayer, church, and the Bible. In fact, this is neither necessary nor required. When these elements are thrown in for the sake of making a story "Christian," the result is usually both stilted and preachy. What matters most to me is that the values of Christianity are exemplified in how the characters act, react, and solve their problems. The way Katy included the spiritual aspects in her story flowed naturally from the situation.

Many stories that I publish make no formal mention of anything specifically religious. They show the Christian principles in action rather than tell of them.

—Susan Reith Swan, Assistant Editor,
Story Friends

Story Friends
4–9 years
725 words

A Lemon Friendship

By Maureen Webster

George daydreamed of birds. He'd already read every library book about birds. Once school started, he walked home so he could linger at the pet store. By October, all the birds knew George.

"Money's tight since we moved, George," said Mom. "I need to pay bills. Can't you find a friend instead of a bird?"

George didn't want a friend. He wanted a bird.

I wonder if I could find a used bird, he thought. George began searching the want ads. They told of cockatiels who hadn't bonded with their owners or were left alone too much. The cockatiels had grown up to be grouchy and unsociable.

No wonder they're giving them away, thought George. *My cockatiel would miss me while I'm at school. As soon as I'd open the door he'd fly out of his cage and sit on my shoulder.*

There was one parakeet whose owner was moving to Florida. "He doesn't like to be touched," said his owner.

"Thanks anyway," said George. *My parakeet would like to nuzzle into my neck while we watch afternoon cartoons,* he thought.

George read another ad for an African gray parrot. It said, "Owner must be able to take risks and make a commitment."

"What kind of commitment?" asked George when he called about the bird.

The gruff owner said, "This parrot could bite off a finger. He's going to need some tough love."

"I couldn't be tough on any bird that lives in my house, even if he's mean to me." George hung up.

One day he found an ad that read, "Found: one lemon-yellow parakeet. Call 555-1134."

George called. No one else had answered the ad. "This parakeet needs me," said George. The finders were glad to pack up the lost parakeet and deliver it to George.

"Lemon," George whispered to the bird. "That's what I'll call you."

Each morning before school, George rose fifteen minutes early to give Lemon fresh water, torn lettuce leaves, and birdseed for breakfast. In the afternoon, he took Lemon out of his cage and stroked his back. By the end of the week, the bird sat on George's shoulder while he practiced his spelling words. Lemon waited patiently while George struggled with his math problems. Lemon chattered when George watched *Super Science Tuesday*. But when *Wild Animal World* came on, Lemon watched just as carefully as George.

"George, Pete's shooting baskets," said Mom. "Why don't you join him?"

"I'm busy with Lemon. Did you ever see him smile?" George asked.

"How can you tell?"

"His mouth sort of quivers and his eyes close up a little. See? He looks happy."

"I'm glad you have Lemon to keep you company," said Mom, "but wouldn't you like to be friends with some of the kids? I almost forgot. I have to leave early for work tomorrow. Can you get yourself to school?"

"Sure," said George. *It'll be the perfect day to take Lemon to school,* he thought.

"You can see what I do all day," George said to Lemon the next morning as he packed his lunch. George placed Lemon inside his zippered lunch cooler. "I'll leave it partly open so you can breathe." Lemon perched on a package of fruit snacks all the way to school. Once there, George unzipped the cooler and tucked his lunch and Lemon inside his desk.

The morning was uneventful until the spelling test. "Panther," said Mrs. Tackle.

Scritch, scratch, scritch, scritch.

"What was that?" Mrs. Tackle scanned the room. George took a deep breath.

Scritch, scratch, scritch, scritch.

Pete turned to George. "I think something's nibbling the inside of your desk."

George cracked the lid of his desk. "Shhhhhhh," he whispered.

Mrs. Tackle continued with the spelling test. Lemon stayed quiet for the rest of the morning.

When everyone went to lunch, George slipped back to the room. It was the first school lunch George had shared with a friend.

Just then, Pete showed up. "I didn't know you were here. I came back for the basketball." Pete stopped and stared. "There *was* something in your desk."

"He's mine. Lemon's his name," said George.

Pete stepped closer. "I've got a parakeet, too, but I've never thought of bringing him to school."

"It's easy. I just set Lemon on my fruit snacks," said George.

"Yeah? I bring fruit snacks," said Pete. "Lemon just smiled at you. Mine does it all the time."

"Hey, Pete," yelled a voice from outside. "What's taking you so long?"

Pete scooped up the basketball. "You want to play?" he asked George.

"Sure," George tucked Lemon back into his cooler. "I won't be long," he said to Lemon. "Guess we both have a new friend." George closed his desk and followed Pete out to the playground.

From the Author

The idea for "A Lemon Friendship" came from my most prolific sources for my writing—my two sons, Ben and Evan. Ben wanted a parakeet when he was ten years old. I'm not a pet lover, but I relented because a parakeet seemed easy to live with. The first two parakeets we bought died (so much for easy to care for). There were many tears shed.

Thank goodness, Lemon, our third parakeet, was healthy and became one of the family. He had a favorite song that he sang when we played it on the tape player. Ben noticed how Lemon "smiled" at us when we were all together as a family. Ben took Lemon out of his cage every day and talked to him, let him fly in the house, and trained him to sit on his shoulder, as well as changed his food and water.

For a long time, he was Ben's confidante and trusted friend when other friends were unavailable. As a person who stood outside of the circle of pet lovers, I observed all these details come together. I had to write "A Lemon Friendship."

I wrote the first draft one day when my son was home sick. I did three more revisions with comments from my writing group. Revisions are the most difficult for me because I can't always see where I'm going with the piece. Critiques from the group helped me shape it into the final story. This story felt very real to me and emotionally satisfying.

I submitted it to eight different magazines before *Story Friends* bought it. One of the form letter rejections I received had a hand-written note on the bottom, which bolstered my spirits. I kept sending it out and was giddy to finally receive an acceptance.

The technical part of writing "A Lemon Friendship" involved many things. The humor in the story comes from seeing a bird as more than a bird. I was able to make him into a well-rounded character because of his human traits.

I wrote the story in third person because it felt the most authentic. In first person, George may have been just an echo of my son. In third person, George became a boy that I grew to know by writing his story.

Dialogue is something I really have to read aloud to others and then revise. It takes work to make people sound authentic. I often start with actual dialogue I have remembered and written down, then I write it down in a stream-of-consciousness style for my rough drafts and often for revisions too, when I am stuck.

Writing fiction for young readers is a challenge for me. I see plot and story ideas, but don't often have the characters to go along with them. I often find I am too wordy and have to cut much of what I wrote in my first draft because it is unnecessary or repetitive.

When I am not writing, I earn a living as a part-time elementary teacher. I enjoy being with children and often find seedlings for stories and essays to add to my writing while I am at school.

—Maureen Webster

From the Editor

I receive many stories about children either wanting pets or losing pets. Most of them deal with dogs or cats. The fact that George wanted a bird was the first thing that made this story stand out from the rest.

Second, Maureen used a fresh approach by having George look for a bird through the want ads. I also found her use of language in phrases like, "My parakeet would like to nuzzle my neck while we watch afternoon cartoons" and "Lemon perched on a package of fruit snacks all the way to school" appealing and just right for my readership.

Maureen gave the story depth by having the relationship grow between George and Lemon and by using Lemon as a vehicle for George to be able to make a friend at school. In addition, readers learn about caring for a pet parakeet without even realizing it.

The story was clean, professionally presented, and needed minimal editing. Since it was for the February issue, I changed the sport from baseball in the original to basketball.

The original ending was a bit abrupt, ending where Pete tells George that his parakeet also smiles. I added what I felt was closure by having Pete ask George to play basketball with George finally accepting.

—Susan Reith Swan, Assistant Editor,
Story Friends

Story Friends
4–9 years
790 words

Marissa's Berries

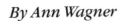
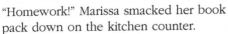

By Ann Wagner

"Homework!" Marissa smacked her book pack down on the kitchen counter.

The next day was Valentine's Day, and for homework she had to draw a picture of something in her house that reminded her of love.

She looked in the refrigerator for a snack, to help her think better. There on the top shelf was a green basket filled with fresh red strawberries. "I could draw those," she thought. "They look like little hearts, and that reminds me of love!"

Marissa set the basket down on the counter and tasted one berry. Its tart sweetness made her mouth water.

When she snapped the lid off her crayon case, Marissa saw that half a green crayon was all she had left. How could she draw strawberries with a green crayon?

Marissa's father burst into the kitchen, waving one sock in the air. "That washing machine must have eaten my other sock!" He leaned on the counter. "Say, those look good," he said, eyeing the strawberries.

"Take some, Dad," said Marissa. "I'm going to draw them for my homework, if I can find a red crayon."

Her father munched on the strawberries as he walked back to the laundry room.

Marissa gazed out the window. Her sister, Beth, whizzed by on her new roller blades—straight into the azalea bushes. Marissa grabbed a handful of strawberries and dashed out the door.

"Are you all right?" she asked, putting the berries into Beth's hands.

"Fine now," Beth said, managing a smile. "I love strawberries."

Marissa sat down next to her. "I need a red crayon," she said. "Do you have one?"

Beth shook her head. "I'll bet Mom has some lipstick you could use, though!"

Marissa found her mother in the driveway, washing the car. "Mom," she began, "could I use some of your red lipstick to draw a picture? It's for school."

"Oh my!" The hose slipped out of her mother's hands and sprayed her, as if it were the trunk of an angry elephant! Marissa tried not to laugh, since her mother looked so bedraggled. She went into the kitchen and came back with the last berries.

"Thank you," her mother said. "These taste so good, I don't mind that crazy hose!"

Marissa walked back to the kitchen There was no need for red crayons or lipstick now. She didn't have any berries left to draw.

On the counter was the empty green berry basket. It reminded her of the berries she gave to her father when he lost his sock, and the berries she gave to her sister when she fell, and the berries she gave to her dripping wet mother.

"That was love, wasn't it?" Marissa thought.

She picked up her green crayon and started to draw green crisscrossed lines inside a square shape.

Marissa called her picture "A Basket without Berries," but it would always remind her of love. ❖

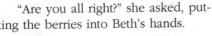

From the Author

Entering contests can be helpful in a number of ways. First, it's a way to get published! Also, especially for new writers, it establishes some rules that help you become more focused and disciplined. You have a deadline, a category, and a reader age-range, all of which help you focus your plot and make every word count. I confess I also have a problem of not finishing stories, but deciding to enter a contest made me overcome that weakness.

The six-to-eight age range wasn't a difficult category for me. I had a niece and nephew those ages, and I was familiar with the way they talked, the things that were important to them, and what problems they faced in daily life.

I also drew from my poetry training to create visual images, and centered the story around my own number-one love: strawberries. Originally, the problem was that Marissa didn't think she had drawing talent; in the end she'd find out she did. But Marissa didn't fit into that problem well. The story wasn't special enough, and the resolution felt contrived. I wanted the story to have a positive, but not sappy, tint.

After numerous drafts, I locked in the conflict, but was horrified to discover the story was 1,200 words long. "I'm sunk," I thought, but did six more rewrites until the final draft was pared to 482 words.

When I sent the story, I thought, "If nothing else, I learned about editing and honing." Having a word limit turned out to be a valuable restriction. It taught me how to edit my own work and analyze what really was necessary in the story.

Since "Marissa's Berries" won the contest in *Children's Writer*, I have continued to write for children. I've had work published in children's magazines, including *Cricket* and *Hopscotch: The Magazine for Girls*. I have also written and performed a number of children's stories for my church for the "Children's Message" portion of the service.

I work as a newsletter/publications editor and writer full-time, but I make time for my real love—writing for children.

—Ann Wagner

From the Editor

Writing to enter contests isn't about luck, it's about honing skills. With "Marissa's Berries," her contest-winning contemporary story for ages six to eight, Ann Wagner advanced her writing abilities by shaping and strengthening through more than six rewrites. The result is a story strong on every front. It engages immediately with the lead, an exclamation we've all made, an action we've all taken—that moves readers right into the plot.

With the second paragraph, the time of year and setting and problem are clear. Deft strokes bring in three additional characters, father, mother, and sister, all with a small obstacle of their own to be resolved. Ann keeps the action gently moving, and tucks in a gentle lesson.

At the center of the action is Marissa, resolving the problems with love, and by her own actions solving her own problem.

All of "Marissa's Berries" is marked by very strong visual images, led by the story's true hook, a basket of strawberries—their color, taste, and the heart shape that Marissa wants to use to represent love, even when the expression of the love has been shared and consumed. Every sentence adds to Ann's story.

—Susan Tierney, Editor,
Children's Writer

Children's Writer
Writers for Children
480 words

Where Does the Water Go?

By Jacqueline J. Christensen
Art by Michael Palan

Have you ever watered a garden and watched the water disappear into the soil? Here's a fun experiment that will show you how plants are able to use water to grow. Ask an adult to help you.

You Will Need:
- Medium-sized glass
- Water
- Red food coloring
- Spoon
- 1 celery stalk with leaves

You Will Do:
1. Fill the glass half-full of water.
2. Stir in enough food coloring to make the water dark red.
3. Ask Mom or Dad to cut 1 inch off the bottom of the celery stalk. Place the stalk in the water, and let it stand overnight.

What Will Happen:
The celery leaves will turn red. There will also be red lines running lengthwise through the stalk. If you break the stalk in half, you will see red dots in the middle of each piece.

Why?
As a plant grows, its roots act like straws, sucking water up the stems or stalks. Tiny tubes inside the stalks carry water further up into the leaves. By making the water red, you are better able to see this. The red dots in the broken celery stalk are the tiny tubes through which the water traveled.

From the Author

"Where Does the Water Go?" was written as Assignment 7 for the Institute's *Writing for Children and Teenagers* course. I had never had any interest in writing nonfiction, and was a little daunted by this assignment. Once I began, however, I was surprised to find myself enjoying it very much. I still prefer writing fiction, but have continued to throw some nonfiction into the mix as well.

The idea for this article started with the celery experiment highlighted in the magazine. Using it as a tie-in to plants and their root systems naturally followed. I did more research than I could possibly use, but that made the article much easier to write. It was a matter of paring down the information, rather than trying to stretch it, and I could easily pick and choose what I felt were the more important facts.

Most of my research came from library books and information off the Internet, which is also a great source of ideas for other articles.

Since this article was about 500 words to begin with, I chose to send it first to *Children's Playmate*. Soon afterward, I received a letter informing me that the editor wanted to hold it for possible future publication in *Turtle*. After the editor shortened the article and made some revisions, it was published about a year and a half later.

I live in Minnesota. During the long, cold winters, I spend my time writing, reading (another of my passions), and painting.

—Jacqueline J. Christensen

From the Editor

I picked this particular piece because I thought it would work well as one of our "Simple Science" experiments in *Turtle*. It was a well-written manuscript, with easy-to-follow instructions that even preschoolers could do with a minimal amount of help.

By conducting this simple experiment, young kids would be able to see and understand how plants act like straws to suck water up through their roots and stems. It would also be easy to illustrate. The only thing I had to do was pare down the manuscript to fit the "Simple Science" format.

—Terry Webb Harshman,
Editor, *Turtle*

Turtle
2–5 years
190 words

How Is Your Horse Talk?

By John L. Sperry • Illustrated by Pam Harden

When a horse talks to you, do you listen? That lone paint pony in the pasture you just pedaled by on your bike had a lot to say to you. Did you catch what he said? As you started by, his head bolted up from the grass he was clipping, and he trotted to the fence. He brought a smile to your face as you rolled along. He kept pace, his ears forward and eyes watching you as he nickered. Then tail high, loping, he circled into the pasture, then back to the fence. But you pedaled on, turning as he whinnied. Out of the corner of your eye, you saw him race up and down the fence separating the two of you.

That pony had a lot to say. Did you catch it? His nicker as he came racing up to you was his way of saying, "Hi! I'm glad to see you." His ears forward and eyes watching said, "You interest me." And loping along, tail held high, swinging out into the pasture, then back to you was his way of saying, "Hey! Come on in and play. Catch me if you can." But you rode on by, leaving him distressed and alone. He told you with his whinny and by racing back and forth along the fence that he didn't want to be alone.

Horses are very social animals; they love company and dislike being alone. It comes from ages ago when survival of a horse depended on his ability to watch and smell a stalking predator, such as the mountain lion lurking in the ledges above where he grazed.

Horses banded together in small herds for safety. What one horse did not see or smell, another would. Out of this need to be safe in a herd, a wonderful language developed that allows horses to warn and express a whole range of feelings and moods to each other and to you, once you understand.

It is doubly nice when you understand horse talk. It's a bit like going to a football or volleyball game. If you understand the rules and language of the game, watching and playing is fun. Watching and being around horses is fun and safer, too, when you understand horse talk.

If you want to know what a horse is thinking or feeling, many trainers and riders who spend hours each day on or around horses tell you to keep one eye on a horse's ears, another on its tail, and your ears listening to its nickers, whinnies, and nose blowing.

Ear language is the easiest to understand. With ears perked forward and an intent look, the horse is saying, "Hummm, pretty interesting. I ought to check this out." With one ear forward, the other back, the horse is keeping one eye on his front, the other to his back. A horse that does this is alert, a good pony, because he'll see the loose, unsafe rocks on a

ANGER

narrow mountain trail. Horses have nearly 360-degree vision. That makes it pretty tough for a mountain lion or you to sneak up on a horse that's got any look-out savvy at all.

If you see a horse with ears turned to the side and slightly back, he's saying, "Aaah, I love this tree's shade. I'm relaxing right here." And if one back leg is cocked with just the tip of the hoof touching the ground, that's the final giveaway; this horse is speaking relaxation and likely asleep. Be careful approaching this sleeping horse or "bang!" He may kick before he realizes that it's just you, his friend. It's not meanness, just his age-old instinct to strike at an unexpected enemy.

There is no mistaking a horse's expressing anger; ears will be flat, back against his head. If his eyes are blazing, lips curled, and jaw snapping, you're looking at a horse that can run chills up and down your back. A horse is naturally fearful of anything he senses danger in, but cornered, an angry horse can strike fear even in a stalking cougar.

A horse's tail, like its ears, can speak to you. A fidgety person will pace back and forth. A nervous horse will do that and switch its tail too. It could just be a fly bothering him. On the other hand, if his tail is switching constantly, look around. Something or someone is likely getting on his nerves.

ALERT

interest

A tail tucked between a horse's legs can mean a badly frightened horse, one that's cocked, ready to kick. Check his ears too. Are they back? The language is clear. Play it safe.

The nickering, whinnying, and snorting are horse talk too. If you crawl over the fence into a pasture of horses unacquainted with you, watch; one may start toward you, ears forward in interest, then stop, snort, and bolt back to the herd. The snort is a fear signal, a warning that danger can be near.

Do you recall ever being lost in a crowd, separated from your friends or family? Did you cry or call out? The whinny or neigh is the cry of the horse. Hear it and know something is wrong in the life of that horse. It could be that a horse's companion is missing or has suddenly disappeared from sight.

The nicker is grand horse talk. It is the "all is well" signal. It may come when an owner turns her horse loose in the pasture after a long ride, or she has come to feed him grain and hay, or to spoil him with a sugar cube.

Our thinking changes when we understand even a little horse talk. Now we know that just like us, horses have moods, needs, and feelings. When these are met, they will, just like good friends, give trust.

From the Author

"How Is Your Horse Talk?" was enjoyable to write because I grew up with horses as part of my life on our family farm. However, the germ for the article came while I was reading Monty Roberts's *The Man Who Listens to Horses*. I knew that as wonderful with horses as horse whisperers are, human beings, young and old, who understand a few vocal and physical signals can get along happily and safely with most horses.

I chose the story format for this article because facts and ideas are best remembered and enjoyed in a story framework. To keep the interest of the 9- to 12-year-old age group, I limited the information to easily observable action and sound characteristics, ear movements, tail switching, nickering, etc.—things that even the first-time horse observer can note and feel. Anything beyond basic horse talk would derail the interest of first-time horse readers.

So, I spent time in the pastures and corrals around our place, visited with those who bred, raised, trained, and showed horses. Then finally, I went to a few texts on horse behavior.

The first writing of "How Is Your Horse Talk?" was in disconnected pieces, with no order of importance in the horse communication signals. By the third writing, I had the signals in order, and the story thread that would carry the reader from one signal to the next was in place. A fourth revision took care of any final word choices and proofing. "Horse Talk" was ready.

I searched *Magazine Markets for Children's Writers* for potential markets for horse stories. I circled *Hopscotch* as my first choice because I liked the theme format, the age group was right, and it had an excellent reputation. Slanting the article for girls was a natural. After all, the majority of riders and horse enthusiasts in our country are girls. I was more than pleased when *Hopscotch* expressed an interest in the article. It was an easy decision for me to say, "Yes, please do keep 'Horse Talk' for the next time you do a horse theme."

I have had the joy of being a teacher and a farmer my entire life. I taught elementary and middle school for several years and now teach and do academic advising at the college level. We have had the good fortune to raise our six children on our three-generation family farm. My first stories were for my children, who were often characters in Christmas and adventure stories.

—John L. Sperry

From the Editor

I chose "How Is Your Horse Talk?" because it went along with our theme on horses. In this issue I tried to include fiction stories and nonfiction articles. This particular article was well written, informative, and I felt it would be of interest to both horse owners and those who will never have the option to own a horse.

Girls who don't know much about horses will learn from this article. As the editor, I learned a few things myself. It was definitely unique compared to most of the "horse" articles we received. The description is excellent and easy to visualize.

—Marilyn Edwards, Editor, *Hopscotch, The Magazine for Girls*

Hopscotch
6–13 years
970 words

Raindrops

By Nancy Roskam

1 One raindrop fell from a cloud.

2 Two raindrops, **3** three raindrops fell, and then, too many to count. The raindrops ran down a hill into a stream. The stream joined a river. The river grew bigger and bigger. It flowed into a large blue lake.

The cloud blew away. The sun came out and warmed the lake. Moist air rose from the lake. It rose high into the sky and formed a cloud. The cloud grew heavier and heavier.

1 One raindrop fell from the cloud.

2 Two raindrops, **3** three raindrops, and then, too many to count.

Illustrated by Len Ebert

From the Author

While the inspiration for "Raindrops" came from a weather unit I was teaching to my second graders, the rebus idea came fom Marileta Robinson, a Senior Editor for *Highlights* and my mentor at the Highlights Foundation Writers Workshop.

A rebus usually targets young children who aren't reading yet or who are just beginning to read, thus the reason for the pictures and easier words. The pictures give the children clues as to what the words might be. It should also be a topic that young children are interested in.

It's more challenging to write a rebus than one would think. I wrote and submitted numerous rebus stories before this one was accepted.

When writing this rebus, every word had to count because I was limited to approximately 125 words.

I followed the guidelines for writing a rebus that I learned in a workshop at the Highlights conference. I chose specific words/vocabulary that I wanted to be illustrated, but the artist *Highlights* chose for my piece made the ultimate decisions along with the staff.

I selected *Highlights* because I enjoyed the conference and one of the benefits of attending was getting to know the staff at *Highlights*, so I was comfortable submitting my first piece of writing to the magazine.

I was thrilled when I found out that my rebus had been accepted. The hard work was worth the effort to see "Raindrops" published in *Highlights*.

—Nancy Roskam

From the Editor

Nancy has done several difficult things well in this story. She has presented a science concept in a way that is meaningful and appealing to prereaders and younger readers.

She is aware of our needs in a rebus story and has used rhythm, repetition, short, simple sentences and familiar, concrete nouns that can be illustrated.

We rarely do nonfiction rebuses, but this one worked so well we couldn't wait to publish it!

—Marileta Robinson, Editor,
Highlights for Children

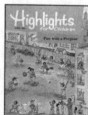

Highlights for Children
2–12 years
94 words

Snapping Snack

By Beth Edwards

Scary, right?

Wrong! Americans eat sixteen billion quarts of this funny food every year. And nobody gets hurt!? **It's Popcorn!**

Popular even with the Indians, who tossed it on hot rocks or popped it right on the cob, popcorn has been a booming success for thousands of years. Samples up to 5,000 years old have been found.

In recent times, street vendors sold it during the Great Depression, and when sugar went to U.S. servicemen in World War II, Americans replaced candy with snacks of tasty popcorn.

There are five varieties of corn. They all have moisture, a starchy kernel, and a hard overcoating, or hull. But only in popcorn does the moisture expand the starch until finally the hull gives way with a loud POP!

Each popcorn kernel needs 13.5 to 14 percent moisture to pop. Unpopped kernels are too dry. Try to re-hydrate them.

Directions:

1. Mark your unpopped kernels, then mix them with some new kernels.
2. Add 1 tablespoon of water, shake well, wait four days, then pop the whole batch.
3. Separate unpopped kernels (every batch has some) and check to see if any are marked. If not, all your left-overs have popped.

From the Author

The idea for "Snapping Snack" originated as a course assignment for the Institute of Children's Literature. Doing the research and making the time to put it together were challenges. Most of my research came from the Internet because finding books on popcorn was difficult. I went to credible sites, such as Jolly Time Popcorn and the Popcorn Board.

I looked for a magazine that isn't overwhelmed with submissions each month. I used the Institute's market directory to find a suitable market, and my instructor approved my choice and encouraged me to send it in—along with the sidebar idea.

I was a little shocked at how much the editors changed my article, including its original title, "Exploding Vegetables." I sent in a 500-word article and they condensed it to less than half of that. I understand they have space limitations, but I almost didn't recognize it.

After I got over the shock of having it shortened so much, I was still proud of it.

—Beth Edwards

From the Editor

Ms. Edwards's 500-word manuscript about how popcorn works fit well in a new feature called "The Green Thumb Gazette," a gardening collection built around a question-and-answer column by a horticulture PhD.

Because the Q&A is the main element, we only had room for about 200 words of Ms. Edwards's original manuscript. We used a good bit of her research and recast the final paragraph as a separate activity about rejuvenating unpopped kernels, but we had to do some rewriting just to fit the space.

—Daniel Lee, Editor, *U*S* Kids*

*U*S* Kids*
6–8 years
190 words

Andrea's Unusual Pet

By Phyllis S. Dixon

Guess what lives in Andrea's backyard! A real turtle. In Arizona it's not unusual to find turtles roaming in the desert, but to have one live in your yard in the middle of Phoenix and to find it at your door begging for food—that is unusual.

One spring about four years ago when Andrea went outside to play in her playhouse, she saw a turtle poking its pointed nose out from a hole under her playhouse. It was brownish in color and its high, pointed shell was about as big as a medium-size plate. When Andrea stooped down to investigate, the turtle backed down into its burrow.

Andrea told her mom and dad about the turtle, and they decided to put out some lettuce and apples near the hole under the playhouse to see what might happen.

The next day all the food was gone. Andrea put out more food every day, which kept disappearing. One day Andrea noticed the turtle come out of its hole and wander around as if it belonged in the backyard.

"I think we'll call him Chomper," said Andrea, "because he chomps down all the food we leave for him. I'm going to look up turtles in the encyclopedia and see what else they eat."

In her encyclopedia, Andrea discovered her backyard resident was probably a desert tortoise because of its short, stumpy, club-like legs, with long claws and a high domed shell. She found out that the desert tortoise lives in the dry desert areas of the Southwest. She also found out that they usually eat plants and live only on land.

When Andrea told her parents what she had found out about Chomper, her dad said, "I wonder how this one got all the way in to Phoenix from the desert."

One weekend Andrea and her mom and dad went away. When they got back home and were eating supper they heard a scratching sound at the back door. Andrea went to investigate and found Chomper standing on his thick, clumsy back legs scratching at the door with his front legs.

"Oh, Mom," said Andrea. "We forgot to leave some food for Chomper."

"How do I check the vital signs of a tortoise through that thick shell?" pondered the vet.

"I'll bet he's starved," said Mom. "Here, give him part of this apple."

Andrea took the apple and cautiously opened the back door, squatted down and held the apple out toward the tortoise. To her surprise, Chomper came right up to Andrea and put out its long pink tongue and licked the apple, then grabbed it with its sharp beak and began to eat.

Dad, who had come to watch, said, "Look at that. I never thought a turtle would eat out of a person's hand." After that, Chomper came to the back door every day for his ration of food.

One day Chomper didn't come and Andrea went to investigate. She found him flopped down outside his burrow with his eyes closed and his head drooping. No amount of coaxing would arouse Chomper so Andrea and her mom took him to the veterinarian. Imagine the surprised look on the vet's face, when he saw that his patient was a desert tortoise.

"How do I check the vital signs of a tortoise through that thick shell?" pondered the vet. "I know, maybe I can check by putting my stethoscope on those big clumsy legs." And that's just what he did. The vet decided that Chomper must have eaten some sort of insect that gave him a tummy ache so he squirted some Pepto-Bismol and a bit of antibiotic down Chomper's throat and sent him home with Andrea and her mom.

Chomper scrambled down into his burrow in a hurry, still trying to spit out the medicine that the vet had given him. In a couple of days, Chomper was back at the door scratching for his usual handout, looking as though he had never been sick.

In October, Chomper came to the door several times every day and ate enormous amounts of lettuce and apples.

"I know what he's doing," said Andrea proudly. "The encyclopedia says that tortoises don't like cold weather and will hibernate during the winter. Chomper is just eating lots to last him through the winter."

Near the end of October, Chomper didn't come to the door anymore. Andrea discovered that Chomper's burrow under the playhouse looked as though dirt had been pushed around so that the burrow had no door.

"Oh, oh, I'll bet you've gone to sleep for the winter, Chomper. I hope you'll be warm enough."

The winter months came and went and soon it was April first. One morning at breakfast, Andrea heard the familiar scratching, and there was Chomper looking a trifle thin and very hungry. Chomper had survived the winter.

"Chomper is back! He made it through the winter," said Andrea excitedly. "He looks thin," said Dad.

"Better get him some food," said Mom as she reached for an apple.

Andrea was happy that Chomper was back. She read that tortoises sometimes live to be one hundred years old and she hoped that Chomper would stay around their backyard for a long, long time and continue to be her wonderfully strange pet.

From the Author

The idea for "Andrea's Unusual Pet" came to me when I was having lunch with friends and one of them told of her granddaughter's pet turtle living in their backyard in Phoenix. I thought to myself, "What an unusual pet—that might make a story." So I asked my friend many questions about her granddaughter's pet: its color, when it came, where it hid, what it ate, and how long had it been around? For research, I went to my trusty *World Book Encyclopedia* and discovered the "turtle" that is actually a "tortoise" common to the Southwestern U.S. I targeted the story for ages 8 to 12.

I revised the piece twice based on suggestions from my instructor at the Institute of Children's Literature. I looked through *Magazine Markets for Children's Writers* for publishers who wanted nature stories and articles that could be enjoyed by the entire family. *Lighthouse* was my first choice, and I was pleasantly surprised when they sent me a contract for publication.

I come from a family of educators and have been an elementary teacher and principal for 32 years. Children have been an important part of my life and now that I'm retired, I thought it would be fun to write stories for children and perhaps give back to them the joy and inspiration they've given me through the years.

—Phyllis S. Dixon

Lighthouse
Story Collections

Lighthouse
Families and ages 8–12
870 words

Feeling Lucky?

By Beverly Patt
Illustrated by John Aardema

Some superstitions have a holy history.

Looking for a way to improve your luck? You probably wouldn't want to try:

- Eating a chopped horsehair sandwich.
- Throwing a shoe over your left shoulder without looking.
- Eating black-eyed peas and hog jowls, cooked with a dime.

Sound ridiculous? Your great-grandparents may have tried one of these superstitions to bring them luck. But before you snicker too loudly, think about your own superstitions.

Have you ever . . .

- crossed your fingers?
- blessed someone who sneezed?
- avoided walking under a ladder?
- shunned the number 13?

These modern-day superstitions are considered little more than folksy traditions. Can you guess what they all have in common? All of them have Christian roots! Take crossing your fingers, for example.

"I hope I get picked for the team," you say.

"I'll cross my fingers!" your friend replies.

Crossing one's fingers was considered to be good luck because it represented the cross. It was kind of like saying, "Jesus be with you."

When you sneeze, someone—even a total stranger—may say, "God bless you!" Years

ago, some people believed that your soul was contained in your breath. By sneezing, you could lose your soul. Blessing you restored it.

Did you ever hear that it was bad luck to walk under a ladder? You might think this became a superstition because you could end up wearing a bucket of paint. Not so! A triangle represents the Christian Trinity: the Father, the Son and the Holy Spirit. A ladder leaning against a wall also forms a triangle. People thought that by walking underneath it, you would "break" the triangle and insult God.

And what about the missing 13th floor on many buildings? Some historians believe this superstition comes from the Last Supper. Jesus and his 12 disciples—thirteen total—ate one last meal together before He was betrayed and killed. To this day, elevators go from floor twelve to floor fourteen!

Of course, eating pig's cheeks and throwing shoes probably never did much for anyone's popularity. After all, who would want to hang out with someone who has hog-jowl breath and dirty socks? However, there is one thing that has been proven to increase your good fortune:

- Fold your hands.
- Say, "Dear God, _____" *(Fill in the blank)*
- Repeat as necessary.

It's called prayer. You might want to try it.

From the Author

While driving and listening to the radio, I heard an ad that mentioned a lucky rabbit's foot. I wondered about the origin of this (it certainly wasn't lucky for the rabbit!) so I went to the library and looked up good luck charms and superstitions. I discovered that many superstitions have Christian roots. Figuring that was a more specific angle than plain superstitions, I went with it. (I never did find why a rabbit's foot was considered lucky!)

I find ideas by being "aware" in my daily life of things that pique my own interest—things on the radio (I'm a National Public Radio junkie), articles in the paper, things my kids say. Also, I've found a great fund of quirky ideas/facts in almanacs that have led to many an article.

For my research, I head straight to my local children's library. I learned early on to shun adult-level books for research—they gave me too much information and jumbled up my pea-brain. Children's books have already been simplified to give concise information in easy to understand terms—why reinvent the wheel?

Using plain notebook paper and recording each book's name and bibliographical information, I'd jot down whatever was interesting or important. I also learned to write down page numbers because I would inevitably want to find a certain passage again and I'd end up wasting time looking.

After the fifth or sixth book, a pattern started to emerge and a few fun ideas began to pop, which I'd write down immediately so they wouldn't escape into the atmosphere of "what was that great idea I had?" After going through all the books, I highlighted the ideas/quotes I wanted to use. Then I formed an outline.

Choosing what *not* to include is a killer. After reading and rereading through my first draft, I can see a few things that stick out, no matter how cool they are. I take them out, promising myself I will do an article just on that one idea someday.

When I drafted my lead I was trying to appeal to kids' natural attractions to gross-ness and wackiness. I like to think of my readers as doing a double-take when they read my introductions. Wacky or gross ideas—like eating horsehair sandwiches—are good ways to achieve that.

I think addressing my readers as "you" makes the information more personal. Reading about "you" and "your grandparents" is far more interesting than reading about some other third person. Putting the reader "in" the article makes it much more exciting!

I'm the type of writer who revises as I go along. I sent the article first to a Christian magazine who liked it but wanted me to cut it from 772 words to 400 words. That was a big chunk! I soon realized I couldn't just take out a sentence here and there—I had to operate. There had been a whole section on black cats that was over 300 words. I axed that and then tried to find sentences that were superfluous.

I sent it back only to wait an agonizing two months before receiving a very nice, but apologetic, rejection letter. After a healthy dose of self-pity, I sent it to Mary Lou Carney at *Guideposts for Kids*.

I think I owe that first editor a big thank you—not only did the cutting make it a better article, it also led me to *GP4K* and *GP4Teens*—publications that I have worked closely with ever since. You never know where one article will lead you. I recently received a phone call from a book publisher—they had gotten my name through *Guideposts* and have asked me to write a book!

One thing I learned the hard way: if you can find only one source to back up a certain fact, either chuck it or call an expert. On two separate occasions, I used a "fact" I found in a book that was incorrect. Nothing is more humiliating (or at least very few things) than receiving a call from an editor with a complaint letter in her hand.

Spice up factual information with humor, wordplay, bad puns—the "badder" the better! Try to find ways your facts may relate to the readers in their own lives—how, for example, a lion killing a gazelle is kind of like the reader going to the local grocery mart. Look for the quirky, oddball facts or challenge yourself to put a quirky spin on an everyday idea. Keep paragraphs on the short side. Add a fun "sidebar" to your article (especially if you have some info that is just too good to leave out!). Sidebars give the editor some flexibility and can be used to draw a reader in. Most important: have fun!

You really have to write for yourself. Write about things that *you* find fascinating or funny or weird. If you're not totally excited after researching a subject, dump it.

—Beverly Patt

From the Editor

Bev Patt is the kind of writer editors dream of finding in the slush pile. Smart. Clever. Original. Articulate. And, perhaps best of all, funny! And not in a slapstick, trying-too-hard kind of way. The minute I read "Feeling Lucky?" I knew it was right for *Guideposts for Kids*. It was entertaining and had great voice, but also presented pertinent information. Like the rest of the magazine, it had a "God" element, but was not preachy or dogmatic.

Not only did I buy that piece, but I actually paid her a higher rate than I normally do for nonfiction articles. (See, editors can be nice. . .) Following her receipt of a contract—and a check—Bev sent me another article right away. (I told you she was smart!) Not only did I buy that piece, I also assigned her a topic I'd been wanting to do in the magazine. She delivered a publishable manuscript, and Bev has been a regular part of my "stable" of writers ever since.

—Mary Lou Carney, Editor, *Guideposts for Kids*

Guideposts for Kids
6–12 years
390 words

Flying Fish

Fantastic Fishes

By B. L. Marshall
Illustrated by Tim Davis

Have you ever heard of fish that can climb trees? Mudskippers can. When a mudskipper gets hungry, it uses its front fins as little legs to crawl out of the water. It then pulls itself up the roots of a tree, but it doesn't climb very high. It is looking for insects to eat.

A mudskipper is able to survive out of water for long periods of time because it has water trapped inside its gill chambers. It can also absorb oxygen directly through the skin of its mouth and throat.

Mudskippers have bulging eyes on top of their head, making them look a little bit like a frog. They also have strong tails to help them scurry across the mud. Mudskippers can be found in Africa, Australia, and Southeast Asia.

Another unusual fish found in Southeast Asia is the climbing perch. During dry seasons, when it doesn't rain for several months, ponds begin to dry up. The climbing perch must find water to survive. It travels by fanning out its stiff gill covers and waddling like a duck.

Climbing perch can absorb oxygen directly from the air by gulping air into their mouths. Some climbing perch have even been found in trees. Do you suppose that's how they got their name?

Hatchet Fish

If you think fish that climb trees sound strange, what do you think about fish that fly? Flying fish leave the water to escape from bigger fish that may want to eat them.

A flying fish has a long, thin body. The fins on the sides of its body form large wings and its tail fin acts like a paddle. When a flying fish wants to fly, it keeps its fins next to its body while swimming swiftly toward the surface. When it emerges into the air, it spreads its fins and flaps its tail in the water for an extra boost. It then holds its fins out stiffly and glides over the water like an airplane.

When the flying fish begins to slow, it drops back down to the surface of the water. It beats its tail in the water to regain speed and then takes off again. The flying fish can glide for 100 feet, or more, at a time. Although flying fish can be found in oceans all over the world, they seem to favor warmer waters.

Hatchet fish can also fly. They are small, almost paper-thin fishes with bodies resembling a hatchet or ax head.

Hatchet fish usually travel just below the surface of the water. When a larger fish wants to eat them, they fly out of the water by flapping their fins. They are found in streams and lakes in South America.

As you can see, not all fish just swim. Some fish do some pretty amazing things!

Mudskipper

From the Author

As a child, I enjoyed reading fiction, but never nonfiction. I always thought it was boring, so I figured if I could find an article topic that would grab the attention of the young reader, the rest would be easy.

One day while reading my local newspaper, I noticed a "For Your Information" tidbit. It was about a certain kind of fish that could climb trees. I thought, "That's it!" I went to the library and checked out a pile of books. In doing the research, I discovered many other fascinating fish.

With a young child in mind, I decided to open with an interesting question to involve the reader quickly. I tried to use descriptive words to paint pictures and to keep the article succinct. I also used additional questions to keep the reader involved. Although the editor didn't ask for any revisions, he did make a few minor changes.

The title was actually easy for me to choose. I've always liked alliteration and "Fantastic Fishes" describes the article perfectly. I chose "fantastic" over "fascinating" because I thought it would be easier for a child to understand.

I decided to send the article to *Nature Friend* magazine after I looked through the *Magazine Markets for Children's Writers* directory. I sent for a sample copy of *Nature Friend* and thought "Fantastic Fishes" would be a good fit.

I advise new writers to not talk down to young readers; just pick an interesting subject, involve the reader, and use descriptive words.

—Brenda Marshall

From the Editor

We look for pieces on unusual animals or unusual characteristics of common animals (birds, etc.). This piece fit that bill.

The title is short and has alliteration. I like both. The text gets to the point and stays there. For a piece of this kind we don't want our readers sifting debris to get to real stuff.

A question is a door to the mind. This piece asks one right away. Only a handful of very minor changes were made.

—Marvin Wengerd, Editor,
Nature Friend

Nature Friend
5–14 years
470 words

Bug Net

Text and Art by Linda Coleman

Something flittered—fluttered—and flew around him. Danny's eyes jumped and rolled as they followed the tiny life. What is that, he wondered. A beetle—a butterfly—a moth—a lightning bug. If I could just catch one!

There among the daisies, it danced within his reach. Danny stepped closer to get a better look, but as he did, it took to the air. Jumping, Danny snatched at the small life, only to have it slip through his fingers.

Like Danny, did you ever try to catch something, only to have it slip through your fingers? With a few simple steps, you can make your own bug net, and the wonders of nature will never slip away again.

You will need:
- Mom or Dad to help
- two pieces of cardboard (a large pizza box works great)
- a ruler
- white glue
- cheesecloth 36-inches square

  Note: Cheesecloth costs about $2.00, and because it is a

Fig. 1

multi-purpose cloth, it is usually found in the cleaning-supply section at your local super-market. Cheesecloth is also used in canning and making jellies.

PART 1
Making the Bug-Net Frame:

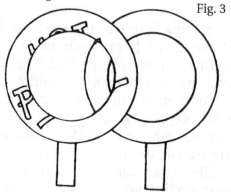
Fig. 2

1. Begin by marking the center of one of the cardboard pieces. Using the ruler, measure out 5½ inches from center, draw an 11-inch circle around the center mark. (Fig. 1)
2. Using the same center point, measure out 4½ inches with your ruler to draw a 9-inch circle inside of the 11-inch circle. (Fig. 1)
3. Using the ruler, draw a handle 4 inches long and 1½ inches wide. (Fig. 1)
4. Cut out the bug-net frame. (Fig. 2)
5. Center and trace the frame onto the other cardboard. Cut out the second bug-net frame. (Fig. 3)

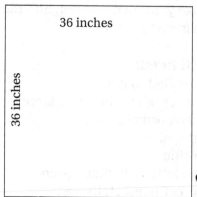
Fig. 3

PART 2
Adding the Netting:

1. Unroll the cheesecloth and measure 36 inches and cut. (Fig. 4)

36 inches

36 inches

Fig. 4

2. Spread cheesecloth out flat and set one frame in the center. Spread glue over entire surface of the frame.

Do not glue handle at this time. (Fig. 5)

3. First, press the four corners of the cheesecloth along the outer edges of the glued frame. (Fig. 5)

4. Then continue to press all the rest of the outer edges of the cheesecloth into the glue. (Fig. 5)

5. Add glue to the handle and to any areas that may have dried.

Match up the second frame, and press onto glued frame. Make sure the handles match up, and let dry about 30 minutes. (Fig. 6)

6. Gather the closed end of the net, one inch from the bottom, and tie with a string or rubber band to add weight. (Fig. 7)

Now the next time something flitters, flutters, and flies all around, don't let it slip away as Danny did.

Grab your bug net. You never know what exciting adventure awaits you in your own backyard. But this time it won't get away!

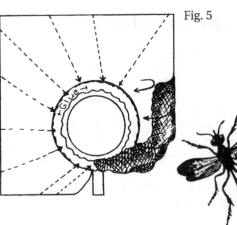

Fig. 5

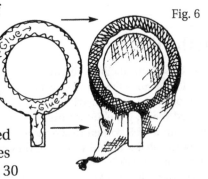

Fig. 6

Fig. 7

From the Author

One summer, my children were desperately trying to catch insects without any success. So, I came up with a way to make our own bug net. Within an hour they were outside catching everything in sight.

It was also at this time I was taking the Institute of Children's Literature's advanced writing course. "Bug Net" became my fifth assignment.

After researching the magazine market, I targeted those magazines that best fit my article.

I prepared a manuscript package, including photos and diagrams. Next thing I knew, I had a check in the mail and a notice of publication for the premiere issue of *Fun for Kidz*.

If I have one important bit of information to pass along, it would be to write so that children can understand the directions. Include diagrams for younger children (a picture is worth a thousand words) and let children test your craft.

—Linda Coleman

From the Editor

"Bug Net" fit our theme, the Great Outdoors. It was an activity and that's also what we look for in our magazine *Fun for Kidz*. I appreciated the way the author treated the beginning with a well-written description of a child trying to catch a butterfly or bug, only to lose it. Everyone has done this.

The activity follows, like a recipe. It lists everything needed and then explains "how-to." Linda also supplied her own illustrations, which was another plus. The materials needed are inexpensive and easy to come by. This is the type of well-written craft we are always looking for.

—Marilyn Edwards, Editor,
Fun for Kidz

Fun for Kidz
5–12 years
240 words

Above, an alligator hatches from its egg. Right, wildlife biologist Walt Rhodes opens a nest of unhatched eggs.

ALLIGATORS ARE REALLY SHY

By Pringle Pipkin

Just ask Walt Rhodes. He catches them.

Imagine finding an alligator hiding under your family's car. What would you do? If you lived in South Carolina, you might call Walt Rhodes, the state's alligator expert. Mr. Rhodes has captured alligators in people's garages, toolboxes, rosebushes, and even swimming pools.

"You have to think about exactly what you're doing whenever you're handling alligators," Mr. Rhodes says.

His main job as a wildlife biologist is to study and protect alligators. For seven years, he has kept records of their births and survival. He wants to see how changes in the weather and the environment are affecting them. "That will help give us answers for management of the alligator to help it survive better in the future," he says.

These large, usually muddy reptiles have been around for millions of years. But now they need Mr. Rhodes and other scientists to help them survive in a changing world. Alligators have been losing much of their habitat as people build houses, golf courses, and shopping centers near their watery homes.

Alligators live in freshwater swamps, rivers, and marshes along the coasts of warm states such as South Carolina, Georgia, Florida, and Louisiana. In the summer, the females build large grassy nests that can hold more than forty-five eggs. Mr. Rhodes uses helicopters and boats to find nests hidden in the marsh.

A Mother's Protection

Sea turtles and many kinds of snakes lay eggs and leave them to hatch on their own. But a mother alligator often floats in the water near her nest. She will pop out to protect her eggs from raccoons, bears, or other hungry animals.

Surprisingly, mother alligators do not confront Mr. Rhodes very often, even when he is digging for their eggs. He sometimes faces a female lurking near the nest or hissing and flashing her teeth. These mothers are trying to scare him away, not attack him. "But you want to keep up your guard because you never know," he says.

That's why Mr. Rhodes always takes a partner along when hunting for nests. One time, he was digging eggs out of a nest in tall grass when the mother came up from behind. His helper shouted a warning. "I bopped her on the nose with the boat paddle, and she jumped in the water," he says.

On a later visit, the same mother refused to back down. Mr. Rhodes kept swatting at her with the paddle while his partner emptied the nest.

Once he has the eggs, Mr. Rhodes hatches the baby-alligator families, which are called *clutches*, in special boxes in his backyard. Hatching baby alligators gives him a way to study them at this precarious time in their lives. Mr. Rhodes always returns each baby to its mother's nest.

As young alligators grow and leave their mothers, they wander away from their homes, looking for food, a mate, or a new place to live. Usually they travel at night. If an alligator is far from the marsh when the sun comes up, it will look for someplace cool and dark to hide, such as under a car. In warmer months, when alligators are busy roaming, Mr. Rhodes is busy rounding them up.

"They are very shy animals, and that's what most people don't realize," Mr. Rhodes says. "The animals view us as a threat. We tower over them."

A Healthy Fear

Some alligators don't slink away. Those that venture into places such as boat landings or golf courses can lose their fear of humans. Too often, people feed the alligators. Expecting food, some of these reptiles have approached people and attacked them. Alligators found in developed areas are often destroyed to protect people.

Once, a big alligator swam into a water pipe and ended up behind a drainage grate at a large store's parking lot. People saw the alligator and called Mr. Rhodes. The alligator was about nine feet down in the pipe.

"I laid down and crawled into the drain up to my belly," Mr. Rhodes says. "Someone held my ankles, and I was kind of bent over in the hole."

Using a long pole, Mr. Rhodes slipped a wire noose, or *snare*, over the alligator's head and tightened the wire around the reptile's neck. He eased the alligator up into the parking lot. Then he slipped a second snare over its snout and let the animal tire itself out by struggling.

While Mr. Rhodes's helpers held the snares in place, he snuck up behind the alligator and squeezed its mouth shut with his hand. Then he snapped a thick rubber band over its snout, lifted the muzzled creature into the bed of his pickup truck, and hauled it away.

"Science is not all lab coats and microscopes," Mr. Rhodes says. "Some of us do get to go out and play and get muddy."

An alligator's camouflage keeps it well hidden in marsh.

Photos by Thomas E. McCarver

From the Author

A friend told me that her husband and lots of other folks here in coastal South Carolina swim in creeks and rivers with alligators. Sometimes, they even swim over to the gators and splash at them to scare the gators away. I wanted to do an article about that for our local newspaper.

The subject of alligators seemed so kid-friendly that I decided to query *Highlights*. (I had always wanted to write for children.) They said they were interested, so I plunged right in. I read *Highlights* all the time to my children, so I was very familiar with the magazine.

When I started talking to folks about alligators, everyone referred me to the *real* gator expert, Walt Rhodes. So I called him and talked to him for about one hour for the newspaper article. In that phone call, I learned enough about his work to know there was good material for a children's science article on Walt and his gator experiences. I set up another interview in person at his office, and we spent about two hours talking.

I had already done a lot of background research on alligators for the first article—I probably talked to about six alligator experts around the U.S. I also interviewed (over the phone) another scientist Walt works with on his research.

I did not make an outline, but I had a general plan. I wanted to teach kids that alligators are not as scary or aggressive as most people believe, and to back that up with Walt's stories of catching alligators. Of course, I also wanted to tell kids that alligators are wild animals and can be dangerous if they're disturbed.

I tried to include the anecdotes that were most dramatic and riveting. I included quotes that weren't full of scientific jargon, but said something interesting in words that kids could understand. I like to use quotes to sum up or support a point that the story is making. I had a word limit that I'd gotten from the *Highlights* writers' guidelines, so I tried to stay within that limit. That forced me to make some hard choices about what to include.

About six months after I submitted the article, an editor wrote back to say he would like me to make some specific revisions and resubmit it. He was not offering to buy it, only to look at it again. But his suggested changes were outlined and clear, and he seemed very interested in the subject. So I worked on it again and sent it back a couple of months later. This time he bought it.

My advice is to read the magazine and see what its editors like in terms of subjects. Also, see the depth of the reporting and type of language. Then try to pick a subject that interests you and give it a similar treatment to ones published in the magazine.

I also like to read my drafts to real kids and get their feedback. I have children, so I usually get them to tell me what they like and what they didn't understand. Then I use their feedback to make more revisions.

I have a background in journalism and wrote for newspapers in North Carolina and Missouri before resigning to become a stay-at-home mother. After selling the article to *Highlights*, I attended the Highlights Foundation Writers Workshop at Chautauqua. I started writing poetry for children and, after about 25 rejections, I sold a poem to *Ladybug* magazine. Also, I am working on more nonfiction articles and a novel for preteen readers.

—Pringle Pipkin

From the Editor

Pringle discovered an excellent subject in alligator expert Walt Rhodes. In his day-to-day job, he interacts closely with a species of animal that's of high interest to our readers. He has a dangerous job, and he has a great attitude about it. So Pringle's first step toward writing a great article for us was her ability to recognize a good story subject when she saw one.

Pringle also clearly has a knack for interviewing a subject. She was able to capture anecdotes and direct quotations that reveal Walt's character, the excitement of his work, and a lot of interesting and worthwhile information about alligators.

That excellent groundwork gave her high-quality raw materials for exercising her craft. She might have tried to write an encyclopedic article based on things she had read. Instead, she offered a peek at the life of a person who has adventures on a regular basis—and along the way, our readers learned something about alligators, biology, and wildlife management.

—Andy Boyles, Science Editor, *Highlights for Children*

Highlights for Children
2–12 years
800 words

When This Cracker POPS, Treats Fall Out!

By Debora Sullivan

Crackers are popular party favors. They were first made in France or England during the early 1800s. At that time, crackers were bags of sugared almonds wrapped in colorful paper with twisted ends. Children pulled the ends to make the bag burst, then treats spilled out.

Later, crackers were made from paper rolled into tubes. They were filled with riddles or small toys. People started using special paper that made a loud *CRACK* when the ends were pulled. Sometimes, a small explosive device was used for a loud *BANG*. Crackers today are much the same as they were in the late 1800s. Make the cracker below, and use it as a party favor, gift, or tree decoration.

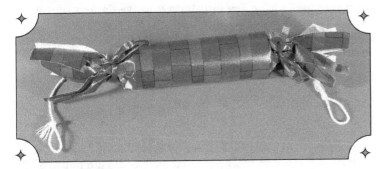

Popping Device

1. Find a cork that fits snugly into a plastic film canister. (Corks are sold at many hardware stores.)
2. Ask an adult to help with this step. Use a ballpoint pen to poke a hole in the bottom of the canister. Use a knife to cut a half-inch section from the cork. Use a needle to poke a hole through the center of the cork section.
3. Cut two 12-inch-long pieces of string. Tie a button onto the end of each string.
4. Poke one string through the bottom of the canister so the button is inside and the string hangs out the bottom. Poke the other string through the cork and pull until the button meets the cork.
5. Push the cork into the canister, button-end first. Tie a small loop on the free end of each string.

Wrapper

1. Cut a 6-inch-by-12-inch piece of gift-wrap paper. Center a 4½-inch-long cardboard tube on a long edge.
2. Tape the paper to the tube, then roll the tube and tape the other end of the paper in place.
3. Put the popping device into the tube so that one string hangs out each end.
4. Gather the paper at the tube end where the string tied to the canister (not the cork) is hanging out. Tie it with ribbon. (The looped string should still be hanging out.)
5. Through the open end, fill the tube with surprises, such as treats, small toys, stickers, messages, and riddles.
6. Gather the paper at the open end of the tube. Tie it with ribbon (with the string still hanging out). Cut the paper at both ends to make fringe.

To *POP* your cracker, put your fingers through the string loops, and pull! The harder you pull, the louder it will pop.

> Test your popping device by putting your fingers in the loops and pulling the cork out quickly. If it doesn't *POP*, you might need a cork that fits more snugly.

From the Author

An article in the Institute's *Children's Writer* newsletter inspired me to try writing a craft piece. The author of the article recommended getting first writing credits by starting small. He suggested studying children's magazines and submitting crafts, recipes, games, and other fillers as a way to get a foot in the door with publishers. The article also discussed the high demand for holiday and seasonal items.

I always loved the tradition of Christmas crackers so I went to my local library and did some research. I also sent away to a company in Canada that makes Christmas crackers to get more information. I decided that children would enjoy learning about the origin of this tradition and could make them as a fun holiday project.

I studied several children's magazines and concluded that *Highlights for Children* was a good match for the piece. I made several prototypes of the craft, which originally was decorative and didn't actually pop, then wrote the piece that included a brief history of Christmas crackers, directions for making them, and ideas for fillers. I submitted the article and was thrilled to receive a letter from *Highlights* asking me if I could rework the craft so that it would pop, and resubmit the piece on speculation.

It took a lot of experimenting to get the cracker to pop using only household items, but after a lot of trial and error I devised a popper using a cork and a film container. I resubmitted the article and it was accepted for my first sale.

When writing craft pieces for children ages 6 to 12, it is important to make as many prototypes as necessary to streamline the directions to their clearest form. I strive to keep craft pieces to no more than five steps.

Since the first Christmas cracker article, I have had many other craft articles accepted by *Highlights for Children*. I have also contributed to *Hopscotch*, *The Parent Planner* newspaper, the SCBWI *Bulletin*, and a book titled *Look What You Can Make with Egg Cartons* (Boyds Mills Press).

—Debora Sullivan

From the Editor

When Debora first sent this manuscript to us, I liked it for several reasons: The craft seemed fun to make; it could serve as a great gift; and some historical context was included.

As I recall, however, in the original manuscript the cracker did not make a popping noise when it was opened. I believe that Debora had intentionally left this out because historically, explosives were used for that effect, and she knew that we wouldn't publish something like that in *Highlights*. Without some kind of popping effect, though, I felt that part of the fun was lost, too, so I tossed the challenge back to Debora to revise the craft so that it would have an acceptable (i.e., non-explosive!) popping device.

She met the challenge with great success and created an ingenious device out of a cork and a film canister that gave a loud, satisfying pop when activated. Best of all, the popping device could be reused (which you can't say about gunpowder!).

She also sent me her backup about the history of "crackers," which was very useful to me when I was checking the manuscript for accuracy. Overall, I was thrilled with her revision; it was a pleasure to buy and publish this craft.

—Judy Burke, Associate Editor,
Highlights for Children

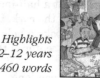

Highlights
2–12 years
460 words

In the F🍊🍊d M🍎🍎d

Can you turn FOOD into FUEL by changing one letter at a time?
Use the hints to help you.

F O O D

___ ___ ___ ___   If you don't eat, you're one of these.
___ ___ ___ ___   The refrigerator keeps foods _____.
___ ___ ___ ___   A black lump of rocky fuel.
___ ___ ___ ___   Wear one of these to stay warm.
___ ___ ___ ___   Water surrounding a castle.
___ ___ ___ ___   A great source of protein.
___ ___ ___ ___   Food energy will let you accomplish a fantastic _____.
___ ___ ___ ___   Build a healthy body from your head to your _____.
___ ___ ___ ___   Eating properly makes you _____ great!

F U E L

(See answers on page 72.)

Answer:

F	O	O	L
C	O	O	L
C	O	A	L
C	O	A	T
M	O	A	T
M	E	A	T
F	E	A	T
F	E	E	T
F	E	E	L

From the Author

Many children's magazines are always on the lookout for creative puzzles, so I started to play around with words. I knew one type of puzzle was to "turn" a word into another by changing one letter at a time. Since *Jack And Jill* promoted health-related subjects, I worked with two, four-letter words that I felt "fit" together: FOOD and FUEL.

The puzzle itself was fun to make. I enjoy playing with words, just as some people enjoy doing crosswords, and there is a great sense of accomplishment when you've actually created a unique puzzle.

Of course, the acceptance of "In the Food Mood," my first publication in a children's magazine, was a thrill. So much so that I'd often wonder, "Oh, I hope no one finds anything wrong with it (despite the fact that my entire extended family had 'proofed' the puzzle for me)."

—Joanna Emery

From the Editor

Ms. Emery's word puzzle fit in well with several other items in our "Puzzle Pages." It was originally titled "Word Ladder," which we changed. The only other work we did with the puzzle was to shorten some of the clues to fit them into the art design.

—Daniel Lee, Editor, *Jack And Jill*

Jack And Jill
7–10 years
75 words

A CHILLING Thrill

Or was it a thrilling chill?

By Karen Dowicz Haas

My new school's ski trip seemed like a good idea to my mom, who was holding up the slick new ski jacket she'd just bought for me. Mom must have imagined me—her seventh-grade daughter, Carly—and my new rosy-cheeked friends sipping hot chocolate beside a roaring fire. Maybe she thought I'd spend the weekend dashing through the snow in a one-horse open sleigh, bells jingling.

After all, she knew I couldn't ski.

"So? You'll learn," she said, conveniently forgetting that I was nearly ten before I could manage a two-wheeler.

"But I don't really know anybody . . . ," I said, afraid to admit the whole truth. I'd been in school for months and still had no friends.

"And what better way to get acquainted?" she said.

Obviously I had no clue.

After hours on the bus with rival boom boxes blaring the entire length of the New York State Thruway, we finally arrived at the slopes. The wind chill made the temperature feel like ten below, so I distributed the tubes of lip balm my thoughtful mother had sent to prevent chapping.

After my classmates smeared on smudge-proof all-day protection, I snapped photos, the proof Mom wanted that I was having fun. My best shot was of some guys on the football team. Their lips had turned hot pink.

My ski lesson went well. I learned how to break skis. Bindings snapped off under my uncoordinated legs.

"It's OK," the instructor said. "That's supposed to happen. Sometimes it keeps you from getting hurt."

"Sometimes?"

He pointed to the plaster cast on his ankle. "Avoid the moguls," he said.

"Real estate moguls? Developers who turn mountains into ski resorts?"

"Nah," he said. "Moguls are mounds of snow. Bumps on the slope."

He repaired my skis and sent me toward a rope that was mysteriously moving up the mountain.

"Stick with the bunny slope," he said.

"Is the bunny named Godzilla?"

My pink-lipped classmates, who were either seasoned skiers or fearless fools, had deserted me and raced for the lift lines to Mounts Denali, Rushmore, and Vesuvius. I shuffled to Godzilla's leash, tucked in my lucky scarf, and grabbed on.

The icy rope slid through my mittens. My frostbitten fingers gripped tighter and harder but to no avail. Fidgety four-year-olds stiffened up behind me. As I turned to apologize, a knot reached my hands and dragged me up the hill with the force of a tidal wave.

It was only fitting that Beach Boys music started blasting out of the speakers in the lodge: "Surfin' U.S.A." Little kids in goofy hats surfed by me on snowboards. Slush swooshed into my face. My nose dripped into my lip balm.

Higher and higher I went up Mount Bunny until I reached the peak from which, theoretically, I would ski down.

I wiped my nose and surveyed the situation. I considered riding the rope back down, but the snickers from the snowboarders would be too humiliating. Peer pressure is a terrible thing, especially from kids half your age.

I reviewed what I'd learned. The instructor had said to point your ski tips

together to stop. He called it "snowplowing." Where I'm from, we use a pickup truck with a giant blade in the front.

He kept saying to "slalom" down the mountain, a term I later realized means to zigzag. Frankly, I thought he'd said "salami." I figured they had a gourmet deli on the hill. All these people would need to eat.

With this wealth of knowledge, I slid off. I followed the tracks of the child who'd gone before me. Since her ski tips eventually plowed together, I stopped. No problem. Turning, however, took some maneuvering. I couldn't seem to do it.

Finally I squatted, figuring

that the closer I was to the snow, the easier it would be to fall. Skis together, aimed directly at the ski-lodge door, I zipped down the hill.

The cold air suddenly turned fresh and exciting. I felt like an Olympic champion. At long last, the thrill of skiing! That my eyes were frozen shut only added zest.

I snowplowed to a stop and entered the lodge. My cheeks tingled from the warmth of the crowded room, and the biggest, most ridiculous smile took over my face.

"I'm still here," I said, practically bragging to the crowd. They didn't erupt with applause, but they didn't pelt me with snowballs either. Actually, nothing had changed. Just my attitude.

Without thinking twice, I

went up to Marie, a girl from my math class. "Hi, I'm Carly," I said. "Fracture anything yet?"

We'd been studying fractions all week, but she missed the common denominator of my joke.

Her face reddened. "They had to stop the ski lift so I could get on," she said. "I wanted to die."

"Aw, that's nothing," said a kid named Joey as he leaned in. He took off his cool sunglasses. "I had to change my name and put on a disguise after the Ski Patrol chased me for going too fast."

"Look what happened to me!" said a guy behind them. He wore a bike helmet, and the exposed hair that peeked out around his face was frozen into stiff, curly ringlets. Matt Hall. We rode the same bus every day but hadn't said so much as "Hi" before.

"I did a belly flop to avoid the tree that jumped into my way," he said with a smile.

Marie and I laughed. And to my surprise, I discovered that my mother was right. I'd forgotten that I was a social misfit. What better way to get acquainted?

Matt, Joey, Marie, and I hit the slopes again.

The ski slopes? No way! Instead, we went dashing through the snow. No horse, no sleigh. We were the kids tobogganing near the lodge on the backs of our ski jackets.

From the Author

An editor at a kids' magazine I'd been submitting to needed a humor piece for a winter issue, pronto. I remembered my first feeble attempt at skiing. I quickly put together something that I hoped might work for her. My first try was pretty much a series of jokes.

I submitted the manuscript to Mary Lou Carney at *Guideposts for Teens*. She rejected my effort, but gave me a clue why. She mentioned the importance of growth and change in the main character.

When I saw *Highlights* had "adventure stories" as the theme for its annual contest, my first thought was that instant thrill that comes from skiing. This time, though, I made sure the character's story came first. I incorporated a few of those hard-thought-out ski jokes, and then entered this story in the *Highlights* contest.

Six months later, I found out it didn't win. However, Rich Wallace, the Senior Editor, told me it was a finalist. He told me what he liked about it, and what he didn't think worked for *Highlights*. He also said the ending needed more detail. At his suggestion, I rewrote. This third substantial revision had a more satisfying ending. Then, we pruned away some of the beginning that didn't serve the story's needs.

I worked from the premise that almost every frightening experience is, in hindsight, extremely funny. I brainstormed and listed all the funny/frightening bits that created my own first skiing experience. I tried to put the funniest parts together into a story that made sense. When that didn't work, I reversed the process. I wrote a story that made sense and then I put the funny parts into it.

My advice would be to think not only about humor, but also about the story you want to tell. While jokes are fun and may be written first, they are actually secondary. Humor must serve the interests of the story.

I chose to write in first person because I think kids like to read stories told in first person. I know I do. Plus, if you look at what magazines are printing, you'll see many first-person stories.

I've been reading *Highlights* almost all my life, both as a child and as an adult. I respect its mission of fun with a purpose. For new writers, there is no better opportunity than *Highlights for Children*'s annual contest.

I am a mother of three school-age children, and I've been concentrating on writing, rather than selling what I write. Alas, at this very moment, I have no other professional credits in the children's market (though I have started to check my messages and e-mail frequently hoping to connect with that lucky editor who will finally recognize my genius). Still, I keep at it. Am I crazy? Stupid? Both? Perhaps so, but I'm also a writer. And I'm happy.

—Karen Dowicz Haas

From the Editor

We immediately knew that this story would appeal to our readers because of its honest, kid-like voice and its humor. The narrator has the same sorts of insecurities and self-doubts that many kids that age must overcome, and she has just enough objectivity to see the humor in her own situation. She pokes fun at herself and others, but not in a mean-spirited way. And her resolution seems very realistic. The narrator takes a few small steps and ends up with a significant gain. Karen created a character that our readers can identify with and thus gain some useful insight into making friends.

—Rich Wallace, Senior Editor,
Highlights for Children

Highlights for Children
2–12 years
980 words

My little brother would believe *anything.*

Herman

By Peggy Tromblay
Illustrated by John Hanley

I shouldered my fishing pole, clutched a battered tackle box packed with lures, and followed my 7-year-old brother, Darryl, out the screen door and into the dark.

"Grandpa said we should get an early start if we want to catch Herman," Darryl said.

"I don't think he meant leaving now," I said, stifling a yawn. "Besides, Herman isn't even real."

"Oh yeah, Stevie? What about Mr. Bailey's scar?"

I rolled my eyes. Darryl would believe anything Grandpa and his friend Mr. Bailey told him.

Yesterday, the first day of our vacation, Grandpa had introduced us to "the folks" in Hermansville . . . there were probably 50 in the whole town. Main Street was only two blocks long and dead-ended at Hermansville's Pond. The story of Herman, the giant fish, was a legend in the town.

When Mr. Bailey met us, he had peered over the top of his glasses and asked our grandpa, "Charlie, you warned these boys about Herman, right?" He held out his pudgy hand. A jagged scar zigzagged along his index finger. "Let me tell you, he's one mean fish. Nearly took my finger once."

I looked up at Grandpa, who's always telling me I'm too smart for a 12-year-old, and winked. But Darryl, poor Darryl, stood there wide-eyed, eating it all up.

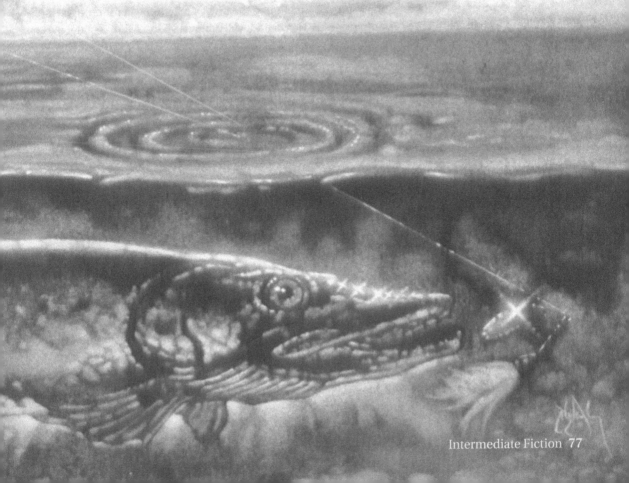

Now, walking to the pond, I reminded Darryl, "Mr. Bailey's a butcher. He probably cut himself. You swallowed that whole fish tale hook, line, and sinker, didn't you?"

Darryl spun and pointed to the "Herman Sundaes" sign hanging over Lowe's Ice Cream Parlor. "Yeah? Then what about *their* scars, huh?" Mr. and Mrs. Lowe had both showed us scars on their fingers and told us they'd gotten them trying to land Herman.

I laughed. "Oh, Darryl, welcome to Hermansville, where *everyone* has a scar." By now we'd reached the pond. "There are probably ten fish in the whole pond. They named the biggest one Herman. Then they made up fish stories about him to keep themselves entertained in this hick town. Any questions?"

Darryl stuck out his lower lip. The morning sun peeked over the horizon.

I slapped him on the back. "Come on. We came here to fish, didn't we? You pick the spot."

Gravel tumbled and spilled into the pond as we slid down to the water's edge. "Here," Darryl said.

We snapped on our lures.

"Let's see if there are any fish in here." I cast my line into the middle of the pond as the sun climbed higher into the sky.

Between casts we slapped away the mosquitoes and horseflies. By noon, the only things we'd successfully snagged were stringy green weeds and rocks.

"Maybe Herman's just sleeping," Darryl said, sounding hopeful.

Didn't this kid ever give up? Then I saw it. "Look!" I pointed. A huge fin sliced the surface and glided through the water. "Now *that's* a fish!"

Darryl scrambled beside me to see.

Aiming, we cast our lines into the pond. Our splashing lures sent a three-foot-long fish leaping from the water where it lingered as if mounting itself on air. Silver scales shimmered like diamonds in the sunlight. Outstretched fins waved, beckoning to us. Then, twisting its head, the fish's beady black eye aimed a dare our way.

"It's HERMAN!" Darryl cheered, watching the fish, the size of a small shark, plunge back into the water. We cast eagerly, again and again.

I was reeling in, about to lift my lure from the water when I felt a yank on my line. Instantly, my pole tip kissed the water and a whizzing sound filled the air. I jerked my pole upward and leaned back as the line ripped from my reel. "I've got him!"

Darryl threw down his pole. "Reel him in, Stevie!"

My line sliced the water, curving left, then right. I was grinning and holding on tight, imagining the town's reaction when I brought Herman to Mr. Bailey's shop. All of a sudden, the pitch of my pole changed. I looked down. Panic set in. "I'm running out of line!" I yelled. "Grab the net! He's going to get away!"

I braced myself, yanked hard, and . . . tumbled backward into jagged rocks.

My lure, leader, and line were gone, swimming away inside Herman's mouth. Staring at the limp line dangling from my pole, I punched the ground. "He got away."

I hugged my knees and rested my chin on my arms. I'd snagged a huge fish, but without proof, no one would believe us.

"Hey!" Darryl said, pointing to my hand. "You're bleeding!"

I rinsed my hand and peered at the gash from the sharp rocks. It hurt, but it didn't look too deep.

Darryl slapped my back. "Welcome to Hermansville, Stevie, where everyone has a scar! Any questions?"

Sometimes Darryl is too smart for a 7-year-old.

From the Author

I discovered "Herman" while mining my favorite childhood memories. That huge fish definitely existed and, for all I know, is still lurking in the depths of that pond. But back then, everyone we told about that monster fish dismissed us and tried to discount our reality with various explanations of what we probably saw. Trying to convince people who haven't seen what you have is nearly impossible, and that's the premise I used for this story.

I tapped into that momentous day and recorded, as my 12-year-old self, every memory, sensory detail, and emotion of a tiny town with a tiny pond and two kids who witness the unbelievable.

First person was a natural point of view for me with this story. After all, I was writing from experience, and I easily sank into the character. The tomboy in me became Stevie and this became Stevie's story.

The biggest dilemma with the early drafts was getting myself to let go of reality and play with "what if" scenarios. My first two drafts rambled on for about 1,100 words. Unfortunately, they also contained more details than necessary and a less than stellar ending—the real one.

This story, as it really happened, didn't contain a conflict or provide readers any resolution. Critiquers challenged me to get the story down to 900 words, begged for meatier characters, and asked for a stronger, more satisfying ending. I did a lot of chin-tapping and rereading.

Keeping the disbelief aspect in the forefront, I worked on various conflicts. First I tried the boys proving Herman's existence to the town. Too broad. Then just to Grandpa. Nothing at stake. Finally I tried Stevie vs. Darryl. Ah hah! And with that decision, I discovered my main character. Revision was fun and exciting once I knew the direction of my ending.

I needed to show readers Stevie didn't believe in Herman and that he thought Darryl was gullible because he did believe in this crazy tale. In a few select sentences, I flip-flopped Stevie's attitude, introduced his age, gave him a little ego, and let readers in on his disbelief—the important ingredient for his upcoming change. Suddenly everything made sense. To heighten the odds, I added the townspeople's tales and scars and suddenly the ending was obvious. Stevie would earn a scar and become a believer.

I used dialogue to showcase my characters' personalities and their points of view. Every word had to sound real, true to character and reveal story details I didn't want to explain in narrative. I found success in speaking the dialogue out loud and typing exactly what I said.

I used narrative for backstory, scene setting, passing time, and providing a window into Stevie's mindset. In later drafts, I reduced narrative to a minimum and sandwiched it between action and dialogue. It needed to appear natural in the story.

Five months later, "Herman" was ready for travel at a whopping 875 words. Time for marketing. After many hours in the library reading various children's magazines, I selected *Guideposts for Kids*. Their fictional stories held humor, great characters, and best of all they were almost always written in first person, like "Herman." I submitted it.

Then I began to chew my nails as that little demon of doubt jumped on my shoulder and began chanting, "Herman's just another fish tale about the one that got away." "Don't get your hopes up." "I can't believe you couldn't come up with something more original."

When my SASE returned a month later, I remember pulling it from the mailbox and staring at the little "YES" sticker on the outside of my envelope and thinking the mailman was playing head games with me. When I opened it I discovered a cheerful contract inside. Suddenly, the YES sticker made complete sense. They want it! I sold it! In that second, I graduated to a real writer.

Since "Herman," my publication credits include the NESCBWI website, finalist in a *Pockets* fiction contest, another sale to *Guideposts for Kids*, and one to *Pockets*. I am a former

Assistant Regional Advisor for the Wisconsin Chapter of SCBWI and belong to several critique groups.

Besides being a writer, I hold a wide variety of "side jobs" including working part-time at an insurance agency, substitute instructional aide, baseball and volleyball coach, and director of the district's volleyball camp. My favorite to-do's include reading/writing, playing, and best of all, laughing.

—Peggy Tromblay

From the Editor

Because I only purchased six to eight stories annually for *Guideposts for Kids*, I could afford to be picky. And I was! We read over a thousand manuscripts a year to cull that half dozen or so.

"Herman" is exactly the kind of story I like— and I believe kids like, too. For starters, adults are only bit players in this drama. The boys are center stage. I like, too, the sibling relationship, which is teasing and tender at the same time. And, of course, when the younger brother turns out to be right, the ending is all the sweeter. Also, I was drawn to the way the author "ties it up" at the end by having Darryl throw Stevie's words back at him *and* having Stevie acknowl-edge that his younger bro is one smart cookie, just like him. All in all, the piece is kid-friendly and compelling, with a strong voice and a well-focused plot. And that's what makes editors cut contracts and checks!

—Mary Lou Carney, Editor-in-Chief, *Guideposts for Kids*

Guideposts for Kids
6–12 years
800 words

Hats Off to Sally

By Nancy Jean Okunami
Illustrated by Ralph Butler

"Jeremy, take off that hat please," Miss Allran said as she passed out quiz papers.

Jeremy complained as he plopped his hat onto the floor beside his desk. A few minutes later, when Miss Allran turned to write on the board, he put his hat back on. Miss Allran didn't notice, but I did because Jeremy sat right next to me, smiling and waiting for me to give him the thumbs up for his boldness. Unimpressed, I went back to working on my quiz.

"Psst! Psst!"

I looked up. Jeremy was pointing to Sally Winfield on the other side of the room.

"If she gets to wear a hat, I get to wear a hat," he said, whispering.

"Sally has cancer, you goof," I said, also whispering.

"So!" he said without feeling.

"So? So, she's

lost her hair—from chemotherapy."

Jeremy looked at Sally, then again at me. He shrugged and shook his head.

"When you have cancer, the doctors give you really bad medicine to help you get rid of it," I said. "It can make you sick to your stomach and stuff like that. But you gotta do it or you could die."

"How do *you* know that?" Jeremy asked.

"My aunt had cancer," I said. "Sometimes she was too sick to leave the house. And when her hair fell out, I remember she cried. I feel bad for Sally."

"Jeez!" Jeremy said. "If she's that sick, I don't want her near me. I'm keeping my hair."

"Cancer's not contagious," I said. "Some people get it and some people don't. But you can't catch it."

Jeremy stared some more. "Hmmm, I'll bet she's probably embarrassed about her hair," he said, sympathetically.

"Don't stare," I said. "When my aunt lost her hair, she said dealing with the weird looks people gave her was sometimes harder than dealing with the way the medicine made her feel."

"Is your aunt OK now?" Jeremy asked.

"She's in remission," I said, smiling. "That means her cancer's gone . . . and her hair's growing back."

I looked at Sally. I wondered if it might make her feel better to know I knew someone who had had cancer and who was getting better. Or maybe if Sally wanted to talk, I could like "be there" for her or something.

I wanted to help, but since I didn't know her very well, I felt funny about walking up to her

and asking a bazillion questions. I did know one thing about her—she was brave. To sit in class and take a test like nothing else was going on in her life, and with her hair missing, well . . . that was braver than I could ever be.

Suddenly I heard Jeremy's hat hit the floor again. Sally must have heard too because she looked over at him and smiled. This time I approved of Jeremy's boldness. He gave Sally a thumbs up and smiled back.

Celebrate

A Hug Is Always in Order

Remission

Go Hat Shopping Together
One place we could go is:

_____

Show You Care
One thing I can do to show I care is:

_____

Talk About It
One thing I could say is:

_____

Ask Questions
One thing I could ask is:

_____

Diagnosis

Questions

1. Have you ever had something happen to you that made you feel like you stuck out (like a bad haircut or a black eye or a broken arm)? How did it make you feel when others stared at you? Do you think it would have made you feel better to be able to talk to them about what had happened? Do you think it would have made them feel more comfortable about you?

2. Smoking accounts for 85 percent of all lung cancer deaths and may be attributed to one-third of all cancers in the United States. Did you know that the companies that make cigarettes are required by law to print on cigarette packs a warning that smoking cigarettes can cause cancer? Why do you think people ignore the warning and smoke anyway?

Activity

People who are fighting cancer often feel frightened and alone. True, you may not be able to walk in Sally's shoes, and you can't completely understand how it feels to be wearing them, but you can walk beside her and help her on her difficult path from cancer to remission. Follow the path at left and stop and consider how Sally might be feeling along the way. Stop at each question and jot down something you could do to help Sally feel a little better.

From the Author

I am a cancer survivor, so I wanted to write something about that. To me, the memory of being told that I had cancer and fretting over the thought of losing my hair to chemo felt bigger than the memory of realizing, "Hey, I could die." I was getting married soon, and it seemed clear to me that I would be a less nervous bride if I could count on having hair to attach my veil to. I had to reprioritize my thoughts, and remind myself that I was an adult and could handle this. The thought of being a *child* with no hair slipped in. I thought about how children sometimes tap into extraordinarily strong places inside of themselves to deal with things. How would their peers deal? What if their peers were harsh? The story took shape from there, and I let it sit until I found the perfect market.

For this story, I began with a character and a feeling. When you have cancer, you have to go through things alone. So, I wanted my character to be alone in her thinking with others looking on. That's why I had her taking a test—also a very solitary thing.

Before taking the Institute of Children's Literature course, I had always written in third person. I took a cue from my instructor's own writing and mixed that with some of her comments and changed my writing style. For me, writing in first person gives me wings. I've toyed with the idea of going back to third person, but I'm just too comfortable to go back again.

The magazine I chose for "Hats Off to Sally" had a completely different style than my own writing. It was strange to write in a way that fit the style of the magazine rather than in a way that fit my own voice. And because I tend to use humor, it felt unnatural to stifle that urge—because this story needed to be more straightforward. But that's what targeting magazine stories is about—targeting. And once you say you can do it, you can.

I offered revisions, but my story was published exactly the way I wrote it. I was pleased with that and like to think that it was because I revised it four times. I usually start with an idea, write whatever comes out (glancing at my word count at key times to make sure I am not writing a 2,000-word story versus a needed 500-word story), and then look at the finished product. I revise first for glaring holes in logic and clarity; then revise to make it smoother; and then do a final flow/punctuation revision before letting it sit for a day or two. Revision number four involves letting my husband read it because he is even more of a perfectionist than I am. I resist the urge to ever say "good enough" and send it out before I feel it's the best I can do.

A children's market guide ran an article about focusing on niche markets. It made sense. The words of Anita Jacobs of *Winner* and *Listen* (in the article) piqued my interest; so I checked *Magazine Markets for Children's Writers* and read more about them. Then I sent away for writers' guidelines and sample copies, read the samples from front to back to get a feel for what they wanted, and made some notes. I pitched six ideas via snail mail hoping Anita would choose one. Anita e-mailed me back choosing THREE. I sold her all three, with "Hats Off to Sally" being the first one they published.

My advice for new writers in crafting stories for this age level is, please, never lecture. Read until you get a true feel for what is successful with that age group, and when you think you understand fully what works, go to a local school and volunteer to read during a library hour. This one act alone will quickly dispel any myths you have about fifth-graders liking Grandma stories . . . unless you have Grandma wielding a baseball bat threatening to pulverize the next person who puts a finger on her antique Brazilian pipe collection. Kids would welcome a Grandma like that into their lives. The cookie-baking-knitting-an-afghan-Grandmas are from *your* memories, not theirs.

I have published over 100 articles and stories (fiction and nonfiction), with more than 50% targeted to children. I am a former Regional Advisor for the Society of Children's Book

Writers and Illustrators and write full-time. My first middle-grade novel manuscript, *1504 Bean Street*, is being considered, while I work on my second novel, *The Decrepit Touch of the Crotchety Baroness Barinoff.*

—Nancy Jean Okunami

From the Editor

When I am looking for a story for *Winner* magazine, I look for it to be relevant to the needs of my 10- to 12-year-old readers and meet the mission of *Winner*, which is to help children want to live a positive lifestyle.

"Hats Off to Sally" fit our needs. Sally has an illness that touches, directly or indirectly, many children across the U.S. This story was a way to teach children that they do not need to fear people with this disease and gave insights into how they should treat them. I felt the author did this very tactfully, but in a way that would hold a child's attention.

Other areas that we approach are family issues: divorce, sibling rivalry, abuse, friendships. And our main focus is on abstinence from abusive substances: tobacco, alcohol, and other drugs.

—Anita Jacobs, Editor, *Winner*

Winner
8–12 years
490 words

On the same team

By Danielle S. Hammelef • Illustrated by Mary Chambers

My legs felt like rubber bricks, and my heart was pounding so loud I had to shout my thoughts to myself. I rested my hands on my knees, gulping air, as sweat dripped from every pore of my body.

"Give me three suicides!" shouted Coach Salinger.

I lined up next to my best friend, John, along the baseline of our high school gymnasium.

"Hey, Kyle," John panted.

"Are you ready for these again?"

I had secretly hoped Coach Salinger had forgotten about this exercise for today's tryouts, or would at least give us a break. After the two previous days' tryouts, I knew why they called them "suicides." I watched as the guys in front of me raced to and from the closest free-throw line, the half-court line, the farthest free-throw line, and finally

to the far baseline.

"If you want to make this team, you have to give 150 percent!" shouted Coach Salinger, as I dashed up and down the court. "You have to work harder than you've ever worked before. Let's go, Brooks! Pick it up!" My chest tightened as I heard him call my name. I wanted to make the school basketball team more than anything, and I didn't want to make any mistakes. My legs just wouldn't give anymore, and I stumbled over my own feet. I pulled myself up and mustered a jog to the baseline.

"Gather 'round," said Coach Salinger. "Names of those who made the team will be posted on my office door Monday, immediately after school. If your name is on the list, there's a brief team meeting scheduled for Monday at three o'clock here in the gym. For those who don't make the team, there's always next year. Have a good weekend."

"A good weekend?" I said, panting, as John and I headed for the locker room. "This'll be the longest weekend of my life. Do you think you made it?"

"Don't know, and I don't want to think about it now. I just want to go home and stare at the TV," said John.

"Well, if I make it and

you don't, I'll quit, okay?" I said. "I don't want to be on the team without you. Okay?"

"That's crazy. If I make the team and you don't, *I* won't quit."

"I just assumed we were friends."

"We are, but friends don't ask each other to quit something they love, just because the other person can't do the same thing. Come on, would you really quit?"

John and I used to do everything together, but since we'd started junior high, John had changed. I guess I hadn't realized how much till now. "See you Monday," I said, and walked out.

After the last bell sounded Monday afternoon, I wasn't the only one to rush for the gym. A crowd of guys was already swarming around Coach Salinger's doorway when I got there. Some left giving each other high-fives. Others looked like their dog just ran away from home. I scanned the list, assuming I'd see my name. *I must have missed it*, I thought. I searched again. I was stunned. I couldn't believe it! I didn't make the cut.

"Hey, Kyle! Did you make it?" asked John.

I tried to answer, but there was a lump in my throat. I shook my head no, and ran from the gym to my bike, chained outside. As I fumbled with the lock, I heard quick steps approach me from behind.

"Hey. Are you okay?" asked John.

I couldn't keep a tear from sliding down my cheek. "No!" I said angrily. "I really wanted to be on this team!"

"I know you did. It's the pits that you didn't make it, but, hey, like Coach Salinger said, there's always next year."

"That's easy for you to say. *You* made the team."

"If it helps, I thought you played well enough to make the team."

"Yeah, well, obviously Coach Salinger doesn't think I'm good enough. I don't think there'll be a next year."

"Oh, don't say that. I've got to go to the team meeting. I really *am* sorry you didn't make it. I'll call you later, okay?"

"Don't bother," I said, under my breath, as John walked away. "Some best friend!"

"Kyle! John's on the phone," my mom shouted, later, from downstairs. I shuffled over to pick it up.

"Hi," I said, without enthusiasm. "How was the meeting?"

"Nothing exciting," said John. I could tell from his tone of voice that he wanted to tell me all about it, but was hesitant. "We got our practice and game schedule. Boy, Coach Salinger's going to work us hard."

"Not 'us', John, remember? Just you. I'm not part of the team."

"Sorry, I didn't mean. . . ." John's voice trailed off.

We sat without saying anything for what seemed like hours. I wanted to ask him why things had changed. I wanted to tell him that I wanted us to want the same things, that I wanted us to do the same things, and most of all, that I was afraid we wouldn't be best friends anymore. But I couldn't say it. Then I remembered the time when I'd won the school spelling bee and John, who had been eliminated from the competition, cheered me on, all the way to the state finals. I realized that now it was my turn to cheer on John, even though it wouldn't be easy.

He finally broke the silence. "Will you come to my games?"

After a long pause I replied, "Only if you come to mine."

"Yours?"

"Yeah. I'm going to sign up for our church's basketball team." I surprised myself as much as I did John.

"It's a deal," he said. I could hear his grin over the phone. ⚫

From the Author

My dream of being a published children's writer came true when I opened the acceptance letter from *On the Line*. No lottery winner has jumped around and shouted as much as I did that day. I called everyone I knew. I wrote a letter (full of exclamation points!) to my Institute instructor who had encouraged me to market "On the Same Team," which I'd completed as Assignment 6. The acceptance letter and copy of my first paycheck as a professional writer hang on the wall behind my computer today.

My main character is a fictional version of myself. In Assignment 6, I had to write a story based on a real incident from my past. I chose a vivid and painful memory from fifth grade—when my best friend made the school basketball team and I didn't. I chose to throw my main character right into the tryouts to hook the reader with an action opening. Once I had the beginning scene, I let the story unfold on screen. Keeping my audience in mind, I decided to use only a few scenes and eliminate any that didn't move the story forward. Sometimes my best ending scenes are those that surprise me.

On the Line had a surprise for me as well when I received my contributor's copies. Originally, my story was written from a girl's first person point of view, but *On the Line* changed my female character to Kyle. I write most of my stories in first person because it allows the readers to *become* my characters.

I like to use dialogue to reveal a character to readers. I always read my stories out loud several times and listen for awkward passages or stilted dialogue. I have someone else read my stories too, because I sometimes fail to see a word or sentence that doesn't fit. I listen to others' thoughts on my work with an open mind, but only make changes that I believe will make my story stronger.

The most difficult part of writing this story was coming up with a title. After brainstorming for days, I put my toddler in a stroller, grabbed a pencil and paper, and went for a walk. About five minutes from my house, my main character told his best friend, "I wish I was on the same team as you," and I knew I'd found my title.

"A Winner! To Market," my instructor's note read at the top of my assignment. This task seemed daunting, but I dug through the *Magazine Markets for Children's Writers* and found my story matched several magazines' needs, including *On the Line*. After receiving several rejections from other magazines, *On the Line* purchased "On the Same Team."

Besides *On the Line*, my stories, articles, and poetry have sold to *Cricket*, *Pockets*, *Horsepower*, *Kids' Highway*, *Devo 'Zine*, and the *Education Center*. I am a Society of Children's Book Writers and Illustrators' Magazine Merit Award winner for my story "Please, Not Daryl!" published by *On the Line*.

—Danielle S. Hammelef

From the Editor

The story was well written, with humor and natural-sounding dialogue. The story line of a boy who hopes to make the team and then has his dreams dashed appeals to kids because it's the type of thing they go through all the time. The added dilemma of Kyle's best friend making the team and how Kyle would decide to react gave an interesting twist to the story. The story ends in a satisfying way, without Kyle miraculously being on the team after all, but with his choosing friendship over pride.

—Mary Clemens Meyer, Editor, *On the Line*

On the Line
9–14 years
950 words

The Great Coat Chase

By Karen S. Hopkins • Art by Elizabeth Rocha

On Wednesday afternoon we were rushing down the highway after a coat! "Hurry, Mom!" I yelled.

It all began when our class started collecting coats for people in need. Twenty coats was our goal. After many weeks, we had gathered 17 coats of different sizes and styles. Our teacher, Mrs. Parker, said she was proud of us. Only three more coats to go!

On Wednesday, after two more were collected, Jessica Graham raised her hand. "I think I can bring in another one!" she said proudly.

"Great!" exclaimed Mrs. Parker. "That will make 20!"

Jessica thought she was so perfect! It made me mad. Did she care about kids who needed warm coats or did she just want to be the one to bring in the 20th coat?

I was still upset when I walked into the house on Wednesday after school. But I stopped fast when I saw what lay on the sofa. A girl's red coat! Mom must have collected it for my class! I grabbed it and ran down the block toward school. Mrs. Parker was still there.

"Tania!" she exclaimed. "Did you forget something?"

"This coat! Number 20!" I said, gasping for breath.

"Thank you very much!" she said, giving me a huge smile.

I skipped all the way home. I had just brought in the 20th coat!

Back at home, I told Mom what I'd done. Her eyes opened wide. "That was Jessica's coat!" she said with alarm. "Jessica just got that coat yesterday, and I was going to shorten it as a favor for her mother."

"I thought someone from your work had donated it!" I cried.

"You should have asked first, Tania!" said Mom. "We have to get it back!"

We hurried to school, but my classroom was dark and the coats were gone. We stopped at the office and left a message for Mrs. Parker to call us immediately.

When Mrs. Parker called back, she told us she had taken the coats to a collection center in Brimby, five miles away. So off we went again.

At the collection center, Mom described the coat to a worker. "I think it was chosen by someone who just left," said the worker. As we looked out the window, we saw a man and a girl driving away in a rusty old pickup truck. There in the back was Jessica's coat!

We rushed to our car and hurried after them.

They stopped at the railroad tracks as the gates began to lower. What luck! A train was coming! Mom honked her horn as we stopped behind them. She tried to shout to the man from her window, but the train was too noisy.

After the train passed and the gates had lifted, the man drove on. They turned into the driveway of a small house. We pulled in behind them.

The man and the girl got out of the truck. As Mom started to explain, the girl reached into the back of the truck for the red coat. She clutched it tightly.

"I'm very sorry," said Mom.

The man shrugged. "Just a mix-up," he said. Then he told the girl to give us the red coat.

Mom and I drove home with Jessica's coat. But I didn't feel happy about getting it back. I felt awful. I had seen the look of sadness in the girl's eyes and I knew it was my fault.

"We better tell Mrs. Graham what happened," said Mom. "I'll hem this coat Saturday. Then Jessica can donate her old coat, and your class will have reached the goal."

The next day at school Jessica said, "I heard what happened. Your mom called my mom last night." But instead of smirking at my mistake, Jessica told me her idea. She wanted to keep her old coat and give her red one back to the girl. I couldn't believe it!

After school, Jessica and I packed the red coat in a box. Mom drove us to the store

where I used my allowance money to buy red gloves and a scarf. We added them to the box on our way.

After we had given the new red coat to the girl, Jessica and I walked back to the car arm in arm.

"You brought in the 20th coat after all," Jessica said with a smile.

"No," I replied as we hopped in the back seat. "It was your coat that was the 20th."

But neither of us really cared who had brought it in. We knew the most important thing was sharing with others.

From the Author

The schoolchildren where I live often participate in fund-raisers and service projects to help those in need. One day, I observed a disturbing trend. Many children were getting caught up in the competition of collecting "the most," or getting some designated "prize," and losing sight of what was important—helping others. That's how the idea for "The Great Coat Chase" came about. I decided to write a story about a girl who gets caught up in the competition of just such a project, and what happens to her because of it.

I selected the first-person point of view (something I rarely do) because I needed the main character, Tania, to tell the story in her own voice, letting the reader in on what she's feeling every step of the way.

After writing, revising, and revising many more times, I still felt the story needed something more, so I let it sit for about a week. As soon as I picked it up again, I got the idea to have Tania use her own money to add a scarf and gloves to the coat box. This helped show that Tania truly understood the meaning of the project.

The final challenge I faced was finding the perfect title. I must admit, none was forthcoming until my husband read the story and immediately told me what it should be called! His title was not only a good "hook," but sounded just like something Tania would use to describe the events of her story.

After studying sample magazine issues, I sent "The Great Coat Chase" to three magazines before it was accepted by *Story Friends*. Six months later, I was thrilled to see my first story in print! I have since had over 30 additional pieces (stories, poems, and articles) accepted for publication by various children's magazines, but that first one will always be special.

—Karen S. Hopkins

From the Editor

Talk about a first impression! Karen's first sentence is a great example of a real attention-grabber. How could I not be compelled to read on to find out why they were chasing a coat down the road? She gets our attention, then goes on to tell the story of how the protagonist got to this point. Too many writers begin with a lot of informational background rather than jumping right into the story. An important skill for a writer is to know how to weave the background naturally into the story.

Karen also did her market research in targeting this piece for *Story Friends*. We look for stories that deal with the Mennonite concern for social issues, especially in the natural way that Karen handled this. It's obvious that Karen kept asking "What if . . . " every step of the way as this story unfolds. Tania, the protagonist, is not perfect—she's real. Her jealousy and competitive spirit get her into trouble. While there is some help from the adults, the girls' choices make the difference and solve the problem. Karen shows through actions and dialogue how Tania discovers that her attitude toward and perception of Jessica has been wrong. She changes appropriately and believably.

Karen did everything right—gave a professional presentation, hooked us with a great opening, created an imperfect protagonist who works to solve the mess she's in, followed all the rules of good story structure, and targeted her market. It all adds up to what this story is— a winner in every sense of the word.

—Susan Reith Swan, Assistant Editor, *Story Friends*

Story Friends
4–9 years
760 words

DISCOVERY trails

FOR KIDS IN SEARCH OF THE TRUTH!

SO WHAT IF PETER DIDN'T HAVE ROLLER BLADES. JEREMY WAS SURE HE COULD WIN.

THE NEW NAME

Illustration by Randy Rider

By Nathalie Ryan

Jeremy and Peter paused in front of the Leisure Center bulletin board on their way home from swimming class. A large, orange sheet of paper caught Jeremy's attention.

"Give our Leisure Center a new name," Jeremy read aloud. "Prize—rollerblades, safety helmet, elbow and knee pads—courtesy of Oak Gardens Mall. Contest open to children thirteen years and under."

"That's a great prize," Peter said, pushing his thick glasses back onto his nose.

"It sure is, and I'm going to win it," Jeremy said smugly. "I bet I can think of a really cool name."

"What would you do with new rollerblades?" Peter asked, frowning. "You got a pair for your birthday two months ago."

"I'll have two pairs, that's all," Jeremy said, shrugging. "I can have two pairs if I want."

"Yeah, well some of us don't even have one pair of rollerblades," Peter said, frowning. "Mom can't afford to buy me a pair. Maybe I'll try to win the prize."

Jeremy frowned. How could Peter compete against him? He put his hands on his hips angrily. "I bet I can think of a better name than you can."

"No, you can't," Peter said. His face started turning red. "I can think of a ton of good names for the Center."

"Prove it," Jeremy challenged. "Come over to my house tomorrow before swim class and show me."

"OK, I will," Peter answered then stomped away.

As Jeremy watched Peter walk away, he felt a knot form in his stomach. *That probably wasn't the way Jesus would have acted*, he thought, dropping his head. *But I've got as much right to win the grand prize as anyone, don't I?* Jeremy slowly turned around and walked home alone.

That night Jeremy lay on his bed, staring out the window at the bright, full moon. *I know Peter wants rollerblades,* he thought. *Maybe I should help him win . . . Nah. He's too clumsy to rollerblade. He should stick with swimming. That's his sport.* Jeremy rolled over to go to sleep. He could feel the knot in his stomach getting bigger.

The next day, Peter arrived at Jeremy's house as promised. He walked into Jeremy's bedroom with a sheet of paper in one hand and his beach towel in the other. "Did you think of any names for the Center?"

"Not really," Jeremy admitted. "I was too busy thinking about winning the prize."

"Well, I've got a whole list of names," Peter said proudly, waving the paper like he would a flag on Independence Day. He stopped waving and smiled. "I'll pick my favorite on the list, then you can pick one too."

"Thanks, Peter," Jeremy said, feeling the knot in his stomach tighten.

"That's OK," Peter said modestly, handing Jeremy the list. "I've got a lot of names. I can't use them all."

Jeremy took the list from Peter and scanned it. There were at least twenty names on the list. Jeremy focused briefly on the first name— Lifetime Leisure Center. *That's not bad.* Jeremy continued down the list. A name caught his eye. It seemed to pop out at him. "I found one!" he shouted, jumping to his feet. "The Fun and Fitness Center!"

"OK," Peter said, laughing. "You can enter that name if you want. I'm going to use Lifetime Leisure Center."

The two boys hurried to the Leisure Center. Before going to their swimming class, they stopped at the office to fill out their entry forms for the contest.

"The winner will be announced a week from today in the gym at 4:00 P.M.," Mrs. Reardon, the receptionist, said as they dropped their entries into the box.

A week later, Jeremy and Peter waited with several other kids for the contest winner to be announced.

Mrs. Reardon stood at the far end of the gym beside a metal table under the basketball hoop. "All the ideas we received were very good," she began. "It's too bad we can pick only one

name. After careful consideration, the new name for our community's Leisure Center will be . . . *The Fun and Fitness Center,* suggested by Jeremy Johnson."

I can't believe it, Jeremy thought. *I won!* He made his way through the crowd. The kids clapped, and some patted Jeremy on the back as he passed.

When he reached Mrs. Reardon, Jeremy turned and searched the crowd. He spotted Peter standing apart from the others, his back against the gym wall. Peter's shoulders were slumped, and he stared at his old running shoes. The knot in Jeremy's stomach felt like it was the size of a bowling ball.

Jeremy swallowed hard. *I don't really need a pair of rollerblades,* he thought. *I can't believe I'm being so selfish. This isn't how Jesus would want me to act.* He said a quick prayer for forgiveness then turned to face Mrs. Reardon.

"Congratulations, Jeremy," she said, shaking his hand.

"The winner had my name on it, but it was my friend, Peter Anderson, who thought of the new name," Jeremy said proudly. "I'd like to give the prize to him, if that's OK." Jeremy felt the knot in his stomach melt away as the words came out of his mouth.

The next day, Peter was holding onto Jeremy's arm for support. "I'll never get the hang of these rollerblades," he said. "I didn't think it would be so hard." Peter's legs wobbled. Suddenly, his right foot shot forward.

Jeremy grabbed Peter with his free hand before he could fall. "You're doing fine," Jeremy told him. "Peter, I'm sorry I was so selfish about the contest. I wasn't acting like a Christian should. I'm glad you won. Now we can rollerblade together."

"I can't be mad at my best friend." Peter wobbled back and forth. "Who would teach me to rollerblade?"

"I think roller-falling is a better name for what you're doing." Jeremy snickered as Peter's legs flew out from under him and he sprawled on the pavement.

"Oh, ha, ha," Peter said, rubbing his backside. "Very funny."

From the Author

The idea for "The New Name" came from a local newspaper article about a contest to rename something. I got the idea that it would work as a children's story if I could think of something plausible that children could rename. That's when I thought of renaming a community/recreation center.

I often start my stories with a situation or event. The next step is to think of a pair of characters that will interact within the situation and decide which of these kids will be center stage. At this point, I flesh out my protagonist by doing an in-depth characterization session. Then plotting the story is usually easy, as with "The New Name."

The first draft generally flows easily after my earlier planning. The number of revisions that I do depends on the story. "The New Name" was revised quickly. Others take a lot of work. Once I'm satisfied with a story, I let it cool for at least a week before doing a final revision. I catch tons of spelling and grammatical errors this way. I also check that my story has a good flow, or rhythm.

When I'm done with the writing process, I make a list of possible markets, keeping in mind the message of the story and word count. If there are magazines on the list that I'm not familiar with, I contact them asking for a sample copy. This is extremely important. *Discovery Trails* was not the first magazine I submitted "The New Name" to. It was the fourth. That's actually pretty good. I now have another story published that took 10 tries before it found a home. Unfortunately, rejection is part of the territory.

My advice for anyone writing for 8- to 12-year-old children is to use lots of dialogue and sneak in sensory language whenever possible. Listening to how kids talk and interact helps a lot. What works for me is having many writing projects on the go at once, so that I can move to something new if a current project isn't working for me on a particular day.

Currently, I'm in the planning stages of my first novel. I'm also working on a sci-fi novella written in diary format. And naturally, I've got three new short story projects in varying stages of completion.

—Nathalie Ryan

From the Editor

We knew rollerblading appeals to this audience. Boys as characters also appeal to the audience, and the characterization of Jeremy and Peter was realistic—easy for boys to identify with them. The story opens in an interest-grabbing decision-making scene and is carried by dialogue and action throughout.

The theme involves friendship and sacrifice for that friend. Selflessness is an example of what Jesus would do. This spiritual emphasis was added as an intrinsic part of the story to show how living for Jesus is a part of how a Christian should act every day. Giving the prize to his friend was done in a way that would not embarrass him and became a part of their joy of learning together.

Some changes were made to shorten the story to fit our space, but the intrinsic story was retained.

—Sinda Zinn, Editor, *Discovery Trails*

Discovery Trails
10–12 years
1,000 words

2 + 2 = Baseball

By Eric J. Teichroew

Mark walked out of the coach's office and slammed the door behind him. Looking down the school hallway, he saw Dan, his best friend, drinking from the water fountain.

"Hey, Mark. What did the coach want?" Dan asked, wiping drips off his chin with his sleeve.

Mark kicked a locker, and the bang echoed in the empty hallway. "He wanted to suspend me from the baseball team—and he did."

"What? *Why?*" asked Dan.

Mark took off his Yankees baseball cap, revealing his shiny head. His favorite college baseball player, Kenny Wills, had shaved his head for the playoffs, and so Mark did, too. He stared down at his feet, and kicked the locker again. "Because I'm failing math," he replied.

"You're *still* failing?" Dan asked. "But I thought you passed your last test."

"Forget it, Dan. I don't want to talk about it." The last thing Mark needed was another lecture. He knew he'd get an earful at home. He kicked the locker door one more time, and turned to leave.

Dan picked up his backpack and followed Mark to the front doors. "So," he said, "what are you going to do? Beating up poor, defenseless lockers isn't going to solve your problem."

Mark laughed and gave his friend a playful punch on the arm. Outside, he breathed in a deep breath of fresh spring air. It felt great after being cooped up in boring classrooms all day. Usually he would be at baseball practice, but Coach

had suspended him from all team activities.

"I have it all worked out, Dan," he said. "I'll be back on the team before you know it."

"What do you have worked out?"

"Promise you won't tell anyone?"

"That's a stupid question, Mark. You know your secrets are always safe with me."

Mark stopped and looked around. "I'm going to make cheat notes for the next math test and ace the thing," he whispered. "Then I'll be passing math and be back on the team."

"Cheat notes!" Dan cried. "Are you crazy? They'll suspend you from school!"

"Not so loud, Dan," Mark said nervously.

They walked in silence for a couple of blocks. "I don't get it, Mark," Dan finally said. "Why don't you just study like everyone else? Only losers cheat."

Mark stuffed his hands in his pockets, and sighed. Dan was a great friend, but he didn't understand Mark's reputation on the baseball team. To his teammates, Mark was "cool," because he never studied for anything. Baseball was his life. He didn't have time to stare at schoolbooks, and he didn't want to, anyway. "It's under control, Dan," he said. "I have to get back on the team, and this is the quickest way."

"Don't you mean the *easiest*?" Dan said angrily. Before Mark could reply, Dan took off down the street, and disappeared down a back alley.

In math class the next day, Mrs. Williams reviewed material for the next test. Mark tried to look busy, like he was taking notes. Instead, he was writing formulas on little strips of paper to hide in his calculator case. That way they'd be easy to get to during the test.

When the bell rang, Mrs. Williams stopped him before he could leave the classroom. "Mark," she said, "I think it would be a good idea if someone helped you study for Monday's test. I talked to Ernie Kraely, and he's agreed to tutor you over the weekend."

Ernie Kraely! Mark tried not to laugh. Ernie was the nerdiest of nerds, and he didn't know a thing about baseball. *Like I'm going to spend time with this guy?* Mark thought. *I don't think so!*

"No thanks, Mrs. Williams," he said, stifling a snicker. "I'll be okay."

"Mark, you're failing math. I think you would be wise to take his help."

"Okay, Mrs. Williams, I'll think about it." He left the classroom, shaking his head. *Ernie Kraely! That's a good one.*

The last bell of the day blared, and Mark raced out of the school. It was going to be a good weekend. The Yankees were playing the Red Sox, and he wouldn't miss it for anything. He looked around the busy schoolyard, trying to find Dan. There was no sign of him.

At nine o'clock that night, Mark tuned the TV to the local sports station. The lead story was about Kenny Wills, but not about his latest game-winning heroics. The reporter was saying Kenny had paid someone to steal exams, which he'd use to cheat on his finals. He was suspended from college, and a hearing was to be held next week. Mark stared at the TV. *Boy, this is too weird*, he thought. *But Kenny cheated big-time. I've only made a few lousy cheat notes. It's not the same thing.*

On Monday morning, Mark bumped into Dan in front of the school. "Hey, Dan," he said, with a big smile. "Did you see the Yankees this weekend? They destroyed the Red Sox!"

"I watched a few innings," Dan said, "but I studied most of the weekend."

"Too bad. You missed some great games."

"You're going to do it, aren't you?" Dan asked, frowning. "You didn't study all weekend, and now you're going to cheat."

"Quiet, Dan!" Mark hissed. "The whole school doesn't have to know about it."

Dan glared at him, and left without saying another word. *He'll get over it,* Mark thought. *Once I'm back on the team, everything will be okay.*

Mark fidgeted as he waited for Mrs. Williams to hand out the math tests. She laid a copy on his desk, and Mark looked up at her with a nervous smile. He stared at the first question, and took a deep breath. This was it. There was no turning back now. He grabbed his calculator.

Fifteen minutes before class ended, Mark was finished with the exam. He couldn't wait to find out his score. He tiptoed up to Mrs. Williams and quietly pleaded with her to grade his test now. She said yes, and Mark crept back to his desk.

The bell rang, and Mark waited for everyone to leave the room. Mrs. Williams placed her reading glasses on her desk, and looked up at him. "Well, Mark," she said. "How does 87 percent sound?"

He jumped out of his seat and shot up to her desk. A big 87 percent was written in bright red ink on the top of his test. "Wow," he said, grinning from ear to ear. "Am I passing math?"

"Yes, Mark. You're now passing math. Well done."

Mark walked out of the classroom, pumping his fist as he went down the hall. Turning the corner, he nearly hit Dan. "Eighty-seven percent, Dan!" he yelled. "Can you believe it? Man, it feels great to pull off a mark like that!"

"Yeah, congratulations, Mark. You cheated your way back on the baseball team. That's real impressive. Now, get out of my way. I have to get to my next class." Dan brushed past him.

"Wait a second. What's the matter? This is good news. I'll be playing ball again!"

Dan stopped and whirled around. His face was just inches away from Mark's. "Good news?" he started to say. Then he looked over Mark's shoulder, and his eyes narrowed. "What are you looking at, Ernie? Get lost. This is private."

Mark wheeled around to see Ernie Kraely, standing behind him.

"Hi, Mark," said Ernie. "I was curious about the math test. How was it?"

"Why should you care?" Dan asked impatiently.

"W-well," Ernie stammered, "I spent the weekend tutoring Mark, and I wanted to know how things went."

Dan stared openmouthed at Mark. "You studied with Ernie?" he asked.

Mark looked down at the floor and shrugged his shoulders. "Thanks, Ernie," he said. "I did great. I got 87 percent. Thanks for all your help."

"Wait a second," Dan demanded. "You *didn't* watch the Yankees play? You *didn't* cheat?"

"Yeah. I guess I'm not as 'cool' as I pretended to be. I couldn't sleep Friday night. I kept thinking about Kenny Wills. I may have copied his haircut, but I wasn't about to copy his suspension."

"You're a nut case, Mark."

"Not anymore, I'm not. Getting an 87 was a rush. Hey, Ernie, how do you feel about the New York Yankees?"

From the Author

"2 + 2 = Baseball" was created while taking the Institute's course, *Writing for Children and Teenagers*. Assignment 5 required a description of a child engaged in an activity, followed by an inner portrait of that child. At the driving range one day I noticed a boy hitting golf balls. He was wearing a Yankees cap and he seemed very athletic. I took note of his actions and mannerisms, and he became the basis for my character, Mark.

Assignment 6 asked for a story using the character from Assignment 5 as the protagonist. I knew the story had to be about baseball, but I needed a conflict for Mark. Because he was competitive, a clear conflict would arise if Mark were prohibited from playing baseball. This conflict would be dramatized if his suspension resulted from his own failure. I decided that Mark would be failing math, get suspended from the team, and his challenge would be to get back on the team. The title of the story came to me before I wrote it. "2 + 2 = Baseball" seemed to be a catchy title that incorporated the story's theme.

My instructor liked my title, but she had numerous revision suggestions. In my original story, I didn't introduce Mark's conflict early enough; he didn't study; he failed his math test, and he never got back on the team. He was left thinking what he should have done, instead of actually doing something to overcome his problem. He would need help and this could be accomplished by adding his teacher (Mrs. Williams) to the story, along with her encouragement for Mark to accept a tutor.

I rewrote the story for Assignment 7. I introduced Mark's conflict earlier, and I put the idea of cheating in his head. I wanted the reader to think that Mark was cheating to solve his problem. This added to the story's climax.

I originally wrote the story in the first person. Because this is a difficult approach to master, my instructor suggested that I try writing the story using the third-person point of view. Third-person writing allows more freedom in storytelling and doesn't restrict the author to the language of the narrator. By changing to third person, I found it easier to adhere to writing's cardinal rule, "show, don't tell."

After my instructor returned Assignment 7, I introduced Kenny Wills earlier in the story and added internal narratives to show Mark's thoughts. I reviewed the *Children's Magazine Market* directory for a magazine that was looking for contemporary fiction for intermediate readers. *On the Line*'s requirements fit my story and its word length. Much to my surprise and excitement, they purchased my story. It was my first submission, and that made it extra special.

I am an accountant, and during my early years of studying and putting in long hours, I let my "writing" dreams fall by the wayside. Thankfully, my wife and son came along, and their encouragement turned me in the right direction.

—Eric J. Teichroew

From the Editor

I needed a story about a boy that was appropriate for spring, and this story fit the bill. In addition, I felt it had a good message for kids about choosing good role models and avoiding the temptation to cheat. The twists of humor, especially the surprise ending, were a plus.

The boys seemed real—I could hear real junior high boys saying the words. With light editing, the story was ready to go.

On the Line is a Christian magazine, and I was happy with the values promoted in "2 + 2 = Baseball."

—Mary Clemens Meyer, Editor, *On the Line*

On the Line
9–14 years
1,400 words

IN WOLF HOWL HOLLOW

By Noreen Kruzich Violetta
Illustrated by Deborah C. Wright

Grandpa walks tall and towering, just like the trees that rocket up above our heads. Grandpa knows a special place; he calls it Wolf Howl Hollow.

"There will be wolves," he whispers.

I smile a shaky grin, but I walk a brave step forward, hold Grandpa's hand a little tighter. I hum a tune, and it evens out my smile.

"Who—Whooooo," rattles a broken tree.

"The dark is full of song," smiles Grandpa.

I hum a little louder. Grandpa hums a little too as he says, "Singing takes away the goose bumps." I bite my lower lip.

My feet stop where the trees line up at the meadow. Tonight I will not turn back before it's time to leave.

Grandpa taps my shoulder. Something moves in front of me—please let it be my feet! Fireflies drift 'round and 'round us like tiny flashlights showing us the way.

We climb the big rock that I know by daylight. By night, it's twice as big. And there we sit like statues. We face a wall of tall, lean timbers that holds our visitors.

Grandpa cups his hands about his mouth and lets go a string of howls that sails to the moon. It's like sending signals. We listen for the wolves.

I sketch them in my head. To me they dot the

forest like checkers on my game board. They slip one by one between the trees and move ahead, space by space, with each whoop and holler Grandpa makes. Their shadows flow like long, black capes.

But Grandpa says real wolves don't dress up like grannies, don't eat Red Riding Hoods, and don't huff and puff and blow your house in. No—Wolf Howl Hollow wolves are real.

For a long, long time, maybe more, I do not move. I am the rock I sit on. And like the field I sit in, I'm wide open to the dark. All around us sings the night. And then it happens.

"Owooo," trickles through me right down into my toes. And straight out of the trees, like a fairy tale come true, the wolf slides out swishing through the moonlit grasses. Two pups are tucked within her shadow and bumping close behind. Their tails turn and heads toss about.

Again, Grandpa calls into the night.

Again, Mama wolf answers.

Grandpa taps my shoulder. I part my lips, but nothing sounds.

Mama wolf with those moons for eyes, looks straight at me.

She lifts her muzzle, closes tight her eyes, and shoots a howl that rings straight past my ears.

I face the moon, close tight my eyes, and pump out a howl to fill the sky.

"Ow—ow," chases my own call.

The pups, with heads rolled back and eyes shut tight, are speaking to the stars with me.

And I begin to dance, but my feet— they do not move.

From the Author

I am an avid hiker and for years have longed to hear the howling of wolves. I can remember wishing to hear them on trips into the wilderness when I was a kid.

After moving to Canada, I made it a quest to hear wolves. I will never forget the first time I heard a whole pack of wolves howl along with the pups. It was a symphony with so many different tones blending together. It took me off my feet. I have heard a pack twice since that time, and it is a rare treat for sure. It's captivating!

I often take a notebook on my treks into the wilderness. I tend to lean toward natural history topics and take notes when I am with experts out in the field or at nature organization functions. I also research what themes magazines have coming up, and target topics of interest to me. I use the same research to write more than one story or article. A nonfiction piece I wrote on wolf howls appeared in the same issue of *Boys' Quest* as "In Wolf Howl Hollow."

Readers have to go there with you, so I tried to create a dramatic moment; one that makes you quiver with anticipation. I chose word pictures that would set the scene and aid in building up the moment.

I felt that this story was stronger in first person and would have more impact on the reader. I didn't want the reader to be watching on the sidelines. First person presents only what the protagonist can see, hear, feel, or think.

I revise until I've molded every word to flow, to fit, to sound like the voice I want. I can't remember how many times I revised this piece, but probably at least a dozen.

I targeted the magazines I knew published nature related topics. I found out that *Boys' Quest* had a "Forest Animals" and a "Night Creatures" theme for future issues. The editor took my nonfiction piece first and then told me later that she wanted the fictional piece as well for the same issue. Of course I was elated! The time between my submission and publication was two years.

Try to remember yourself at the age you're writing for, and make sure your writing voice doesn't sound like the adult perspective on the topic—especially in fiction. Ask yourself, how would a child see this? You'll find it's different than how you would describe it as an adult. Find a fun angle to a story, a unique twist. And don't hand young readers encyclopedia jargon.

Know the magazines you pitch to. I go out and buy magazines that I want to target for articles/stories. I look them over for content, style, word count, etc.

I've been writing most of my life, but only recently for children. Currently, I am the Regional Advisor for the Canada Chapter of the Society of Children's Book Writers and Illustrators. I juggle my time between writing magazine articles for both adult and children's publications.

—Noreen Kruzich Violetta

From the Editor

"In Wolf Howl Hollow" fits the theme on "Night Creatures." Instead of using a great deal of dialogue, the author's descriptions make it easy for the reader to visualize the moment. You feel like you are the young boy present with his grandfather. I also like the idea of the boy going out on an adventure with his grandfather and perhaps overcoming some fear of the wolves.

—Marilyn Edwards, Editor,
Boys' Quest

*Boys' Quest
6–13 years
480 words*

It Takes Time

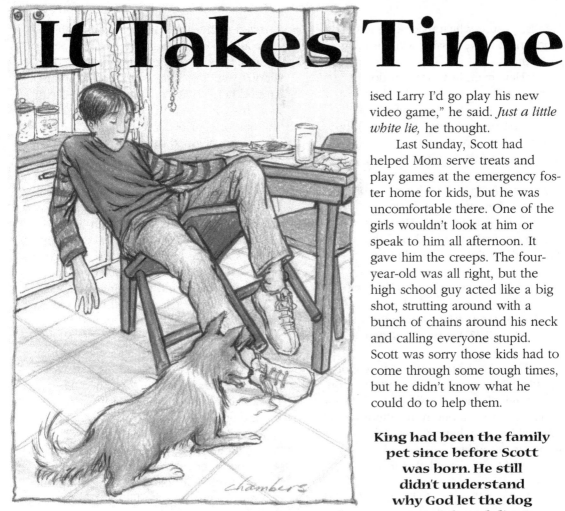

By Lael Hoerger
Art by Mary Chambers

Scott Thompson closed the screen door without making a sound and tiptoed across the back porch. His wiry frame glided noiselessly down the steps. *If I'm not around, she can't ask me,* he thought. He combed his dark brown hair back with his fingers and sighed.

"Scott," his mom called, "are you coming with me?"

Scott froze. "Not today, Mom. I prom-ised Larry I'd go play his new video game," he said. *Just a little white lie,* he thought.

Last Sunday, Scott had helped Mom serve treats and play games at the emergency foster home for kids, but he was uncomfortable there. One of the girls wouldn't look at him or speak to him all afternoon. It gave him the creeps. The four-year-old was all right, but the high school guy acted like a big shot, strutting around with a bunch of chains around his neck and calling everyone stupid. Scott was sorry those kids had to come through some tough times, but he didn't know what he could do to help them.

King had been the family pet since before Scott was born. He still didn't understand why God let the dog get sick and die.

At least visiting the children's home had taken his mind off King for an afternoon. It hurt to think about his dog. King had been the family pet since before Scott was born. He'd never known a day without the dog until last month. He still didn't understand why God let King get sick and die. He'd tried to pray about it, but he felt like God had forgotten him.

With his head down and his hands jammed in his pockets, Scott shuffled over to Larry's house, kicking a stone along the way.

He wasn't sure which made him feel worse right now, missing King or lying to Mom.

"Hey, man, how are you doing?" Larry asked as he opened the door. "How about some help with my curve ball?"

Scott pushed past Larry and plopped down on the sofa. "Got any new video games?" he asked, ignoring Larry's question. *Being with Larry is a lot better than spending time with those weird kids,* Scott thought. He focused on having fun with his friend, and thoughts of King and the lie soon faded away.

"How can you even think of having some sick dog come here, after King suffered like he did?" he blurted out.

When he came home from school Tuesday, Scott overheard Mom talking on the phone. "Tomorrow? Well I . . ." she hesitated. "How about in the afternoon? My son will be here then." Quiet. "Thank you so much. Good-bye."

"What was that all about?" Scott asked.

"I was talking to Collie Rescue," Mom said. "It's an organization that nurses neglected or abused collies back to health and finds good homes for them."

Scott couldn't believe his ears. "How can you even think of having some sick dog come here, after King suffered like he did?" he blurted out.

"It won't be a sick dog," she said. "The Collie Rescue people take care of collies till they think it's safe for them to be someone's pet. Of course, the dog will still have a way to go; and being in a different place might set him back a little."

Scott's face turned red, and his eyes filled with tears. This was more than he could take right now. He wasn't going to accept Mom's logical explanations. "I don't want any dumb, sick dog whining around here. That's asking for trouble," he said, his voice cracking. "This is definitely not one of your better ideas, Mom."

Mom stepped toward him, to put her arm around his shoulders, but Scott pushed her hand away and bolted up the stairs.

He lay on his bed, arms behind his head, and stared at the photograph across the room. He and King had been happy on the day that picture was taken. They'd spent the weekend in the country with Gram and Gramps, exploring the woods and following the creek. Scott always felt safe and happy with King by his side. He wanted to feel that good again, to get rid of this empty feeling.

Scott was in a gloomy mood at school the next day. He slouched in his seat, chewed on his pencil, and watched the clock. Larry tried to cheer him up at recess, but it didn't work. At lunch, Scott couldn't eat. After a while, he shoved his untouched tray in front of Larry, who took it greedily.

"You're a bottomless pit," Scott said.

"Pits need to be filled," Larry said, with his mouth full.

After a few bites, he thought he felt something tugging on his foot. Dropping his chair back on all four legs, he looked under the table.

When he finally got off the school bus, Scott was relieved. At least he didn't have to be with all those dumb kids for a while. He headed straight for the fridge. "The cafeteria food was really gross today," he told Mom. "They called it Texas Hash, but I'd call it Texas Trash." He made himself a baloney and cheese sandwich and scooped three mounds of chocolate ice cream into a dish. "Now, that's *real* food," he said. Just as he took his first bite, the doorbell rang.

Mom walked quickly to the front door. "Three?" she said, in a surprised voice. "Oh, all right." She held the door open, and three collies and the Collie Rescue Team trooped into the living room.

"We want to see how each dog interacts with the family, and then make the best match," said the man in charge.

"Scottie, come and see this!" Mom called.

"In a minute," Scott said irritably, taking a bite of sandwich. Deliberately he ate slowly, tipping his chair back on two legs and looking out the window. He couldn't bring himself to go to the living room, and he wasn't sure why.

"Come on, you fearless tugger," he said softly. "It's okay, boy."

After a few bites, he thought he felt something tugging on his foot. Dropping his chair back on all four legs, he looked under the table. There was a fluffy tan and white collie, with a shoelace clenched in his teeth. The dog tossed his head from side to side, tugging with determination.

"What do you think you're doing?" Scott asked, fighting back a grin. He reached down to feel the collie's soft, thick fur. The dog jumped away from his hand. "I won't hurt you," Scott said. He took a piece of baloney from his sandwich and held it out to the dog. "Come on, you fearless tugger," he said softly. "It's okay, boy."

Scooting on his belly, the dog slowly advanced, sniffed the meat, and then gobbled it up. He licked Scott's hand, enjoying the last bit of flavor. "Hey, that tickles," Scott said, smiling.

That was the beginning of a new relationship. Tugger was the perfect match for Scott's family. At first, the collie cowered when someone raised an arm or spoke loudly. Sometimes, he did strange things like bark at his own shiny metal dog dish or back away from his chew toy, but Scott was patient with him.

A month later, in church, Scott heard the pastor say that God never leaves or forsakes us. He prayed a silent prayer, asking God to forgive his anger and doubt. *And, thanks, God, for sending Tugger to us,* he added. Scott smiled at the thought of Tugger. He was becoming quite a friend. Someone had treated Tugger badly. It would take a while for him to get over it, but Scott would be there for him, to see him through the difficult times.

Later that day, Scott stretched out on the living room floor. Tugger came and stretched out next to him, his nose resting on Scott's stomach. The two lay motionless for a few minutes.

"You're quiet today, Scott," said Mom.

"Mom, I've been thinking," Scott said. "Are you going to the children's home today?"

"Yes. They count on me," said Mom.

"I haven't been there for a long time. I think I'd like to come with you today."

"That's great, Scottie," said Mom. "The kids will be glad to see you there."

"I know," said Scott, as he ruffled Tugger's fur. "I understand now how important it is to be there when someone needs you. I guess if it takes time and patience to build trust with a dog, it's the same with people."

From the Author

The idea for the story came to me when my son's family adopted a dog from Collie Rescue. Much of the behavior of the dog in my story came from the actions of Bailey, my son's dog. Because I am mainly interested in writing for Christian publications, I tried to think of ways to use the story of a dog's recovery from abuse to encourage understanding and acceptance of children in similar circumstances.

At that time, I served as a relief caregiver at a home for abused children who were separated from their parents. The two situations were uniquely alike, and I began to put them together in a story.

I had noticed in the editors' comments in *Magazine Markets for Children's Writers* that some magazines were asking for stories about boys, rather than girls. That's how I decided on Scott as my main character. I worked from a story plan rather than an outline, although I rewrote the story at least four times. I worked on scene shifts and eliminating unessential material and characters. At one point I decided that with such a heavy subject, I had better introduce a bit of humor. So, I worked on that.

I enjoy writing dialogue, and feel it makes the story *real*. It's also fun to get into a person's head and write his or her thoughts, making the person come alive.

I am a former elementary and preschool teacher, Sunday school teacher, and for many years a "Story Lady" to preschools. I serve the community and church in various volunteer ways. Along with my husband of 47 years, I have four married children and twelve grandchildren.

—Lael Hoerger

From the Editor

Losing a pet is something most kids have to deal with sometime. This story addresses the natural feelings of a boy who's lost his dog—sadness, questioning, and not wanting to replace the dog with a new one.

The story makes a nice tie-in between the abused and neglected collie Scott's family takes in and the kids at the emergency foster home where his mom volunteers. Scott doesn't want to be around either the new dog or those kids. But the collie wins Scott over and helps him see that it takes time and patience to build trust.

This story was well written—I did just minor editing. Dogs always appeal to kids, and Scott's questioning of why God let his pet die was something they could relate to—and learn from.
—Mary Clemens Meyer, Editor,
On the Line

On the Line
9–14 years
1,340 words

Dear Dedyshka

By Cynthia Fletcher Rothstein

Illustrations by Eris Klein

Dear Dedyshka,

　　I hate America!!! I don't know why Mama and Papa thought living here would be better than in Russia. Why did they make me come here? I think all the time of our cozy apartment with you and Babushka in Moscow. I can smell Babushka's cabbage and apples simmering on the stove! How I miss you both! English is so difficult. At thirteen I am too old to learn a new language. I am not doing well in school. I cannot even speak to the other girls in my class. They stare at me as if I were from Mars. Life was so much easier in Russia.

　　　　　　Your miserable granddaughter,
　　　　　　Yelena

My dearest Yelena,

　　Life in Russia easier? The quality of life here is improving, but it is not easy. As for cozy, today Babushka is wrapped in three blankets to stay warm. The building owner has decided to turn off the heat during the day to save money. And it is only March! There was no tea at the market, so she sips hot water instead—but from her grandmother's delicate teacup. So, life is not so bad.

　　I am sending you a book to lift your spirits. Although it is a book for children, I think you will find it amusing. It is about a bear from Darkest Peru who finds himself in a foreign land. He is befriended by a kind family who finds his behavior unusual but endearing. Tell me what you think of this Paddington Bear.

　　　　　　Your chilly Dedyshka

Dear Dedyshka,

Thank you so much for the wonderful story of Paddington, the adorable bear from Peru. I found his behavior delightful! The best thing about the book is that it is Russian! I am sick of the tedious English books I must read. I must use the dictionary to understand almost every word.

I am sending Babushka my woolen scarf. I don't wear it because it prickles my neck and makes me sweat. No one at school wears one. Now, when Mama demands to know why I do not wear it, I can say it has been put to better use. Warmth and kisses to Babushka.

Your enchanted granddaughter,
Yelena

My dearest Yelena,

Surprise! The author of A Bear Called Paddington *is not Russian. The book I sent you was a Russian translation from the original English. Go to your library in America and find a copy of it. Now that you know the story, the English should not be so difficult to understand.*

I am glad you found Paddington so delightful. Readers from all over the world have enjoyed his unintentional oddities.

Babushka thanks you for the scarf and tea bags. As April sheds its winter coat, we hope for many warm spring days.

Your clever Dedyshka

Dear Dedyshka,

You are so cunning! I read the whole book of Paddington in English without looking up one word!

When the librarian saw my Russian copy of the book, she showed me a special section of books tucked away behind the staircase—all in Russian! Some are translations from other languages, but some are written by Russian authors.

I am reading a Russian translation of *The Adventures of Huckleberry Finn* by the American author Mark Twain. When I am finished, I will read the original version as well. Huck is a mischievous boy who is always trying to avoid his chores. His adventures are quite entertaining but often lead him into trouble.

Your amused granddaughter,
Yelena

My dearest Yelena,

I am delighted that you have found many Russian and English books to entertain you. As you read more books in English, you will feel more comfortable with the language. Now you must try to speak to your classmates at school.

Your loving Dedyshka

Dear Dedyshka,

Today my English teacher read my homework assignment aloud to the class. I was so nervous, I could not swallow! I thought the other students would laugh at my awful English, but they liked my story! It was short, but Mrs. Cohen said it is the best story I have written.

There is a girl in my class named Katelyn. She is so beautiful, she could be on television. Her hair hangs like a golden, velvet rope down her back, and her blue eyes sparkle like jewels. Everyone at school likes Katelyn, especially the boys. Today, when Mrs. Cohen read my story, Katelyn looked at me and smiled.

On my way home, I walked through the park where Katelyn and her friends go after school. Katelyn called out, "Hey, aren't you the Russian girl in my English class?" (I am also in her science class, but I don't think she has noticed.) I answered, "Yes."

She asked me what my name is. When I replied, "Yelena," she could not understand what I said. "Elaine?" she asked. I was so nervous, I just smiled. She said, "O.K., Elaine, see you tomorrow."

Can you believe it, Dedyshka? This girl, whom everyone adores, talked to me! I think she wants me to be her friend. So you see, I am talking to the girls at school.

Your (soon to be) popular granddaughter,
Elaine

My dearest Yelena,

How nice that you are making friends in school! And your schoolwork is improving, too! Your new friend, Katelyn, sounds lovely. And are you making other friends as well?

Your proud Dedyshka

Dear Dedyshka,

Katelyn is NOT my friend! I will never speak to her, or her horrible friends, again! They are so cruel.

Last week my science teacher, Mr. Lopez, assigned Katelyn as my laboratory partner. I was trying very hard to think of something to say to her; I was so nervous. (My English is still not so good.) I decided to tell her about the book I am reading. I asked her if she knew of Mark Twain. She answered, "No, what grade is he in?"

Dedyshka, I thought she was making a joke. I laughed so hard, tears were running down my cheeks. I'm afraid I disturbed the entire class because Mr. Lopez asked me to tell everyone what I found so funny. So, of course, I had to say what had happened. The whole class laughed, not just me. Even Mr. Lopez was smiling, although I think he was trying not to.

Then I looked at Katelyn. She was not laughing. Her face was as pink as the geraniums in Babushka's window boxes. She ran out of the classroom and did not return. Dedyshka, I'm afraid she really thinks Mark Twain was the name of a boy at our school!

After school I went to the park to find Katelyn and explain. She and her friend Rebecca were sitting on a bench, drinking sodas. When I approached them, Katelyn's eyes blazed, and she announced for the whole world to hear, "Here comes Elaine, the Russian brain. She thinks she's so smart and she can't even speak English." Her sharp laughter was almost a shout. Rebecca laughed, too, like a high-pitched chorus accompanying her.

Dedyshka, I was so hurt. Katelyn did not see me, Elaine. She saw a foreigner, Yelena, a peculiar little bear from Darkest Peru with a strange accent and annoying habits. I did not mean to embarrass her, but she is blaming me because she does not understand. She does not try to understand me because I am different—too different to be her friend.

Your strange granddaughter,
Elaine

My dearest Yelena,

What is strange to some is special to others.

Your devoted Dedyshka

Dear Dedyshka,

Today my teacher, Mrs. Cohen, asked me if I would like to prepare a display on Russia for our International Night celebration. I told her no. I think she was surprised that I refused; many students are preparing displays on countries from which their grandparents and great-grandparents came to America many years ago. Dedyshka, they do not understand what it is like to leave their homeland and live in a foreign place. Why should I give them a reason to laugh at me?

Your cautious granddaughter,
Elaine

My dearest Yelena,

May I send you something from Russia for your display?

Your helpful Dedyshka

Dear Dedyshka,

The strangest thing has happened. Today at the library, I noticed a girl watching me. It was Katelyn's friend Rebecca. I tried to pretend I did not see her, but she approached me and said hello. I mumbled something and turned to leave, but she put her hand on my arm and said, "I'm sorry that I laughed at you in the park the other day."

I did not know whether to believe her. Then she continued, "Sometimes Katelyn expects people to laugh with her."

I said, "Yes, but she does not expect people to laugh *at* her."

Rebecca smiled sadly. "No, she doesn't. She likes to be the one to make jokes about other people."

"I did not mean to make a joke," I explained. "I thought she knew who Mark Twain was."

"I'm sure she does, but she wasn't thinking about books at the time. She spends most of her time thinking about boys. It embarrassed her to sound so foolish."

I wanted to say that was no reason to embarrass me, but I stood looking at my feet instead.

"Are you really from Russia?" Rebecca asked me.

I did not know what to say. Was she also thinking how strange I am?

"My grandmother came from Russia when she was a little girl," she explained. "She used to live with me and my family, but she died last year. I really miss her. I often asked my grandmother what it was like to live in Russia, but she wouldn't talk about it. She would just shoo me away and tell me she was too busy to answer such questions."

"Sometimes it is difficult to explain to someone who has never been there," I said.

"I'm sure it is, but I would like to understand what it's like. My mother told me that Nana was too proud to discuss her life in Russia. Mom said Nana worked so hard to be an American and fit in when she first arrived in this country that she forgot what it was to be Russian." Rebecca looked right into my eyes and said, "Can you imagine erasing your past, your heritage, like that? It's like pretending your family before you, and all they lived through, never happened."

"No," I whispered. "I cannot imagine."

Rebecca's face brightened. "I can't wait to see your display at International Night."

I looked away, and she asked, "You are making a display on Russia, aren't you?"

Dedyshka, until that moment I was certain I was not going to make the display. But my heart spoke for me. "Of course I am," I assured her. "I must never forget my heritage."

So, Dedyshka, tomorrow Rebecca is coming to my house to see some of my treasures. I will show her the nesting *matryoshka* dolls you sent me, Babushka's flowered Ukrainian headdress, my poster of St. Basil's Church, and a photograph of my dear Dedyshka.

> Your lucky granddaughter,
> Yelena

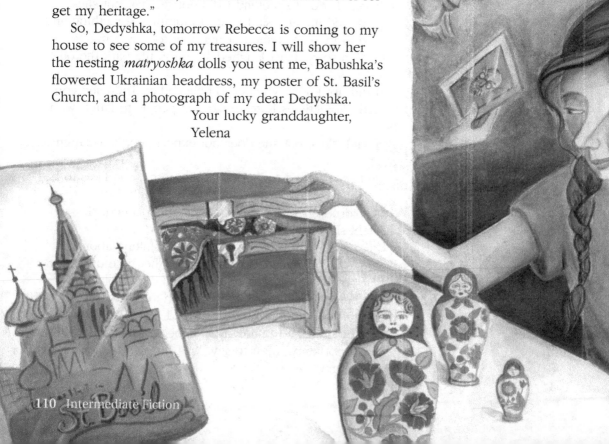

From the Author

The idea for "Dear Dedyshka" originated when I was sitting at the skating rink while my sons had their skating lesson. I was watching one girl practice skills the skating instructor had shown them. This particular girl was by herself, working on her turns. All the other children in the class chose to practice in pairs or small groups, laughing and joking with their friends. I couldn't help but wonder, why is that girl all by herself?

At the time, I was working in a middle school library in a town with a sizeable immigrant population. I would marvel at the progress these children made in learning to speak English in the nine short months of the school year. At the beginning of the year, they would come in alone. They couldn't understand my questions, but they would check out book after book. By the end of the year, they would come in, confidently, with new friends and ask me for certain books.

I put my two observations together: perhaps this young skater couldn't speak English and had isolated herself from her peers because of a language barrier. Eventually I realized I didn't know enough about skating to write about it in detail, so I focused instead on Yelena at school.

Yelena's self-isolation made it difficult for me to write a readable story. Every story needs dialogue, but to whom was Yelena going to speak if she had no friends in America? I hesitated to use a letter format because it can seem so contrived, but in this case I decided it was necessary. And when I decided to whom she would be sending letters, her insightful grandfather in Russia, I realized the exchange could be the solution to the conflict.

The letter format was actually quite easy. It was dialogue, which I find very easy to write. And because letters usually summarize only the high points of the action, I found it easy to keep the plot concise. Only the essential bits of information were exchanged.

First-person point of view is manageable in a letter format. We always write letters in first person. Yelena's letters were about her experiences in America. Dedyshka's letters were, of course, from his point of view, but they were brief, in comparison to Yelena's letters, and only responded to her plot line.

I worked the entire plot out in outline form before beginning to write. I don't always write that way, but this story was an Institute of Children's Literature assignment. The assignment was specifically to write a plot outline before beginning. It worked very well for me.

I never think "theme" before writing, but all my stories end up having one! When I began writing my story plan, I was thinking conflict and resolution. I knew the conflict would be that Yelena was not comfortable in her new home because she couldn't speak the language and didn't have any friends. Having friends is the most important thing to any 13-year-old girl. I liked the universality of that issue. I wanted my readers to realize it doesn't matter what culture you're from or what language you speak; kids from all over the world feel the same about so many things. I was hoping that after reading my story, my readers would be more empathetic the next time they encountered someone who didn't speak their language.

Realistic dialogue is not difficult to create if you can get inside the heads of your characters. You have to understand who your characters are. Yelena is partly me. I have been in her shoes. I lived in Germany for two years, and knew the isolation of not being able to speak the language and the struggle with trying to learn it. If your character is not like you, then it helps to do an intensive character study to learn to think like your character. Once you know your character, you begin to talk like your character.

How I begin my stories depends on the original idea. Sometimes I think of an intriguing character and figure out a way to use that character in a story. What is his or her purpose? How can he or she make a difference in the lives of my readers? Most of the time I think of a situation, usually an odd situation that I want to try to explain. What could be a possible explanation for something odd you observe?

The creation of scenes in "Dear Dedyshka" was determined by the conflict/resolution pattern of the plot. Each scene or pair of letters furthered the conflict/resolution process. Every sentence has to take the reader one step closer to the resolution. There should be almost no "padding" in a story. If a detail does not further the plot or help to explain a character's motivation, then take it out. I try not to have more than four to five scene changes in a short story; otherwise, scene changes are too distracting for the reader.

The best way to acquire a voice that young readers can relate to is to remember what it's like to be the age of your main character. My childhood memories are very vivid. I can remember different stages in my childhood and recall my feelings and reactions to situations. I also read a lot of children's literature to recall aspects of my childhood that may not be as clear.

Dialogue is an excellent way to make readers connect, if it sounds real. As soon as I find myself writing something that sounds phony, I know I've lost my voice. I delete it and begin again, focusing on what sounds real. It also helps to have children of one's own or to hang around other people's children. Volunteer in a school and listen to how the kids talk to each other today.

When I submitted the story to *Cricket*, the editor had about a dozen rephrasing suggestions. Most were reasonable and didn't change the story in any way. I only disagreed with two suggestions, but not strongly enough to insist they publish it my way. I wrote a letter to the editor explaining my reasons for using the words I had chosen, but deferred to her editorial expertise. She left one the way I had written it, and changed the other one!

I was ecstatic, but totally unprepared, to receive fan mail! I couldn't imagine what the fat envelope from *Cricket* was, and couldn't believe it when I discovered I had fans. Two of the girls told me it was the best story they had ever read. A couple of others told me that they had been through similar experiences, and it was so comforting to read of Yelena's experience. Literature has had that impact on me, but I never dreamed I could create that feeling of connection for someone else. Wow!

—Cynthia Fletcher Rothstein

From the Editor

"Dear Dedyshka," by Cynthia Fletcher Rothstein overcame a bumpy path through editorial review on its way to publication. Most publishing houses have a set group of standards by which submissions are evaluated. In our case, we consider the following: Are the characters believable? Does the story flow smoothly? Is the writing fluid? Does the plot line draw the reader in, truly engaging his or her interest and making the child sympathize with the protagonist and want to continue reading to see how the action or drama is resolved?

"Dear Dedyshka" met the standards for narrative flow, engaging protagonist, and character growth, but some of the editors were not entirely comfortable with the epistolary format and felt that it was not well suited to this story. Others were unfamiliar with the complex emotional reactions to assimilating into a new culture that Yelena, the child protagonist, experiences, and they didn't consider it entirely believable.

Cricket Editor-in-Chief Marianne Carus's and my own experiences of assimilating into foreign cultures came in handy in reassuring the other editors that Yelena's situation was not only believable but also quite common. During final evaluations, Marianne Carus, who is always the final arbiter in evaluating manuscripts, allowed the story to pass editorial review and continue along its path to publication.

—Julia Messina, Associate Editor, Carus Publishing

Cricket
9–14 years
1,850 words

"I'll tell you if we need to bail out," the flight instructor says as he adjusts your parachute straps. "On second thought, you'll *know* if we need to bail out."

With these cheerful words fresh in your mind, you walk to the airplane and struggle into the front seat. The instructor buckles you in and tightens the belt across your lap.

"This feels a bit snug," you say.

"Believe me, it won't when you're upside down." He climbs into the backseat.

This Super Decathlon airplane is different from the training planes you're used to. For one thing, it's an "aerobatic" plane, designed for the stresses of loops, rolls, spins, and other extreme maneuvers that regular airplanes can't handle. The instructor sits behind you, not at your side. You can't see him—he exists mainly as a voice in your headphones. And this plane has an old-fashioned tail wheel rather than the nose wheel "tricycle" landing gear you're used to. You've heard horror stories about how easy it is to crash these tail-draggers upon landing.

You go over your pre-engine-start checklist and review the bailout procedure. The hot, cramped cabin, the parachute digging

By Brian Bakos
Illustrated by Charles Shaw

into your back, and the tight lap belt all add to your discomfort. But every item on the list must be checked, and you mustn't rush.

"Ready to go anytime you are," the instructor finally says.

"Clear prop!" you yell out the window. You turn the ignition key, and the engine starts perfectly. You're off down the taxiway. You steer using the rudder pedals, keeping a sharp lookout for other aircraft on the ground.

Near the end of the runway, you stop and review the items on the pretakeoff checklist. Flight controls free and correct, instruments set, engine firing properly—everything must be right, or the flight will be scrubbed.

Finally you're set for takeoff. The sky is clear of other aircraft. You announce your departure over the radio and taxi into position, right on the runway's big white arrow. Throttle to full power, feet off the brakes—the runway races by, and the tail comes up off the ground. You're on the main wheels now, dancing on the rudder pedals to keep the plane on the centerline. You ease back the stick and become airborne.

Today you'll practice spin entry and recovery. If time allows, the instructor has said he'll also teach you some basic rolls. Of course there's enough time. He's only giving you an easy way out if your nerves—or stomach—fail, and you want to quit early.

Spin-outs cause many serious crashes each year, but spin recovery isn't taught during standard flight training. You only practice how to avoid a spin, not how to get out of one once it starts. So you decided to take an extra lesson in an aerobatic plane to round out your training. Besides, flying aerobatics sounds like fun. At least it did back on the ground. Up here, you're not quite so sure anymore.

"Take us to that little round lake to the northeast," the instructor says, "and level off at 5,500 feet."

You head toward the lake.

In order for an airplane to spin, the wings must first become stalled. A wing stall isn't the same as an engine stall, such as might happen when a car won't start. A wing stall occurs when the angle of the wing to the "relative wind" becomes so great that the wing can no longer provide any lift. This angle of the wing to the relative wind is called the "angle of attack."

To get an idea of relative wind, picture a car stopped at a red light. The car has a little flag hanging limp from its antenna. Once the car starts moving, however, relative wind begins from straight ahead. The flag now flutters straight back. You can feel relative wind

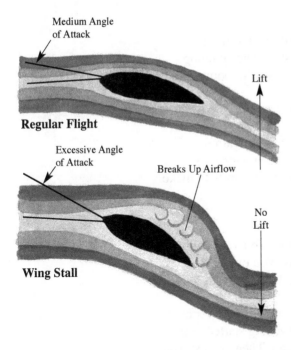

Medium Angle
of Attack

Lift

Regular Flight

Excessive Angle
of Attack

Breaks Up Airflow

No
Lift

Wing Stall

while riding a bike or even while running, if you go fast enough.

An airplane flying straight has relative wind flowing from directly ahead. If the wings are at a proper angle to this relative wind, air flows smoothly around them, giving the plane lift. However, if the angle of attack is too steep, the air swirls around, and the wings provide no lift: this is a wing stall. Without lift, a plane will come down in a belly flop like a falling leaf. If the pilot destabilizes the plane by dipping a stalled wing, he or she may cause a spin. If the pilot can't recover in time, the plane will crash. Such accidents most commonly occur on takeoff, on final approach to landing, in poor visibility, and when pilots try stunt maneuvers near the ground.

"**R**eady to try a spin of your own?" the instructor asks.

"Sure." You try to sound confident. The instructor's demonstration spin was scary enough. Now it's all up to you.

"Recover after two turns," the instructor says.

"O.K." Your calm voice surprises you.

You close the throttle, and the engine roar drops off to almost nothing. Then you pull back on the stick, farther and farther, until it's pressing into your midsection. The nose of the plane pulls up into a steep angle. You can no longer see the horizon ahead, just blue, cloudless sky.

"More back stick," the instructor says.

You pull the stick back still farther, until it's really pressing into you. The plane shakes as the wings begin to stall.

You hesitate a moment, wishing you were someplace else. Then you press the left rudder pedal all the way down and pull back even farther on the stick. The plane veers left and heads down into a spin.

Outside the windshield, the whole world has gone nuts. The ground is whirling around and coming closer. Fields and roads whip by; a red barn comes and goes. The little round lake comes back into view.

"One turn!" you call out.

The world continues to rotate as if you're in a dream. The lake comes into view again.

"Two turns!" you call out.

You release the left rudder pedal and push down the right one. Then you move the stick forward to break the stall. The spinning stops, and you release the rudder pedal. But now you're pointed straight down, and the ground is rushing up.

You pull back a bit too hard on the stick, and gravity presses you down in your seat, as though you were on some crazy roller coaster ride. The plane's nose comes up, and you can see sky again.

"Take it easy. This isn't a dive bomber," the instructor says.

You level the plane out and add power. The world starts to make sense again.

"Piece of cake," you say casually.

Forty minutes later you're back on solid ground. You've done plenty of spin recovery practice, along with a few rolls. You even got to fly upside down for a couple minutes. Yes, that lap belt did seem loose as you dangled like a side of beef in a meat locker.

You feel pride mingled with relief now that the flight is over at last—and you feel a real thumper of a headache getting started. You take off your parachute and hand it to the instructor. Then you ask yourself: I wonder what it would be like to bail out with one of these things.

From the Author

I originally wrote "Spin-Out!" for Assignment 7 of the Institute of Children's Literature's *Writing for Children and Teenagers* course. The assignment called for a nonfiction piece. As a private pilot, I thought I could draw on my own experience to tell the readers something about the excitement and adventure of flying.

Writing "Spin-Out!" was very easy, as it drew entirely on my own experience with acrobatic flight training. Even the dialogue, including the opening line, came directly from real life. I used a second-person viewpoint to draw the reader directly into the action, but the whole thing was a presentation of my own thoughts, emotions, and sensory impressions.

I needed no article plan or conscious application of fiction techniques, as the story flowed from my memory. I added some technical information from the FAA Flight Training Handbook and the piece was finished. I wasn't sure if it was exactly an article any longer. It seemed more like a work of historical fiction.

I submitted the full story, without query, to *Cicada Magazine*. I had intended the story for older readers and thought that *Cicada* would be the best choice from among the Cricket Group publications. John Allen, Senior Editor, wrote back saying that the story would work better for younger people—the *Cricket* readership. He suggested that I resubmit a revised, simplified version. I did so. Mr. Allen accepted the piece, and, after one pass of editing, it was ready for publication.

The title was my own choice. The sidebar comments were added by the editor; I had not suggested any. I was pleased with the art work, but rather amused to see that the wing struts had been eliminated from the airplane. This bit of artistic license made for a better view of the airplane's occupants, but any attempt to actually fly the thing without its wing struts would not have been wise.

—Brian Bakos

From the Editor

Although "Spin-Out!" was published in *Cricket*, Brian Bakos originally submitted the manuscript to *Cicada*, our literary magazine for teens. While the story wasn't right for *Cicada*, the editors enjoyed the white-knuckle excitement and the scientific underpinnings of the piece. Furthermore, the author mentioned in his cover letter that he's a general aviation pilot and that his story, while fiction, was based on personal experience and had been thoroughly researched. All these factors led us to recommend that the author rework his piece for a younger audience and resubmit it to *Cricket*.

In terms of revision, we suggested that he simplify the language and provide easier-to-understand explanations of the science. He complied, and *Cricket* accepted his manuscript for publication. The author wrote back to wish us "happy flying"!

—Deborah Vetter,
Executive Editor,
Cricket and *Cicada*

Cricket
9–14 years
1,230 words

"*I*f you pass this last test, Kalyr, you'll have all the powers of a master wizard. Fail, and . . ."

"I know, Master Bokul. You have told me many times that in the final test I risk my very life. But I am ready." Kalyr sat in the testing chair, pulling her black braid out from under her long legs.

"You're the first apprentice I've ever had who has come this far." Master Bokul's paper-white skin crackled as he patted Kalyr's smooth, brown hand. "Remember the lessons you have learned. I'll not help you after the test begins." He stroked his wispy, gray mustache and strode to his desk. He unrolled a scroll, then began to mutter and to stroke his bald head with both hands.

Kalyr closed her eyes, calming herself. After studying with Master Bokul for half of her fourteen years, she knew she had a few minutes to think while he muttered. The final test. What would it be?

Every test so far had surprised her. The easiest had been finding her own mother in a crowd of identical beekeepers that Bokul had conjured up. Not allowed to look beneath their veils, Kalyr had finally noticed that, while the other women smelled of wildflowers, only her mother smelled of honey.

The hardest test yet? When Bokul had taken a fatal, withering poison and had sent Kalyr into his den of potions to find the antidote. She'd been terrified that he would die. First Bokul's skin had turned pale blue with cold, then it dried up like an old wasps' nest. His breath rattled like winter leaves blowing across frozen ground. Kalyr realized that an orange potion, the color of sunshine, would warm him. Shaking the three orange potions, she'd chosen the one that sounded like a cleansing rain to counter the dryness. She'd given the cure to him just in time.

"Ready, Kalyr?"

Kalyr opened her eyes. Master Bokul

raised his arms. The room dimmed, and the walls seemed to breathe.

"Ready."

The room disappeared. Kalyr stood in a meadow surrounded by tall trees. Around her feet, thousands of flowers bloomed. The mingling fragrance of the purple, red, yellow, and orange blossoms made her smile. Kalyr tasted a hint of sea salt in the clear air. The sun stood just above the treetops. Judging from the dampness of the ground, she guessed it was midmorning.

I am standing in a meadow somewhere near the ocean in a quiet forest, Kalyr thought. What's it to be, Master Bokul? Dragons? Demons? A pack of wolves?

Kalyr heard Master Bokul's reply in her mind. "Nothing so easy. You must discover the problem and solve it by sundown, or you'll be stuck there forever."

Kalyr turned slowly. A slight breeze caressed her face but did not disturb the silence. Eerie silence. Had she gone deaf?

"Is that it?" she asked aloud. No, she could hear herself. Why so quiet, then? She paced around the meadow. A mouse darted across her path, and a swallow fluttered above her into the treetops. Kalyr watched the bird. It left the trees and circled above the meadow, then returned to a branch. Its actions seemed aimless. Kalyr twisted the ring on her finger. The ring was a gift from her mother, and it brought some comfort.

Kalyr followed a narrow path into the trees. Shy, white bellflowers nodded in the shade of the tall pines and rustling birches. The path meandered around boulders and under fallen logs. Kalyr saw no tracks in the dirt, but small piles of scat told her that deer walked the trail.

She stopped when the path ahead of her curved around a giant, dead tree. Halfway up the great pillar of its trunk, a cavernous hole yawned. Such a hole had once housed her mother's bees. Kalyr froze, every muscle tightening with fear, her skin itching. "If I don't move, they won't hurt me," she whispered. She waited for the bees to fly out of the hole and attack. But after a long time, when nothing moved, Kalyr took a shuddering breath.

She pivoted on the path, walking slowly away from the hole in the tree. She felt it watching her. Her back prickled. When the path had turned enough to hide her from that threatening black hole, she ran until the meadow opened in front of her. It was well after noon.

The flowers bloomed less brightly now, and their leaves fell back against drooping stems. They looked thirsty. Kalyr dropped to her knees. The ground still held moisture, so something else must be wrong with the plants.

"Master Bokul!" she shouted. "What kind of test is this?" Her words faded into the oppressive silence.

Kalyr twisted her ring again, thinking of her mother. A fierce anger flushed her cheeks. She would not die here, alone in this place that Bokul had magicked. She could not leave her mother alone, struggling to survive by tending her six beehives, selling honey at the market, and taking in mending during the winter. And for the first time in her long apprenticeship, Kalyr began to wonder if she'd made the wrong choice. She had wanted to become a wizard, but what if she failed this final test? Perhaps she should have followed in her mother's profession and tended bees.

Bees. Kalyr looked more closely at the meadow. No bees flew through the air; none gathered pollen from the thousands of flowers. She parted the flower stems in front of her to examine the ground. No ants, no beetles, no insects of any kind wandered among the plants.

The silence, that was it. Without insects, this world could not survive. But how could she make the insects reappear?

Kalyr looked up. She had a few hours of daylight left. The meadow looked more diseased now. Leaves turned rusty, and petals fell to the ground. Kalyr thought hard about the spells she knew. Never had she learned to create something from nothing, but Bokul had once taught her how to transform a paper flower into a living blossom. Could she change a bee-shaped ball of mud into a life-giving bee?

She gathered a small bit of mud, trying to think of a bee's most important characteristics. All that came to mind, however, was the terrifying morning from her fourth summer when Mother tended the annual swarm.

Kalyr had stood at the edge of Mother's meadow, watching. Deep inside the wide, spiraling tower of bees, Mother stood very still, her tall body swathed in her protective covering and veiled hat. The roar of the swarm vibrated in Kalyr's head.

"Mother!" She bolted into the edge of the swarm, thinking her mother was in danger.

"Stop!" Mother shouted.

Kalyr stopped but could not hold

Without insects, this world could not survive. But how could she make the insects reappear?

still. Several bees landed on her, and others buzzed around her. The weight of every crawling step of each bee seemed to dent her skin. She clenched all her muscles against her urge to run. She stifled her screams to a whimper. "Mother, help me!" she begged.

Slowly, Mother moved from the center of the swarm toward Kalyr. Bees walked over Kalyr's head and face, their sticky feet tugging at her hair and skin. Kalyr trembled, instinctively flapping her arms and dancing in panic. One bee stung her under the arm, then another on her leg. Bile rose in Kalyr's throat. Then Mother lifted her, crushing several bees against Kalyr's skin, where they stung. Mother carried her to the river and immersed her for a few moments. Then her mother left her, dripping and shivering, to gather the swarm from the tree and guide it into the hive. While Kalyr waited for Mother, she counted her wounds. Fourteen stings.

She'd been sick afterward, despite the poultices Mother had made. Since that day, Kalyr had helped her mother with the honey but always avoided the hives. And now, somehow, she had to make a bee from this mud in her hand. Her skin still twitched with the memory of all those crawling bees.

Why this? Why not something—anything—else?

Even her fear when Master Bokul took the poison hadn't run as deep as this. Kalyr glanced at the sky. The sun moved ever closer to the trees. She must make the bees return very soon.

With her free hand, Kalyr rubbed salty sweat from her eyes. Saliva rushed into her mouth, and she swallowed hard, trying not to think of how those tiny, sticky feet would feel on her palm. Remembering the way bees collected pollen and traveled unerringly from the flowers to the hive, she wrote the spell in her mind. Then she cleared her throat and whispered:

Sturdy wings and pollen sacks
Always follow unseen tracks
Yellow jacket striped with black,
Now I conjure all bees back.

Kalyr blew gently on the mud, but nothing happened. The sun sank more quickly than she thought it should.

"Don't rush me, Master Bokul," she muttered. Her heart beat faster. There must be essential qualities about bees that she hadn't put into the spell. Mother always said that bees were sweet if you knew how to handle them, though Kalyr had never dared to learn. As sweet as honey. As sweet as nectar. Sweet but noisy. For a moment, the roaring of the swarm filled her ears, and she looked up, expecting to see thousands of bees filling the air. The noise faded. It was all in my head, Kalyr thought.

She picked a blade of grass and gathered pollen from the dying flowers. The work tired her back, but she kept adding pollen to the cold sweat on her palm, chiding herself for her fear. After all, Mother never feared the bees. Only a child would shudder so, but the horror of her memories remained. Surely true wizards never felt such terror over insignificant things like this. Perhaps, Kalyr thought, that's why my spell failed, because I can't overcome my fear. But she knew she must try again if she hoped to ever leave this withered land and see her mother again.

When at last she had a small ball of pollen in her palm, she inhaled deeply. The sun stood only a finger's width over the treetops as Kalyr closed her eyes, remembering her mother's tender care of the bee stings and her equally tender care of the bees. Kalyr knew that Mother would not lie to her; and Mother had told her that bees could be gentle.

Sturdy wings upon your backs
Nature's key in pollen sacks
Angry buzz protects the hive
Kalyr breathes the bees alive.

With new understanding, she released her breath in love, not fear, over the pollen. Slowly the ball shifted, grew wings, legs, antennae, and a stinger. Kalyr flinched, knowing how awful it would feel. The bee crawled sluggishly toward the edge of her palm. But as she watched it walking, instead of menace, she felt each tiny step as a caress. The bee tested its wings and lifted off.

It flew from flower to flower and from each blossom another bee rose up and flew away. The rust faded from the leaves. The flowers straightened and opened new blooms. Every petal on the ground transformed into a beetle, a line of ants, or a grasshopper. The swallow swooped from a tree to gather its meal. The sounds multiplied until the meadow flourished. As she watched and listened, Kalyr laughed with joy.

"I've done it, Master Bokul!" she shouted.

"Well done, Master Kalyr." The walls of Master Bokul's study grew up around Kalyr as the flowers of the meadow melted into his carpet.

"Master Bokul, I was so afraid. I was ashamed to have you see my fear."

"And you will fear again, Master Kalyr. But the tests you face will be your own. You've passed the last of mine by bringing the meadow alive."

"Master Bokul, did I really do that, or was it only an illusion that you created for me?"

Master Bokul pointed to her sleeve. A bee crawled along it. "Well done, Master Kalyr. Well done."

From the Author

I'd always hoped for a phone call from an editor saying, I love this! I want to publish it! Though my acceptance by *Cricket* didn't happen that way, there were some wonderful, fantastic moments in the process.

I first wrote the story for Assignment 2 of the Institute of Children's Literature's *Writing for Children and Teenagers* course. The assignment was to choose five words from a list and write a short story. I began a story, but realized when I reached the word limit that I'd begun a novel. So I put it aside and tried again.

I struggled with the assignment. Finally I came up with the idea of a wizard's apprentice passing her test. With no outline or story plan, I began to write. (I am a "plodder" rather than a "plotter." I start with an initial idea and write the story to see where it takes me. Often in the revision process I need to cut or add scenes, but this way works best for me.)

I didn't begin with a theme other than "passing the test." Through the revision process the theme of facing one's fears emerged. The opening scenes came easily, but I had no idea what the test itself was. After grappling with it for a few days, I ran across a reference in the newspaper to the dwindling population of honeybees in North America. That gave me the idea for her test.

I ran the story through my critique group and revised it based on their comments. Then I sent it to my instructor, who wrote a wonderful letter back suggesting that I revise "The Silent Meadow" because the protagonist lacked an inner conflict. So I wrote about Kalyr's phobia, weaving it into the story and editing the whole thing again.

My instructor liked the revision. She urged me to submit it to Deborah Vetter at *Cricket*. At the same time, the deadline for the Southwest Writers Workshop contest was approaching. I submitted "The Silent Meadow" to Deborah and to SWW. Several weeks later, I received a form rejection from *Cricket*.

SWW announced that Deborah Vetter would be one of the faculty members for that year's conference. Since I knew the faculty judged the finalists in the contest, I pinned my hopes on at least having a chance to discuss it with her.

"The Silent Meadow" was a finalist in their Children/Young Adult Short Story category. I met Deborah Vetter at the awards banquet and learned I'd won second place. As part of judging the contest, Deborah had written a one-page critique of the story. The ending needed fixing, she wrote, and when I re-read the story, I agreed.

The next day I worked up all my courage to ask her whether she'd be willing to read the story again if I rewrote it according to her critique. She agreed.

I sent her the fourth draft. After five months the story came back. My heart sank as I pulled it from the mailbox. I wanted the skinny envelope with the letter saying, "Here's your contract." Or even better, "Here's your check." If the manuscript came back, that meant rejection. But when I opened it, I found a kind letter from Julia Messina, Associate Editor, who said that Deborah had passed the manuscript on to her. My heart skipped a beat when I read that Marianne Carus, Editor-in-Chief, Deborah, and Julia had all discussed the manuscript. Marianne Carus bore that same title when I subscribed to *Cricket* in 1974-79. I couldn't believe that she had read my story. That was when I felt I had arrived as a writer.

I was invited to consider the changes suggested and resubmit on spec. So I knew they were interested, which was wonderful, but they hadn't accepted it yet, which tempered my excitement.

The real challenge came when Julia Messina at *Cricket* suggested places I needed to expand, but reminded me that I had a 2,000-word limit on the story. Since the story was already 2,000 words long, expanding in some places meant cutting in others. With the help of my critique group, I found ways to tighten the writing to stay within the word limit, cutting unnecessary words or expressing an idea more succinctly. In all, I revised the story seven times. I revised it four times under the direction of editors at *Cricket*.

Seven months and two drafts later, Julia Messina accepted it for publication, but still wanted one more revision. I was very happy, but by then the news was not unexpected, so I didn't shriek and holler the way I'd always thought I would.

The most exciting moment was when I saw "The Silent Meadow" in print. The illustrations were so beautiful, so detailed, and so attentive to the images I'd created with words that I knew I had to thank Julia Messina for sending my story to such a wonderful artist, and I had to find a way to thank Leah Palmer Preiss. I found her website, and e-mailed her my enthusiastic thanks. The illustrations are perfect.

I like to write about strong female protagonists, because there weren't enough of them in literature when I was growing up. So I started there, and Kalyr evolved with the story.

If you want to write fantasy for this age group, read a lot of fantasy, both for young readers and adults. Fantasy doesn't appeal to everyone, and I think you have to love it to write it well. For me, having a number of different critiques from different people helped me see the strengths and weaknesses of the story, which helped me create a publishable piece out of a rough draft.

—Laura K. Deal

From the Editor

Our Executive Editor, Deborah Vetter, awarded "The Silent Meadow" second place at a writers' conference and encouraged the author to resubmit it to *Cricket*. However, prior to submitting it, Debby recommended that the author make some revisions, such as tightening the narrative flow by deleting unnecessary information. In editorial review, we decided that we wanted the author to clarify some of the challenges that Kalyr, the apprentice wizard, found before her, and I worked with her on these revisions.

By the time the revised story was ready for publication, it was in great shape. The main characters were full of life and engaging; their relationship was one of mutual respect and personal growth. Kalyr was depicted as a thoughtful, intelligent individual who experiences universal emotions of fear, doubt, and wavering self-confidence when faced with the challenge of her life. The effective depiction of these universal emotions connects her to the readers, who share the same feelings when faced by challenges. By the end of the story Kalyr has used all of her considerable intellectual and emotional resources to overcome the challenge before her.

Leah Palmer Preiss's illustrations perfectly matched the fantastical setting and even reflected the thoughtful atmosphere and gentle pacing of Laura Deal's story.

—Julia Messina, Associate Editor, Carus Publishing

Cricket
9–14 years
2,000 words

GHOSTS IN THE NIGHT

By Helen Correll

After a busy day playing on the beach, most vacationers go to bed tired and happy . . . and completely unaware of the ghosts prowling the seashore at night! With swift, flitting movements, pale bodies crisscross the dark sand throughout the night leaving only tiny tracks in the morning light. What am I talking about? Ghost crabs! If you take a flashlight onto a beach after dark, you can see what I mean. It's fun watching these harmless crabs go about their nightly business. Be still and look carefully.

Unlike other crabs, ghost crabs are not scavengers (creatures which feed on dead plants and animals). A moonlit beach offers a beautiful buffet of live creatures for ghost crabs to choose from. They use their pincers (PIN-sers), their large front claws, to harvest savory hoppers and mouth-watering mole crabs. And delicious donax, colorful clams the size of a fingernail, are always close at hand . . . er, pincer.

The ghost crab is in a large group of animals called crustaceans (krus-TAY-shuns), creatures which have an external skeleton or "crust." Other familiar members of this group are lobsters, shrimp and crayfish. They also have jointed legs, antennae and they molt, which means they regularly shed their outer shell as they grow. Female crustaceans lay eggs in the water.

In the flashlight beam, you will see the ghost crabs scurrying across the sand toward the water. Their shell, or carapace (KAR-a-pis), is a two-inch box the same color as the sand, covered with small bumps. Their two black eyes stick up like a space alien's antennae and

Illustration by Helen Correll

can rotate 360 degrees to see all the way around. On either side of their body are four jointed, hairy legs tipped with claws. With these, a ghost crab can move forward and backward, but it usually moves sideways. What a funny sight: a little tan "box with legs" scurrying sideways across the beach. And sometimes they move fast—a full-grown ghost crab can run as fast as 10 miles per hour. That's why their scientific name is *Ocypoda*, which means "swift-footed."

The ghost crab's two pincers could be called its "grabbers." They use these pincers to seize their prey and drag it across the beach and down into their golf ball-size holes in the dry sand.

You can recognize a ghost crab's home by its resemblance to a moon crater.

Once, on an evening walk, I startled a determined ghost crab dragging a fresh jellyfish twice his size toward his hole, leaving a ten-foot track in the sand behind him. He was so close to home he must have felt courageous because, instead of darting into his hole to hide, he looked me in the eye and put up his little pincers to fight! I didn't want him to feel threatened, plus I had no interest in his dinner of jiggly jellyfish, so I walked quietly away. But I couldn't help wondering how in the world he planned to squeeze that four-inch blob into his two-inch hole!

You can recognize a ghost crab's home by its resemblance to a moon crater. Sand clumps and crab tracks run out in every direction. From the two-inch hole, a tunnel leads down three or four feet to a burrow in the deep, damp sand. Just as a wet sand castle is stronger than a dry one, the damp sand ensures that the cave won't collapse. This burrow is protection from enemies such as birds, raccoons and cats, as well as from the sun because ghost crabs have to keep their gills wet.

Surprised? Yes, ghost crabs appear to be landlubbers but they, like fish, have gills and "breathe" oxygen from water. Even though it's dangerous, they must sneak from their hole several times during the day to dash to the ocean and let gentle wavelets wash over their bodies. Then they dash back to hide until it's dark and they're safe from attack by the shorebirds, such as seagulls, who have settled for the night. In the winter, ghost crabs are able to hibernate for up to six weeks by storing oxygen in special sacs near their gills.

You won't find ghost crabs on over-crowded beaches or at fancy resorts that rake the sand every day, but you will find them along Atlantic shores from New Jersey to Florida and around the whole Gulf Coast to Texas. So, if you're lucky enough to visit one of these beaches, be sure to tell your family about the "ghosts" that come out at night. They'll probably be a little skeptical and say, "No way!" That's when you grab your flashlight and show them your ghosts!

PEEK-A-BOO, I SEE YOU: A GHOST CRAB TAKES A QUICK LOOK OUT OF HIS SANDY HOME.

From the Author

Because I am an artist, when I decided to take the Institute's course on writing for children, the only kind of writing I had in mind was stories for the picture books I planned to create. I suppose I didn't know myself very well, or just had a narrow vision, because writing for magazines had never occurred to me, much less writing nonfiction.

Luckily, the course opened my eyes to both possibilities and helped me find my niché and get published. I've found a way to write and illustrate part-time while keeping up with two teenage sons at home. Of course, being published will be an advantage when I finally have my first picture book manuscript (probably nonfiction) ready to submit to book editors.

The inspiration for "Ghosts in the Night" came during a trip to the beach with my family. I was sitting close to the water when I saw a little ghost crab sneaking past me. As I watched, he tippy-toed into the water until all I could see were his two black eyeballs above the tiny waves. My curiosity came alive. What was he doing? Isn't he a sand crab . . . so, what's he doing getting wet? That night I looked up ghost crabs in my travel bag of field guides and nature books. One month later, when I received Assignment 7 (The World of Nonfiction), it was easy to decide what to write.

The first thing I did was make a list of questions I thought a child would ask about ghost crabs: where do they live, what do they eat, and especially, why do they go into the water when they live in the sand? The questions helped me come up with an outline for the article.

Next, I went to the library for research. I stayed in the library for hours and let one book lead me to another. Upstairs, downstairs, to periodicals and the children's department I went, comparing sources and information, all the while keeping a list for a bibliography. I also went online to an Internet search engine and typed in "Ghost Crabs" to see if anything new would turn up. It didn't. I already had all the information I needed. This supported my belief that a good library is still the researcher's best tool.

When I felt like I knew, or had at my disposal, much more information than a child would want to know, I started writing. I'd already come up with the title that I thought was appealing because it sounded a little spooky, so it seemed natural to grab the readers' interest with a "ghost story," one children could connect with. Then, I tried to make it fun by writing as if I were talking to a child and using lively words like "crisscross," "blob," and "scurry," and alliteration like "crazy crabs" and "jiggly jellyfish."

I do believe, though, that my passion for nature and personal fascination with the crabs also played a part in the article's success. I have found that the writing process is so much easier when I'm excited about the subject . . . the excitement seems to bubble up through the words.

After studying my market guide, I made a list of several magazines that I thought would be a good fit for my article. When I read about *Dolphin Log*, the editors' philosophy, their desire for "biological illustration" (a strength of mine), and that it is published by the Cousteau Society, I was hooked. It was definitely my first choice.

I included a brief cover letter with the article and mailed it directly to the editor of *Dolphin Log*. When she called a few weeks later to ask for permission to use the piece I was thrilled! I offered to illustrate it and sent some sketches to the art director. It all went quite smoothly with only a word or two changed from the original manuscript. Since then, two more of my illustrated articles have been published in *Dolphin Log*.

I write for other science publications as well, and have finally concluded that I simply have a nonfiction brain; a love of science, a fascination with facts, and a desire to help others become aware of the world around them. If that reminds you of yourself, you should definitely try writing nonfiction. It's very satisfying!

—Helen Correll

From the Editor

Helen wrote an appealing query letter. It was cheerful and upbeat, plus, from the title she had chosen for her piece, "Ghosts in the Night," I immediately knew she had an excellent grasp on what would appeal to kids!

Helen also had something else in her favor—she was an illustrator as well. She offered to design and illustrate her article for us. Obviously, most writers do not have this gift, but it was a definite plus to know that someone was going to draw exactly what we needed for this story. Any time writers tell us they can provide photographs or artwork, it is a huge plus!

I believe we sent Helen sample issues of *Dolphin Log* to read before she sent in her article. It was in very good shape when we received it. She did not need to do a rewrite.

Any revisions needed (a few minor cuts and rewording to fit our audience's age range) were done in-house.

Helen's work was so good we have used her again for a few other articles, and we always get excited when Helen sends us a new query.

—Lisa Rao, Editor, *Dolphin Log*

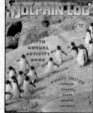

Dolphin Log
7–13 years
770 words

The Kids Who Fought Smallpox

By Mariana Relós

"**P**rincess María Luisa has smallpox, the red death!"

In 1798 panic struck the palace where King Carlos IV of Spain lived with his family. The doctor didn't have a medicine to cure the princess. Terrified, the king could only wait for the outcome of the disease.

Smallpox, or *variola*, was the most terrible disease of the time. It caused a deadly epidemic every ten to twenty years.

The disease was caused by a type of germ called a virus. Since most adults were survivors of past epidemics, their bodies had built up defenses against it. As a result, the virus was caught mostly by children. They developed high fever, chills, nausea, aches, and itchy red spots over their bodies. Many of them died. In the survivors, scabs formed and then fell off, leaving permanent pits and scars. Some survivors were left blind.

Princess María Luisa survived smallpox, and the king of Spain protected the rest of his family from the disease. He used a new method that was slowly becoming accepted.

A Cow Disease

In 1796, Dr. Edward Jenner of England showed that making people sick with cowpox would protect them from smallpox.

Cowpox is a disease of cows that can also affect humans. The cowpox and smallpox viruses are related, and the spots they cause look similar. But in humans, cowpox neither kills nor scars nor blinds.

To give cowpox to healthy people, Dr. Jenner used a method called "arm-to-arm transfer." With a tiny knife, he took liquid from a cowpox sore on a cow or person.

Orphaned boys carried a life-saving vaccine to the New World

Then he scratched the fluid into the skin of a healthy person, giving that person the cowpox virus.

The healthy person soon had a harmless case of cowpox. A few weeks later, the cowpox went away, and the person's body had built up a defense against cowpox—and against smallpox.

Dr. Jenner called this process *vaccination*, from the Latin word *vaccinus*, which means "related to cows." Dr. Jenner's was the first safe vaccine used to protect people from a dangerous disease.

Across the Atlantic

King Carlos IV did not stop with vaccinating his family. At his government's expense, he mounted a program to take the vaccine throughout the Spanish Empire.

He commanded the physician Francisco Xavier Balmis to take Dr. Jenner's vaccine to all the settlements of the Empire, from North to South America (and later to the Spanish Philippines).

To make the program work, Dr. Balmis had to carry the cowpox virus across the ocean and then from town to town. Somehow, he had to keep the virus alive through years of travel.

He tried two ways. First, he took liquid from a cowpox sore and sealed it between glass slides. Most of the time the virus died and did not work.

A Human Chain

The second way was to use people, much as Dr. Jenner had done. But a person is sick with cowpox for only two to three weeks. To make the long journey, Dr. Balmis needed a "human chain."

For the human chain to work, it had to be made up of people who had never had cowpox or smallpox. Most adults had already had one or the other, but many kids had never had either disease.

The government arranged for twenty-two orphaned boys, ages three to nine years old, to be the human chain. As they crossed the ocean, the boys were infected with cowpox, one after another, using the arm-to-arm transfer.

Thanks to this effort, more than one hundred thousand people in Latin America were vaccinated between 1803 and 1807. It was by far the largest vaccination program of its time.

After the program was completed, the government continued to care for the orphans and paid the cost of their schooling in the Americas. They lived in Mexico, and local citizens adopted most of them. These children should be remembered for saving thousands of people from smallpox.

Starting in 1967, a team of doctors led a worldwide program to wipe out smallpox forever. Today, all of the known samples of the smallpox virus exist only in laboratories. No one has recorded a case of smallpox anywhere in the world since 1979.

How a Vaccine Works

A vaccine teaches the body to build a defense against a disease.

The body naturally makes such defenses each time it fights the germs that can cause an infection. The fighting is done by the *immune system*, which is an army of cells and molecules that work together to kill invading germs.

While the immune system is working against the infection, some special immune cells are also being trained to quickly recognize and destroy the germ that caused the infection.

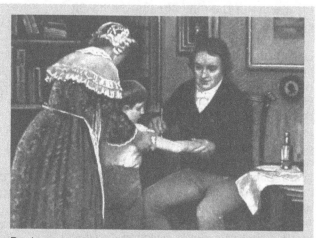
Dr. Jenner uses the arm-to-arm transfer to vaccinate a boy.

If the person recovers, the immune system keeps its best fighting cells ready to find and destroy the germs as soon as they appear. If the same kind of germ infects that person again, the immune system can destroy it so quickly that the person may not even feel sick. The person has an *immunity* to the disease.

Dr. Edward Jenner realized that a cowpox infection gives an immunity to smallpox. Cowpox trains the immune system to attack the cowpox virus—and viruses like it, including the smallpox virus.

Since Dr. Jenner's day, new vaccines have been developed to protect people from many deadly diseases. Today, vaccines are made in special laboratories. Each vaccine contains weakened or killed germs for a particular disease. These germs cause the immune system to be trained to attack them, but without causing an infection. Usually the vaccine is injected into an arm or leg. Most people don't even feel sick after taking the shot, and they are protected against a dangerous disease.

From the Author

"The Kids Who Fought Smallpox" was one of my assignments at the Institute. I wanted to write this article from the moment I read about the vaccination expedition in a science journal. In the science report, the author only briefly mentioned the expedition and its goals, but that was enough for me to get hooked on the story.

I wanted to know more about the expedition and the children, so I contacted the scientist who wrote the report in the science journal. We talked about the vaccination expedition, and a few days later I received a copy of an original publication about the expedition and a list of references. This material gave me a good start in my bibliographical research. Primary references proved to be the most helpful. They were packed with details and also offered the unique perspective of individuals directly involved in the expedition.

The vaccination expedition was an opportunity to combine science, history, and children in a wonderful story. The science behind an effective vaccination against smallpox explained why children had to be in the expedition. This story also provided a good opportunity to show how much science and technology have improved since the expedition's time. Today massive immunizations are easier and safer than two hundred years ago.

It was hard to decide which facts to include and which ones to leave out. I kept the facts that directly moved the action forward. For instance, it was hard to decide if I should include the fact that one of the orphan kids was adopted by one of the nurses before the trip. This showed how much the people from the expedition cared about the kids. But I finally left it out. It did not contribute directly to the way the expedition was conceived and planned, and how obstacles were overcome.

I develop my articles from a plan. At the top of my plan is the problem that has to be solved through the story (in this case: "smallpox epidemics strike the Spanish colonies killing thousands"). At the bottom of my plan is the solution ("children carry the vaccine to the Spanish colonies and save thousands from the deadly disease"). In between, I write in short sentences the events that occurred sequentially to reach the solution. With this plan in hand, I start to write the article by putting together interesting facts and details about the people, the time, and the place. I believe there is a "story" behind each important historical and/or scientific event. There has to be because *people* lead those historical or scientific adventures!

I sent my article to *Highlights for Children* because they are interested in nonfiction articles, especially in science and history for 8- to 12-year-old readers. A few months after I submitted my article, I received a postcard from Andy Boyles, *Highlights*'s Science Editor. They loved my article and I had made my first sale!

Making my first sale was one thing, but having the article published was another story. With *Highlights*, fact checking is a thorough process. Many editors read my article and asked questions about it. I received more questions than in a final comprehensive exam! I pulled my research files and double-checked all my answers with my references before I sent them back to *Highlights*. To complete the article, Andy Boyles asked me to write the sidebar on how vaccines work. This was a great addition because it explained some issues mentioned in the article. There was simply no room in the main text to talk about vaccines in detail.

Editing was next. Andy Boyles worked with me revising my article. The hardest part was to include all the relevant facts, and to tell the story in no more than 800 words! It took a few drafts, but at the end I think we were happy with the result. *Highlights* honored my article with the "History Feature of the Year Award 2000."

Before becoming a children's science writer, I was a scientist for about twenty years and taught biology, biochemistry, and immunology courses to graduate and undergraduate college students.

If I ever have any doubts about the value of a good editing process and of thorough bibliographic research, I just look at my list of publications. Since "The Kids Who Fought Smallpox" appeared in *Highlights*, I have published about thirty more articles in children's magazines and four more are in press.

—Mariana Relós

From the Editor

"The Kids Who Fought Smallpox" has some unusual qualities that captured our imagination and convinced us that it would be valuable for our readers. The story of Dr. Edward Jenner and his use of the first safe smallpox vaccine is important, but it has been told over and over.

The novel angle that Mariana took—focusing on one of the vaccine's earliest and most dramatic deployments—created an excellent doorway to take our readers into this subject. They not only learn about vaccination and this landmark vaccine, but they get a glimpse at what life must have been like at the beginning of the nineteenth century—including recurring epidemics and the lives of orphans.

We had many questions about details in the story, but Mariana's training as a scientist, her thorough and professional response to our queries, and her mastery of the subject inspired confidence.

—Andy Boyles, Science Editor,
Highlights for Children

Highlights for Children
2–12 years
950 words

The Candy Woman Can

By Sara Francis Fujimura

Is this a new Nickelodeon game show? No, it's only a small part of food scientist Michelle Frame's job description.

"I am Willy Wonka," says Michelle, gesturing to the piles of bagged candy littering her desk. "And no one yells at me when I play with my food."

Michelle invents candy for a living for Just Born, Inc.— best known for its Marshmallow Peeps and Bunnies™. Her specialties: jelly beans and marshmallow creations.

Although she has always liked food, Michelle found science boring. Even in college, Michelle didn't enjoy the required basic chemistry classes, but she pushed herself on anyway. Later, when she began to see how chemistry related to her love of food, it became more interesting to her.

Michelle says the most important subject in school for future food scientists is math.

"I use math, specifically algebra, every day," she said. "Sometimes pages and pages of it!"

For example, she frequently converts recipes from pounds to kilograms to meet other countries' imported food laws.

Food Science is a rapidly growing field as more people are looking for pre-made and frozen meals at the grocery store. Food companies need more food scientists to develop new foods and expand the current selection.

Now it's your turn to be a food scientist like Michelle Frame. Make a batch of marshmallow bunnies to share with your family and friends. But first, use the key to convert the ingredients from metric to U.S. measurement. Remember to ask an adult for help when working in the kitchen.

On a typical day, I get really gooey and covered in marshmallow.

Homemade Marshmallow Bunnies

INGREDIENTS:

_____ = 75 ml water

1 envelope unflavored gelatin

_____ = 1.5 dl granulated sugar

_____ = 1.25 dl light corn syrup

pinch of salt

_____ = 5 ml vanilla extract

_____ = 60 ml cornstarch

_____ = 75 ml fine, colored, crystal sugar

small bunny cookie cutter (or different shape)

KEY:
2/3 cup = 1.5 deciliters (dl)
1/2 cup = 1.25 dl
1/3 cup = 75 milliliters (ml)
1/4 cup = 60 ml
1 tsp. = 5 ml

How to Make 'Em

Pour water into a small saucepan. Sprinkle gelatin over water and let soak for 5 minutes. Add granulated sugar. Stir and cook over low heat until the gelatin and sugar dissolve.

In a large mixing bowl, combine gelatin mixture with corn syrup, salt, and vanilla. Beat for 15 minutes on high speed until soft peaks form.

In a separate bowl, gently stir together cornstarch and crystal sugar. Lightly grease an 8" x 8" baking pan, and sprinkle 1 Tbs. cornstarch mixture into it. Tilt pan in all directions to coat sides and bottom.

Spread marshmallow mixture into pan, smoothing down the top. Let stand 2 hours.

With a wet knife, cut marshmallow mixture into quarters. Sprinkle remaining cornstarch mixture on a baking sheet. Put marshmallow blocks onto it. Using a wet cookie cutter, cut out marshmallow bunnies. Press both sides and edges of bunny into cornstarch mixture.

Allow marshmallows to dry, uncovered, overnight. Store in an airtight container.

To see how Marshmallow Peeps and Bunnies™ are made, take a virtual tour of Just Born, Inc.'s plant at ww.marshmallowpeeps.com/factory.html

MEASUREMENTS ANSWERS

1/3 cup water
1 envelope unflavored gelatin
2/3 cup granulated sugar
1/2 cup light corn syrup
pinch of salt
1 teaspoon vanilla extract
1/4 cup cornstarch
1/3 cup colored sugar

From the Author

I worked as a technical/science writer for several years, and while working on a large project about food additives, I became interested in the chemistry behind how complex-flavored gourmet jelly beans are made. Further research sent me to Just Born, Inc. (best known for its Marshmallow Peeps) in Bethlehem, PA, and into the lab of food scientist Michelle Frame.

Michelle was such an intriguing and witty woman, that the story quickly changed from a science piece into a biography profile. I transcribed my notes as soon as I got home. Then I sat on it. Two years and two babies later, this piece finally came to fruition when I suddenly needed an idea for an Institute course assignment.

Because the piece was originally supposed to be about the chemistry of jelly beans, my journey began at a food additives trade show. A sales representative informed me that one of his clients, Just Born, was only an hour drive from my home. Next, I called Just Born's PR department. I inquired about a tour and specifically asked if they had any female food scientists. My trip to Just Born included not only a face-to-face interview with Michelle Frame but also a tour of the facility. How many people can say that they've eaten a Marshmallow Peep straight off the assembly line?

To prepare for the interview, I researched the company's website and read the PR pamphlets sent to me beforehand. Then I wrote up questions in the mindset of, "What would your average teenage girl want to know about this unusual occupation?" Though I had prepared a set of detailed questions, some of the best quotes came when Michelle digressed. Choosing quotes was easy, because Michelle is extremely witty. I picked quotes that made me say, "Wow! Really?" For example, Michelle disliked her science classes, especially chemistry, throughout high school and college until she saw how it directly related to her love of food.

My editor found and made the recipe. My job was to take the poorly written original recipe and transform it into one that your average sixth grader could understand. Doing the math was the hardest part for me. Now I understand why food scientists work solely in the metric system!

One reason it took me so long to write this article was because I couldn't decide which was the better format to use. The original narrative-style felt flat, so I struggled to rewrite it in a Q&A format. When *New Moon*'s editors inquired about the piece, their first request was to change it back into narrative form. Even more of a challenge was cutting down the piece to almost half its original size.

I studied the sample copy of *New Moon* thoroughly. Who was its readership? What was its style? Then I pictured myself sitting down with these girls and telling them Michelle's story in only five minutes. What would they find most interesting and keep their attention? Everything else had to go.

My idea-collecting system has several different forms. I like to take a piece that interests me and look at it from a child's perspective. I also like to take adult stories and give them a kid spin.

I have a specific writing notebook where I jot down ideas for stories, snappy titles, quotes, and questions I want to eventually look up. If an idea really moves me, I start both an electronic folder and paper folder. Rough drafts, character sketches, and notes to myself go into the electronic one. Marketing ideas, research materials, correspondence from sources, and the article/picture/etc. that prompted the idea are put into the paper version.

I am a full-time mother and a part-time writer and dance teacher. I have been published in *New Moon*, *The Writing Parent* e-newsletter, and *Woman's Day*. I'm currently working on a novel about Japanese picture brides coming to Hawaii at the turn of the twentieth century.

—Sara Francis Fujimura

From the Editor

We published "The Candy Woman Can" because in every issue of our magazine, we have a hands-on science experiment. Girls are typically not encouraged to pursue science, so we like articles that encourage girls to explore science.

We liked this article for several reasons. It was about a woman who uses science in her job; it had a science experiment for girls to try at home; and it made science fun.

The article came to us complete, but the author worked with our Girl Editorial Board and adult editorial staff to make the revisions that we required.

At *New Moon*, there's a real back-and-forth process between our writers and our editorial staff, especially with the Girl Editorial Board comprised of girls ages 8 to 14.

—Deb Mylin, Managing Editor, *New Moon: The Magazine for Girls & Their Dreams*

New Moon
8–14 years
500 words

Creepy, Creative C🎃stumes

Text and art by Joanna Schorling

You may be looking forward to a spooky party, but the cost of your costume doesn't have to be scary. You can make your own for less than $5.

The following ideas use common and inexpensive materials. Look for supplies in craft and party supply stores, garage sales, and in your own home. Attics and basements are often great places to look, too. Make sure you get permission before using old clothes or sheets.

SWAMP MONSTER

You need:
Old green sheet,
green fabric, or green felt
Safety pins
Green face paint
Green pants and shirt

Directions:

1. To make "swampweed," cut the fabric into strips of uneven lengths and widths.
2. Safety pin the pieces to baggy green clothes. Place most of them near your shoulders, allowing them to hang down. Pin from the inside to conceal the safety pins.
3. Clip a few pieces of fabric into your hair with a barrette. To finish the costume, cover your face with ghastly green makeup.

MAN IN THE MOON

You need:
2 sheets of white poster board,
each about 24 inches by 30 inches
Stapler
White felt
Safety pins
White or silver face paint
Black pants and shirt

Directions:

1. Draw a large crescent moon on one sheet of poster board, and cut it out along the lines.
2. Trace the first moon and use the tracing as a pattern to cut out a second moon from the other sheet of poster board.
3. Match the two moons together. Staple both sides of each crescent point a few inches away from the tip.
4. To wear, slide your head and one arm through the center hole of the moon. Let one end point toward your ear, while the other curves up toward your hip. If the moon is too large, trim it to the size that fits you best.
5. To wear a "starlit sky," cut stars out of white felt. Safety pin the stars to a black shirt and black pants. Pin from the inside to hide the safety pins.
6. Use bright white or silver face paint to make your face glow like the moon.

From the Author

The ideas for "Creepy, Creative Costumes" came from my own experiences, and from time spent working in an arts and crafts store. I remember the store-bought, 70s-era costumes made out of flimsy vinyl that usually tore before a kid could actually get the costume on (to this day, the smell of a new shower curtain liner reminds me of Halloween). My family and I began making our own costumes out of whatever materials we could find around the house. The fun was not only in the process of crafting our own costumes, but that the possibilities were limitless. Halloween is a time when children can transform themselves into whomever or whatever they want.

With this idea in mind, I began the article. I devised ten costume projects using materials that could be easily obtained, and tested each one to make certain the costume could be constructed by a child with little help from an adult. I used the Institute's *Children's Magazine Market* to find a suitable market, and decided to begin with *Child Life*. The age range was appropriate, and they accepted both craft and seasonal material.

I sent off the manuscript and prepared myself for a rejection by compiling a backup list of magazines to submit to, but instead I received an acceptance letter from *Child Life*'s editor within a few weeks. I was further delighted when their sister publication, *U*S* Kids*, sent me a letter (and an additional check!) informing me that they would also publish my article.

When I received my contributor's copies, I saw the editors' plan: out of the ten costume ideas I had written for the article, *Child Life* published two of those projects and *U*S* Kids* chose another two for their issue. I was completely pleased with the outcome in both magazines.

My original goal, like many new writers, was to publish fiction, but I've since learned that writing nonfiction is also a creative process—words and ideas are chosen just as carefully. And with more opportunities available in the nonfiction market, it's a great place to begin acquiring those writing credits.

—Joanna Schorling

Child Life
9–11 years
340 words

Mind your manners when speaking to this gorilla.

GORILLA Etiquette

By Kathryn Jankowski

I t's well established that primates have feelings similar to those of humans. Take Koko, the renowned gorilla who communicates via American Sign Language and computers. She grieved when her beloved kitten died. Yet Koko can be lighthearted and playful, thumping her bent knee before rampaging down the side of her cage in her own game of "tag," then hooting with pleasure at her cleverness.

But what about other gorillas? Chaka, the lowland silverback at the Philadelphia Zoo, loves to interact with visitors. Will he respond positively to your smile? Should you look directly into his eyes? Or thump your chest in jest?

Take this True/False quiz to find out if you know how to behave around gorillas, or if you need to brush up on your "gorilla etiquette."

1. **True or False?** — Gorillas understand you're being friendly when you greet them with a smile.

2. **True or False?** — It's better to stand below or at the same level as a gorilla, rather than above.

3. **True or False?** — The best way to attract a gorilla's attention is to beat on your chest and hoot loudly.

4. **True or False?** — When a gorilla approaches you, you should make direct eye contact.

5. **True or False?** — If you encounter a charging gorilla on the loose, you should stay perfectly still.

Go to page 140 for the answers.

Answers to "Gorilla Etiquette"

1. **False**—Showing your teeth to a gorilla is an act of aggression. Even if there's a glass wall between you and the gorilla, avoid potentially upsetting actions.
2. **True**—Gorillas respond best when they're treated with respect. Don't stand above them if you can avoid it, or they'll feel threatened.
3. **False**—Gorillas don't like rude noises any more than humans do. Remember, they're sensitive creatures and become stressed when visitors harass them. Startling, mocking motions are hostile. A gorilla is more likely to respond favorably to you if you stay in its line of sight, and move slowly and deliberately.
4. **False**—Staring at a gorilla, especially a male, is considered a challenge. If a gorilla approaches you—and it could happen if you're quiet, respectful, and patient—look down, nod your head, and slowly look up. You can try short periods of direct eye contact, but be prepared to look away if the gorilla becomes agitated.
5. **True**—While gorillas rarely escape from zoos, if you panic and try to run away from one, it might bite you. Scientists who study gorillas in their natural environments report that a charging ape will run past you if you remain stationary and calm.

Overall, kindness and respect—good manners, basically—will show gorillas that you mean them no harm, and allow for greater freedom in observing them. Besides, other visitors can learn from your example, and zoo keepers will thank you for keeping the gorilla habitats peaceful.

From the Author

In my query to *Odyssey* magazine for its "Passionate about Primates" issue, I proposed a story about a gorilla refuge and mentioned a possible sidebar: a True/False quiz about gorilla etiquette.

As a teacher, I know interactive activities are enticing to *Odyssey*'s targeted age group (10- to 16-year-olds). I was delighted when the editor called to discuss my idea. The fact that *Odyssey* chose to go with this approach reinforces my belief that it's always good to suggest a sidebar or two for any article idea you submit. You never know what will tickle an editor's fancy!

The title was prompted by a website that discussed minding your manners around primates, as well as my desire to decrease the obnoxious behavior I've witnessed around gorillas at zoos. This article was based on information from books, the Internet, personal visits to the San Francisco gorilla habitat, and a once-in-a-lifetime visit with Koko.

I'm pleased that *Odyssey* published this piece, not only because it brought me into the children's market, but because I've learned that engaging children in positive learning activities can have more lasting effects than rattling off rules.

Presently, I teach in an elementary school, but I have also worked as a journalist. Teaching is a consuming profession; time for writing is precious. Therefore, I focus on my passions: nature and social studies.

—Kathryn Jankowski

From the Editor

When I saw the "Gorilla Etiquette" query, I knew it would be perfect for our upcoming issue on primates. It complements a more serious story on zoo habitats and engages the reader by presenting the information in the form of a quiz. It also references Koko, the gorilla who is featured in the issue. The proposed piece was short, on target, and certainly worth taking a chance on an unknown writer.

—Elizabeth Lindstrom, Senior Editor, *Odyssey*

Odyssey
10–16 years
470 words

When Katie L. Bates was nine years old, her mother gave her a small red notebook. Katie's first entry was, "I am writing, scribbling rather, just for fun." She went on, "The lines are to short for good rhymes. Storys take up two many pages."

As Katie grew up, she continued to write in notebooks and diaries. Her spelling improved. She even became an English teacher. And she wrote lots of rhymes and stories.

One of those rhymes became an anthem that we sing today—more than one hundred years after she wrote it. The song is "America the Beautiful."

Bates wrote the poem in a notebook during her first trip west in 1893, when she was thirty-three years old. She was headed for Colorado College in Colorado Springs to teach a summer class. At that time she was Miss Katharine L. Bates, a professor at Wellesley College in Massachusetts.

Traveling by train, she stopped in Chicago to visit a friend. While there she spent time at the World's Columbian Exposition. The Exposition was a celebration of the four hundredth anniversary of Christopher Columbus's arrival in the New World. No matter that the fair was a year late—it was spectacular. Many of the buildings were white, and the fair became known as "The White City."

By the fourth of July, Bates was in western Kansas. She noted its "fertile prairies" in her diary. When she finally arrived in Colorado, she wrote that she had begun teaching "under the purple range of the Rockies."

Summer session lasted only a few weeks. When it was over, the teachers wanted to celebrate. What better way than to go to the top of nearby Pikes Peak, the best-known mountain in the Rockies?

Katharine Bates wrote that her group was "not vigorous enough to achieve the climb on foot nor adventurous enough for burro riding." So they made their way

From Scribbles to Spacious Skies

By Donna D. Feeney

huddled in prairie wagons.

On the tailboards of the covered wagons were signs saying "Pikes Peak or Bust," the same slogan gold prospectors had used years before. Horses took the group halfway up the mountain. Mules pulled the wagons the rest of the way.

"We were hoping for half an hour on the summit," wrote Miss Bates. But when the teachers got to the top, two of them became faint from the thin air. The group was quickly "bundled into the wagons" for the "downward plunge."

Katharine Bates said that there was hardly time on the peak for more than an "ecstatic gaze." She added, however, "it was then and there, as I was looking out over the sea-like expanse of fertile country spreading away so far under those ample skies, that the opening lines of the hymn floated into my mind."

As she put the poem on paper, she also recalled the gleaming "White City" of the Exposition. She expanded on it as "thine alabaster cities."

By the time Bates left Colorado Springs, the four stanzas of "America the Beautiful" were penciled in her notebook.

When she returned home, she was so busy at school that she laid the notebook aside. It wasn't until two years later that she submitted the poem to a publication. It first appeared in *The Congregationalist* on July 4, 1895—a perfect date for a patriotic poem.

But that version isn't exactly the same as the one we sing today. It began:

O beautiful for halcyon skies,
For amber waves of grain,
For purple mountain majesties
Above the enameled plain!

Most people liked her poem, but some suggested changes. Miss Bates considered the ideas, which came from all over the United States. Over time, she rewrote parts of the poem. A new version was published in 1904. Later, changes were made to the third stanza, and "America the Beautiful" became the poem we know today.

Even as she was revising it, the poem was being sung to many different tunes. In 1926 a contest was sponsored by the past presidents of the National Federation of Music Clubs to find an appropriate melody for "America the Beautiful." Almost nine hundred compositions were submitted, but none of them was selected.

The National Federation of Music Clubs and the National Hymn Society wanted the poem to become the country's national anthem. But it was "The Star-Spangled Banner," which had been sung by the public and the armed forces for many years, that became the official national anthem five years later, in 1931.

Today, "America the Beautiful" is usually sung to the hymn "Materna," written by Samuel A. Ward. Ward, who lived from 1847 to 1903, was a church organist, choirmaster, and music-store owner in Newark, New Jersey.

Throughout her life, Katharine Lee Bates never stopped filling notebooks with her "scribbling." She wrote many poems as well as travel books, textbooks, and children's books.

But it is the poem she wrote 401 years after Columbus first came to the New World that continues to remind Americans of the sweeping beauty and majesty of their country. It is no wonder that "America the Beautiful" has been called the unofficial national anthem of the United States.

From the Author

When I was 10 years old, my piano teacher gave me a book called *Famous Hymns with Stories and Pictures*, by Elizabeth H. Bonsall. Although I was supposed to learn how to play the music, I was more fascinated with the stories (typically a paragraph or two) behind the songs. As it happens, "America the Beautiful" was included in the book.

I've always been curious as to what inspires a writer, composer, or artist to create his or her work. I've written a few other (unpublished) stories about women who've written enduring lyrics, including Julia Ward Howe, who wrote "The Battle Hymn of the Republic." The fact that these patriotic songs were written by women also tweaked my imagination.

I've always loved history, and I want to share the past with readers by making it come to life for them. Since I was interested in this topic at age 10, I thought that others in that same age group would be as well. Also, since "America the Beautiful" is sung regularly in schools, youngsters have a frame of reference.

I also liked the idea that a woman who became an English professor and the creator of such a well-loved song couldn't spell very well when she was nine. I thought that would be inspirational to young, "not-so-hot" spellers.

I did a lot of research, starting with the *Companion to the United Methodist Hymnal*. From there I went to the local library and eventually utilized the New York Public Library. I used such books as *American Women Writers* *from Colonial Times to the Present* and the *Women Who's Who of America 1914–1915*, but my best source was a book written by Dorothy Burgess, Katharine Bates's niece. She used family documents, diaries, and letters owned by her aunt. My biggest thrill in the research was finding the issue of the July 4, 1895, *Congregationalist* (in which "America," as it was then called, first appeared) on microfiche at the New York Public Library.

I don't use a plan or outline. The number of words permitted by the publication determines the length. However, in this article, I knew I wanted to include something about Bates's childhood, her career, and why she wrote the poem. I use quotes when the subject's words move the story or explain something better than narration would. Again, in this article, I wanted to quote her misspelled diary entry to make a point.

I don't know how many revisions I did, but my folder is thick. After I've written and rewritten, I show my work to my writers' group and then re-work it again. Most of the time, and I believe this was such a case, I take the re-rewritten work back for further critiques.

I submitted this article to *Highlights* because the magazine features a variety of work, including historical nonfiction, and it also covers the age group I hoped to reach. I thought most youngsters eight and older would be able to read the piece, and hoped that younger ones would like to hear it read aloud.

—Donna D. Feeney

From the Editor

I always get a little suspicious when I get a nonfiction submission from an author and it's thin. I enjoy receiving really thick packages, full of copies of research, a juicy article, a detailed bibliography, and a thoughtful but short and crisp letter of introduction. This is what greeted me when I received "From Scribbles to Spacious Skies" by Donna D. Feeney. I hadn't heard of the author so I didn't know what to expect, though by the thickness of the query I knew I probably wouldn't be disappointed.

When I opened Donna's package I went straight to the cover letter to see what I was in for. The story of the writing of "America the Beautiful" didn't exactly thrill me, but the title of the article and the author's passion for the subject captivated me. I went to the bibliography and copies of research to see if the author's passion for the subject was matched with thorough research. Luckily it was!

I read Donna's article without any hesitations, at least as far as the research went. So many times articles can be well researched but fall flat in style, direction, and tone. It's really hard to be a great researcher and creative writer at the same time.

Like the cover letter and bibliography, Donna's article was first-rate. It was not only well written, but it also placed the subject in a historical context. I understood the times in which Katharine Lee Bates lived and how her early love of poetry and English led her to write this important work.

After having read the article I knew the author was really serious and that she would be easy to work with. I tend to be in touch with authors on a regular basis, working on rewrites, more research, contacts with experts, and photo research. Donna was always willing to help out. She, like me, wanted to make the article even better—to make it work within the framework of *Highlights*. This back and forth with the author can take several months and Donna was right there—and eager to boot!

Working with her on this article made me want to work with her again. She's the kind of author editors dream of.

—Carolyn Yoder, Senior Editor,
Highlights for Children

Highlights for Children
2–12 years
850 words

The Secret Life of Sea Turtles

By Carol A. Barre

On a hot, humid August night, Sam Stitt, 17, and a few friends crouch in a North Carolina sand dune. They're guarding a nest of about 100 eggs laid two months earlier by a loggerhead sea turtle.

In between swats at mosquitoes buzzing their ears and biting through their long-sleeve shirts and long pants, the boys debate whether the eggs will hatch tonight.

They're anxious, because their next job is to ensure the hatchlings get safely from their nest to the Atlantic Ocean, about 50 yards away.

Sam, an Eagle Scout, has volunteered more than 100 hours with the Topsail Island Turtle Project. The project's goal: to study—and save—the secret life of sea turtles.

Trouble on the Beach

Sea turtles are in trouble. All seven species and one sub-species are endangered or threatened (see "Turtles in Trouble" box). They have been killed for soup, meat and shell products. Shrimpers and fishermen accidentally drown turtles when the animals get caught in nets. But people like Sam Stitt are helping in small ways to even the score.

Sam and the Topsail Island volunteers protect the nests from turtles' natural enemies—rats, foxes, coyotes, raccoons and dogs that eat the leathery eggs and tiny hatchlings—and from people who unknowingly endanger the animals. This August night, for example, Sam intercepts a jogger and asks him to avoid the area.

"It's Starting!"

When Sam gets back to the nest, another volunteer whispers, "It's starting!" The volunteers strain to see in the red glow of their shaded flashlights.

Tiny avalanches of sand fall toward a small pit in the middle of the nest.

A black, pea-sized head appears, quickly followed by a disk about the size of a silver

TURTLE TECH

Studies of nesting, captive or injured turtles provide only a little information about their normal life at sea. Now technology is helping to fill in the gaps in the secret lives of sea turtles.

• At nesting beaches, scientists inject a tiny microchip ID tag into the female turtle's shoulder. When the turtle comes ashore again, they read the chip with a hand-held scanner, like the ones stores use to read product labels. By knowing how often the turtle comes ashore, scientists help measure whether conservation projects are working.

• Miniature satellite transmitters help track sea turtles.

• Researcher Scott Eckert uses time, pressure, and depth recorders to study how one species, the leatherback, survives at depths that would crush a human being and in water so cold it would kill us in minutes.

• Dr. Dave Nelson works with the U.S. Army Corps of Engineers, using an electronic beacon to monitor turtles resting in channels. That way, the Corps can schedule its dredging projects for seasons when they will not injure or kill turtles.

---

dollar. The turtle scrambles from side to side, baffled by its sudden freedom. It is rapidly joined by four nestmates. Suddenly, the nest boils with hatchlings faster than Sam can count them.

The leaders scramble toward the surf, down a "runway" Sam's team had smoothed in the sand. They leveled footprints and sand castles to make the hatchlings' journey easier, saving the turtles' energy for their long swim.

Be the Moon

Hatchlings follow the moon's light. Tonight it's cloudy, though, so Sam wades into the water holding a flashlight "moon." As the turtles scramble toward Sam's light, he sees a stray. "That one's headed for the pier!" Sam says, and a teammate guides the hatchling back, holding a towel to block the light from the pier.

Another turtle has

TURTLES IN TROUBLE:

All sea turtles, seven species and one subspecies, are listed as endangered or threatened.

Olive Ridley (Lepidochelys olivacea): About 22 to 28 inches long and less than 100 pounds. Small, hard shells and relatively large heads. Nesting populations in Mexico are endangered, threatened elsewhere in its Pacific range.

Flatback (Natator depressa): About 39 inches long and 198 pounds. Flat shell. Found in Australia.

Kemp's Ridley (Lepidochelys kempii): Smallest sea turtle, about 22 to 28 inches and 77 to 93 pounds. Broad, heart-shaped, gray to olive green shell. The most endangered of all, breeding only on a small beach in Mexico.

Hawksbill (Eretmochelys imbricata): About 30 to 35 inches long and 95 to 165 pounds. Elongated oval shell, mostly brown. Endangered. Found in the Atlantic, Pacific and Caribbean.

Green (Chelonia mydas mydas): About 4 feet long and 440 pounds. Heart-shaped shell. Nesting populations are endangered on the east coast of Florida and the Pacific coast of Mexico, threatened elsewhere.

Leatherback (Dermochelys coriacea): Largest sea turtle, 5 to 8 feet long and 640 to 1,300 pounds. Leathery skin. Endangered. Most widely distributed, found in open oceans from Alaska to Africa.

Loggerhead (Caretta caretta): Sea turtle most commonly seen in the Southeast. Grows to about 200 pounds, sometimes up to 1,000. Characterized by its large head and blunt jaws. Threatened.

Black (Chelonia mydas agassizii): A subspecies of the green turtle. Grows to about 39 inches long and 220 pounds. Heart-shaped black shell. Found in the Pacific tropics.

SAVE THE TURTLES

Eagle Scout Sam Stitt helps out at the Karen Beasley Sea Turtle Rescue and Rehabilitation Center, known around Topsail Island, NC, as the Turtle Hospital. In a typical day he might clean tanks, fish for the patients' dinner or hold a turtle for a change of bandages.

Check out how the patients are doing on the Internet: **www.seaturtlehospital.org**

Like Sam, Scouts in many coastal communities work for sea turtle survival:

• On Long Island, NY, and other northern beaches Scouts patrol in autumn and early winter to recover cold-stunned sea turtles. Loggerheads, greens and others can die if they stay too late in northern waters.

• Saving the dunes of nesting beaches is critical to saving sea turtle populations. Scouts plant old Christmas trees along beaches to serve as sand traps, helping the wind build new dunes.

• Any Scout project that reduces water pollution or waterborne trash may help sea turtles in the long run. Rivers wash into the sea. Sea turtles often eat plastic bags or dead balloons, mistaking them for jellyfish.

• Scout troops can "adopt" a turtle by raising funds for a research or rehab facility like the one where Sam Stitt volunteers.

Find out more in the "Fish and Wildlife Management" (BSA Supply No. 33307, phone 800-323-0732) and the "Reptile and Amphibian Study" (No. 33288) merit badge pamphlets.

Or look on the Internet: **www.turtles.org**: Turtle Trax has a Kidz Korner and lists volunteer opportunities.

www.cccturtle.org: The Caribbean Conservation Corporation in Gainesville, FL, offers detailed information about sea turtles and how you can help them.

this beach in 20 to 40 years. Weighing 250 to 500 pounds and with shells two feet to nearly five feet long, they return to land to lay their eggs.

What happens in all that time in between? Scientists are curious. But it's hard to study animals you can't see for more than a few hours a year.

For now, about all the turtles have is the kindness of a few volunteers like Eagle Scout Sam Stitt.

For More Information
For detailed information on sea turtles, check your library or bookstore for these titles:

• "The Sea Turtle: So Excellent a Fish," by Archie Carr (1986, University of Texas Press)

• "Sea Turtles," by Jeff Ripple (1996, Voyageur Press)

• "Search for the Great Turtle Mother," by Jack Rudloe (1998, Pineapple Press)

stopped. Three nestmates rearend it. Momentarily stunned, it scrambles up and continues its journey. The team laughs, then cheers it on.

Crabs in search of an easy meal descend, but Sam and his team shoo them away. By now volunteers line the runway, and the leaders of the nest plunge into the sea.

The Mystery Begins
In less than an hour the last stragglers disappear into the waves. The males may never again walk on land. The loggerhead females may return to

From the Author

"The Secret Life of Sea Turtles" began as an article outline for Assignment 8 of the Institute's course. Jean Beasley, the manager of the all-volunteer Topsail Island Turtle Project, lives next door to my mother in NC. Mom had volunteered with the project for several seasons, walking the beaches to spot signs of turtle nesting. Since my husband Jim and I were "camped out" in our 34' motorhome in Mom's driveway that summer, the Turtle Project seemed a natural subject.

A brief interview with Ms. Beasley, attendance at a public information session, and some background reading were enough to help me write the outline. For purposes of the assignment, finding three possible markets for an environment/wildlife article was easy with *Children's Magazine Market*. I sent for guidelines, read some sample copies at the library, and requested others.

I learned from Jean Beasley that the Turtle Project had an Eagle Scout candidate, Sam Stitt, working with them that summer. Scouts = *Boys' Life*, right? I read *Boys' Life* at the library, sent for guidelines, then contacted Sam's mother for permission to interview him and follow him on some of his activities.

When my instructor responded with great support, "If *Boys' Life* doesn't buy it, I'm sure you could market it elsewhere," I was ready to go. I took a deep breath, tuned up the query and sent it off with outline and bibliography—just for practice. I figured they'd probably say no, but why not start at the top?

A month later, I found a package at the post office: an assignment from *Boys' Life*, a contract, and in-depth guidelines! I was in shock. Then I read the letter more thoroughly. The article that Editor Michael Goldman was requesting was not *quite* the one I had already written, and not the one already reviewed by my instructor but something more ambitious, requiring more about current sea turtle research. My query had led the editor to believe I was a *real writer*. Was I?

My library and the Internet yielded too much information for an 1,100-word article. After several false starts, I selected one research aspect that I thought would grab 12- to 17-year-olds—tracking turtle migration via satellite—and hung the rest of the article around that. I added two sidebars, one on Sam's work with the Topsail Island Project and one about human threats to turtle survival. I revised the title to "The Secret Life of Sea Turtles" and sent a final draft for review to Sam, Jean, and two of the researchers whose work was described.

Boys' Life has a reputation for accuracy, reinforced by their assignment guidelines: every fact should be backed up by original sources. This article was packed with facts, but I felt I couldn't just send the fact checkers a box of printout and books and make them wade through it all. So I created a footnoted version just as if it was for a term paper or an adult journal. Then I photocopied the source pages with penned footnotes directly on the source text. Even so, the packet I sent was over an inch thick. And it was in by deadline.

Shortly after New Year's, I got the letter: "We would like you to take a shot at reworking . . . " My first reaction was, "I am sick of sea turtles. I don't WANT to write it again." But the letter was also complimentary about my research. Mr. Goldman seemed to feel I could shift Sam back into the lead.

I gave myself permission not to decide for three days. By then I had cooled off. I reread the original assignment letter, the suggestions for revision, and two earlier *Boys' Life* articles Mr. Goldman had included, as samples of what he had in mind. I also reminded myself that the contract included a kill fee. So if I gave the rewrite an honest effort, at least I'd salvage 25%, and then I'd have three articles to sell elsewhere. I e-mailed my intention to try again.

Fortunately I had kept my earlier drafts, and among them was a lead that focused on Sam and a group of volunteers waiting for a turtle nest to hatch. The advantage of this lead over the hospital scene I'd used in Assignment 8 was that it tied in more quickly to the research I wanted to include.

I found that I was tempted to fictionalize: to make Sam do or say things in the scene that he *might* have done or said, but that I didn't have evidence or witness for. I wanted to make it more dramatic. I hesitated though, and decided I'd better check on editorial policy. Mr. Goldman responded with a very helpful clarification. In order not to lose some of the juiciest bits of research info, I reworked the sidebars and suggested photo captions.

A month later I e-mailed my writing group: "*Boys' Life* sent a check for the whole amount!" My next communication from *Boys' Life* was in May—a call from the fact checkers. They wanted to clarify whether there were eight species of sea turtles or seven. From the fact checker I learned that publication was scheduled for the August issue.

Knowing that many publications hit the stands a month before the cover date, I began haunting the library in July, but my copies came from *Boys' Life* before the library got theirs. The editorial team had cut quite a lot of my narrative, but they captured the essence and did a great job with layout and photo selection.

I never did query other markets regarding turtle articles, but the original Assignment 9 version took Third Place (with a cash prize) in a nonfiction contest at *ByLine Magazine*. Who knows? Now that I've dug into the material again to work on this "story behind the story," maybe I'll brush off the files and send out some fresh queries.

—Carol A. Barre

From the Editor

Carol Barre certainly knew to whom she was pitching this article. (Number one piece of advice to first-timers: Know your market.) Instead of offering a generic look at sea turtles, she focused her pitch and knew to center the piece on a boy—in this case, an Eagle Scout—who worked with turtles.

Boys' Life features need to have this personal angle. We don't print reports; we print active, interesting, and entertaining tales of life. Ms. Barre provided such a tale. And with the detailed, scientifically accurate, and well-researched sidebar on sea turtles, we more than met our goal of educating the reader while entertaining him.

—Michael Goldman, Senior Editor, *Boys' Life*

Boys' Life
6–18 years
1,055 words

SEATS-OF-EASE

By Joe J. Simmons III • Illustrated by Craig Spearing

If you want to relieve yourself . . . you have to hang out over the sea like a cat-burglar clinging to a wall . . . Take a firm grip of the wooden horse's mane; for if you let go, he will throw you, and you will never ride him again. The perilous perch and the splashing of the sea are both discouraging to your purpose, and your only hope is to dose yourself with laxatives.
—Eugénio de Salazar, 1573

In the passage above, a sailor vividly describes what it was like to go to the bathroom aboard a ship crossing the Atlantic in the 1500s. One of a very few firsthand descriptions that detail the experience, it is important to anyone studying the history of old sailing ships.

Actually, disposing of human waste overboard into the sea seemed an efficient, commonsense approach. Sailors used waste buckets or a small platform that gave them greater access to the sea.

With the development of compasses and improved nautical charts in the 1200s and 1300s, captains began to venture farther from shore. Shipbuilding techniques advanced as well, and vessels were better able to withstand the rigors of deep-water navigation. One development, the increase in the number of decks, offered added protection from the elements and helped improve seaworthiness, but it also created problems.

WHERE VERMIN ABOUND

More decks meant less air could flow to the spaces between and below decks and less light and more humidity at lower deck levels. The addition of decks

This illustration shows how, in centuries past, shipwrights fashioned an external toilet on the starboard (right) side of the stern of an Arab dhow (type of ship used along the coasts of the Indian Ocean).

Dig Data
"Head," the common name for a ship's toilet, traces its origin to the word "beakhead," a projecting structure on a ship's bow. These structures were often used as a platform or place to stand or sit by sailors needing to relieve themselves.

also created a birdcage-like environment in which every imaginable bit of debris, filth, and human waste from the decks above gravitated to the bilges, the bottommost interior part of the vessel. The result was a rich organic compost in the lowest, foulest reaches of the ship that was a breeding ground for great numbers of rats, lice, weevils, fleas, and cockroaches.

Captains, shipowners, and shipwrights developed new ideas to improve the unhealthful conditions below deck in the sailors' quarters. They believed that, in terms of sight and smell, it was better for human waste to be eliminated directly into the sea rather than to the interior of the hull (the body of the ship). The fact that the ship would also be a healthier place for the crew was not a consideration since the connection between filth and disease was not yet fully understood.

Hanging on to the rigging near the bow of a ship may have worked in good weather, but just imagine the difficulties in stormy weather.

SEATS-OF-EASE AND PISSDALES

The development of external toilets was helped by changes in northern European hull design. By the late 1600s, these features had fully developed, and most were kept with little or no modification until the early 1800s.

What made these external toilets possible was the construction of platforms at the bow (front) and stern (back) of a vessel. The platforms consisted of overhangs and projections on which toilets were built that emptied directly into the sea. Projecting shelves and chain supports for the mast rigging on a ship's side provided other structures on which toilets could be fitted.

The 1600s witnessed major developments in shipboard sanitary facilities. One, known as seats-of-ease, was placed within the structure of the beakhead (the bow or forepart of a vessel). Drainage channels directed the waste into the sea. Fore turrets, or small "towers" in the front part of a vessel, were a French design. Access was through a door in the beakhead or forward part of vessel, and there was often a small porthole for ventilation and light.

Another type of toilet was the piss-dale. Installed in the beakhead and in the middle of a vessel, it consisted of a simple urinal channel equipped with lead pipes that extended directly through the platform at the bow or through the sides of the ship. The piss-dale offered no privacy or protection from the elements. With the advent of iron-hulled ships in the mid-1800s, the bow of a ship became a poor place for a sailor's "potty" and it was moved to the middle of the ship.

'RELIEF' IN THE STERN

Studies of 1400s ships suggest various possible designs for sanitary facilities in the stern—these would have been used by the officers. They included barrel-like attachments, closet-like additions, and structures that closely resemble castle turrets. Improvements and changes were made through the centuries. All, however, offered more privacy than the accommodations offered crew members. The first flushing water closets were installed in the officers' quarters of British naval vessels in 1779.

From the Author

I wrote "Seats-of-Ease" at the request of Rosalie Baker, the editor of *Dig*. The article was based on material researched and developed for my master's thesis. The original research took two to three years, but adapting the facts for the article went quickly. I worked from an article plan—organized thematically. The article's original length was twice that of the published version—the editor cut to fit the magazine's specifications. The editor came up with the title—one of the catchy names for ships' toilets in the bow of the vessels.

I am an underwater archaeologist, principally researching early Contact Period Spanish shipwrecks of the late fifteenth and early sixteenth centuries. Areas of special interest are nautical hygiene and early modern wrought-iron artillery. I switched careers to general dentistry, where my excavations are smaller but no less wet.

—Joe J. Simmons III

From the Editor

For each issue of *Dig*, work begins first on researching the theme and deciding the topics to be included. For "The Scoop on Poop" issue, I wanted to cover a range of areas—geographically, chronologically, and topically. My research and conversations with archaeologists led me to add an article that would trace the development of toilets—"heads"—on boats. The writer would have to be someone familiar with boats and archaeology.

An educator/archaeologist, who had written for *Dig* and also for *Calliope*, a magazine on world history published by Cobblestone Publishing, suggested Joe Simmons. I called Joe and explained my ideas. He was very willing to tackle the topic, and his article is a great addition to the issue.

"Seats-of-Ease" has the three ingredients I feel are key to a good article: pertinent information, the ability to hold the reader's interest from start to finish without any "sagging" areas, and clarity in presentation.

—Rosalie Baker, Editor, *Dig*

Dig
8–12 years
665 words

GOALIE'S GOLD

By Shannon McMahon

She wears a mask and a helmet, straps pads to her shoulders and legs, and fights off flying objects with a stick. Is she a cartoon superhero?

No, she's Sara DeCosta of Warwick, Rhode Island, and an Olympic gold medal winner in the sport of ice hockey.

Sara grew up with hockey-playing brothers and a dad who coached the sport. Ice hockey seemed as right for her as for anyone. To Sara, it didn't matter that most girls didn't play ice hockey. Sara played, and she played well. She liked "the competition, the speed of the game, and the team atmosphere."

"People, mostly boys, would ask me why I had to play on the boys' team where I didn't belong. I told them if they had a girls' team I'd be on that too," Sara remembers. At that time there were no girls' ice hockey teams that Sara could join. So even though she was teased and had to work hard, she tried her best to play well.

Sara began practicing with her family when she was six years old. Soon she was playing on an A-level team of all boys. When she got to high school, she was the only girl on the ice hockey team. Not only was she the only girl, but she was the goalie, one of the toughest positions to play. Sara

kept practicing and playing when she entered college and was selected for the 1998 U.S. women's Olympic team that won a gold medal at the Winter Olympics in Nagano, Japan.

Capturing the gold was a dream come true for Sara. Even making the team was a challenge for her, having just recovered from a serious injury. Overcoming obstacles like these and being part of a team have taught Sara valuable lessons. She has learned "not to give up, and to count on your teammates and take responsibility when they're counting on you." She does admit, though, that it's difficult when everyone expects her to be perfect on the ice rink. She feels pressured and overwhelmed at times about her hockey performance.

Sara still attends college and trains all year long, even off-season, to stay competitive. She hopes to be part of the Olympic team again in Salt Lake City, Utah, in 2002.

Until then, she works hard as the national spokesperson for seat belt and bicycle helmet safety. She travels throughout her home state, teaching children about the importance of both these safety rules. She hopes to get her message to teenagers as well. She thinks they're "the hardest group to reach." Sara may not be a superhero on television, but she is a hero in the world of hockey and to all the people she helps throughout her state.

From the Author

"Goalie's Gold" was written as an Institute course assignment in nonfiction. I was hesitant about writing nonfiction, as I had written mainly fiction and poetry in the past. When thinking about a subject, I remembered the standard advice to "write what you know." Sara was a hometown hero for a number of years even before her Olympic experience. She was known as an outstanding athlete in a typically male sport. The more I heard her story, the more confidence I had in writing this piece. What could be better? It included sports, overcoming obstacles, and achieving a lifelong goal.

Sara was busy with hockey, college, and community activities at the time, but was gracious in working with me to complete the piece. Sara was often traveling so we never met in person, but did all our corresponding through mail and telephone.

I submitted "Goalie's Gold" to several publishers before it was finally accepted by *On the Line*. I realize now that a market analysis is crucial in deciding where to submit. It may seem like a good idea to submit to the well-known, more prominent publishers. In the end, an author saves time and effort by narrowing the choices by genre and audience. It doesn't matter if it's a publication you may not have heard of in the past. By researching the types of magazines, an author is much more likely to have success or at least get more specific feedback, even if it is a rejection. The editor did not request any revisions for "Goalie's Gold."

I often scribble notes for story ideas or jot down humorous incidents and stories. I am hoping that the time and love I spend with my five young children will someday be seen in stories that I can share with others.

—Shannon McMahon

From the Editor

I was looking for a winter article that would appeal to kids ages 9 to 14. Since part of our readership is Canadian, I knew hockey would be a good subject. Hockey is a growing sport in the U.S., too, so having an American hockey player profile was great.

This article promoted the themes of *On the Line* by encouraging females to try nontraditional activities, and by highlighting someone who worked with spirit and determination against the odds. The fact that she was a gold medal winner was a plus! The article needed few changes.

—Mary Clemens Meyer, Editor, *On the Line*

On the Line
9–14 years
460 words

White Stallion Ballet

By Margo Myler

When you think of horses, do you imagine them dancing? Have you ever seen a stallion kicking his hind hooves in mid-air? The white horses of Vienna have been taught the French classical art form of "dressage" for centuries.

Dressage is a French word that means "to train" in a systematic and gentle way. After years of practice, the graceful movements of these horses resemble those of a ballet dancer.

Horses are taught to perform on command the moves they do naturally. A floating trot, or "passage" looks like a horse trotting in slow motion. An excited horse will naturally "piaffe," or trot in place. Young stallions rise on hind legs, or perform a "levade," to challenge and play with each other.

In medieval times, stallions were taught war exercises, or "airs above the ground," like "caprioles." A straight leap in the air, with hind legs striking out forcefully, cleared enemy foot soldiers.

In Europe, Spanish-bred horses were in great demand in the 1560s. This led to horse experts buying and transporting mares and stallions from Spain. The Austrians also desired the finest horses for instructing Viennese nobles in the fine art of horsemanship.

However, importing Spanish horses became costly, so a stud farm was set up in Lipizza, a small village in the mountains of Austria. The foals born at the Imperial horse farm were called Lipizzaners.

Snowy Austrian winters stopped outdoor training for horses and riders. This led to building an indoor arena in 1735 called the Spanish Riding School.

The frisky dark brown colts gallop up and down the mountainside, developing their lungs in the clean mountain air. By three and a half years of age, the best stallions are taken to the stables at the Spanish Riding School. The Lipizzaner's coat, now gray, will turn pure white within a few more years.

Of course, the young colt must first become familiar with his new home and learn to trust his trainer. For 8 to 10 weeks, the horse will be trained on a lunge line. Moving in a circle around his trainer on a long rein, the young stallion learns balance and coordination in three areas: walk, trot and canter. A sugar pocket can be found in the tail of every trainer's riding jacket for rewarding the horse.

Now, the stallion is ready to feel the experienced rider's weight on his back. The horse must learn to balance not only his body, but the trainer's as well. The rest of his first year, or Lower School, is spent developing his mind, muscles and coordination. During the second phase, or Campaign School, he learns to use his body more, performing exercises that flex, or stretch his joints.

Just like a ballet dancer, the horse's muscles are strengthened and toned, preparing him for the final phase, or High School. The movements learned in the High School are the most difficult—and daring. The "airs above the ground" are performed with at least two legs, often all four, off the ground.

At the Spanish Riding School, training methods pass down by word of mouth from one generation to another. The school chooses its riders carefully and all positions are filled by men 15 years or older. The new student begins his training on an experienced horse known as a "professor." The untrained rider must first learn to balance himself, without reins or stirrups, on the lunge line. After 10 to 12 years of practice, the student will learn how to create movements that look easy.

The rider must be aware of

▲ **Some of the stallions are long reined.**

the Lipizzaner's needs. If a stallion resists, he's not being stubborn; he may not understand what the rider wants him to do. The trainer's job is to make it easy for the horse, to make him comfortable. In dressage, the horse should never be forced to do anything. The rider must have patience, kindness and understanding.

Few people have the patience and commitment needed to earn the title of "bereiter," or certified trainer at the Spanish Riding School.

The Dancing Lipizzaners tour the world, performing in some strange places. But in the grand setting of the Spanish Riding School they are the masters. Eight horses "half pass," or zigzag through the large white pillars of the school. They "passage" proudly, floating above the ground in a slow trot, each mirroring each other's actions. The white "professors" gracefully present the magic of the stallion ballet.

◄ **The stallions perform in shows all around the world.**
Photos: Bob Langrish

From the Author

The idea for "White Stallion Ballet" began with an interview I set up with a friend who trains horses in the art of dressage. She loaned me videotapes of Lipizzaners trained at the Spanish Riding School in Vienna. As I witnessed the graceful maneuvers of the white stallions I decided to focus my article directly on them.

My research process began at the public library. I studied many books on the White Stallions of Vienna and the art of dressage, becoming familiar with their background and early history. The videos were also a great resource in learning the names of maneuvers and dressage techniques. As I researched, I scribbled down many notes, documenting each source in a notebook.

I worked from an article plan. A catchy opening would excite the reader into learning more about these unique animals. A brief history of their origin, and the terrain and weather of Austria were all factors in training them in the classical art form of dressage. Ending with the stallions performing would tie in with the opening paragraph.

I decided the article would not exceed 800 words, therefore, I spent time revising and polishing, focusing on facts that would be interesting and informative to middle-grade readers.

I wrote a query letter to Lesley Ward, Editor of *Young Rider* magazine, asking about interest in this type of article. I learned that timing can play a huge part in marketing a piece. Three days later she phoned me. One of their photographers had just returned from Vienna with pictures of the Lipizzaners at the Spanish Riding School. She described what she wanted for the feature article, and I felt the piece I had written matched her current need. I mailed it to her. She phoned three days later, accepting the material with no revisions.

My articles have been published in *Young Rider* and *Spider* magazines. I also had work accepted by SIRS Publishing, for online use as well as CD-ROM Discoverer. I am currently writing short stories and articles for middle-grade readers.

—Margo Myler

From the Editor

Although *Young Rider* is primarily a practical, "how-to" magazine, we like to include a "horsey interest" feature in every issue. These features are generally done by freelancers, so we can publish a diverse group of features.

There is a traveling Lipizzaner show that many of our readers might go and see, and I thought they would be interested in a feature about the Dancing White Stallions. When Margo sent in her query I checked with one of my photographers to see if he had slides of the stallions and he did, so I commissioned Margo's feature.

All of our freelancers have read *Young Rider* and require very little editing. We are very specific about the magazine's style, and we make sure the writer understands it before she/he sends in the feature. "White Stallion Ballet" required little or no editing.

I rarely have to edit any commissioned freelance material. I sometimes have to shorten things. If something needs major editing, it's unlikely that I will use the writer again.

—Lesley Ward, Editor, *Young Rider*

Young Rider
6–14 years
730 words

Moroccan Good Luck Hands

By Diane Primrose Farrug

Have you ever had a rabbit's foot, a four-leaf clover, or a horseshoe? Do you believe that these objects can bring you good luck? In Morocco, there is a different kind of good luck charm—a hand. Many Moroccan people wear silver hand pendants around their necks. They hang embroidered hands in their homes, and they even paint hands on the outside of buildings or on the back of trucks.

Moroccans call the hand *khamsa*, and it is a symbol of strength, power, and generosity. It also represents the number five, which some Moroccans say has magical powers of protection against the Evil Eye, a vicious stare thought to bring bad luck, illness, or even death. An extra hand helps people feel safe. After all, khamsa charms do not depict just any hand. It is the hand of someone very special.

Muhammad had one beloved daughter, Fatima. Fatima was a beautiful and virtuous young woman. Although she was wealthy, she chose to lead a simple life, and she was always generous and compassionate. Muslims call her the "Lady of Light." They believe in her purity and protection, and they look up to her as an ideal daughter, wife, and mother.

Fatima died when she was only 18 years old, but it is her hand that offers protection for all time.

Khamsa, or Hand of Fatima, pendants are pieces of silver jewelry adorned with amber or other semiprecious stones. Silver is highly prized in Morocco, especially in the countryside. According to oral tradition, silver has magical qualities and represents purity. The palm of the silver hand is engraved with fancy patterns to depict Fatima's hand decorated with *henna*.

Henna is a paste made from a henna plant and smoked over a charcoal fire. Since ancient times, Moroccan women have applied this paste to their hands and feet in lacy, geometric patterns. It dries and stays on for a week or more. Henna decoration is used for special occasions such as weddings or religious holidays. At first glance, you might think a Moroccan woman is wearing a pair of fancy gloves! Fatima's hand is beautiful, as well as protective and lucky.

Whether or not you believe in luck, you can learn a lot about the culture of Morocco through the khamsa symbol. The next time you feel you need a helping hand, try a Moroccan "Good Luck Hand."

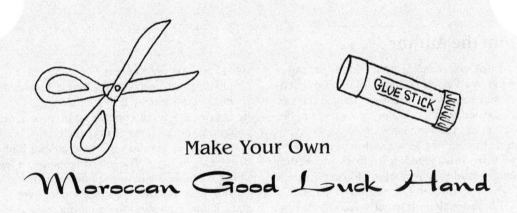

Make Your Own

Moroccan Good Luck Hand

You Need:

construction paper
aluminum foil
glue stick
scissors
pen
sequins

1. Glue a sheet of aluminum foil to a sheet of construction paper. The paper should be just slightly larger than your hand.

2. Trace your hand onto the foil and cut it out.

3. "Engrave" the foil using a ballpoint pen. Decorate with geometric shapes such as lines, circles, squares, diamonds, hearts, stars, or curlicues. Remember the number five.

4. Glue sequins to your "good luck hand" so that it appears to be adorned with jewels.

5. Find a special place to display your khamsa.

From the Author

I like to research material that I can use in my job as a French teacher. I often find article topics by requesting magazine theme lists, and was pleased to see that Morocco was to be featured in an upcoming issue of *Faces*. I began sorting through my files, and found some very brief notes I had jotted down from a workshop: "Hand—good luck symbol in Morocco. Number 5." That was the kernel I needed to get started.

I began with an Internet search to find out if there was much information out there about the hand symbol. Fortunately, there was quite a bit. I used some online information (in both English and French), and then went to the library. I needed to better educate myself about Islam and Moroccan culture in order to have a more solid background to write the piece. Research can be fun, but it can also become unwieldy. I had to focus on the specifics of the symbol and how it related to the culture.

Whenever I teach my students about other cultures, I emphasize the similarities. I find writing nonfiction to be like teaching on paper. All of the same techniques still apply—make the information relevant, interesting, meaningful, and personal. I used "you" because it's how I would address my students.

I had to cut, cut, cut! Each time I went to revise, I could usually find something that could be condensed or cut completely because it deviated from the purpose of my article.

I probably revised my article at least four times, maybe more. The editor requested a few minor changes. Some of the information I included about Morocco was not necessary since it was addressed in other articles in this issue.

I did submit the sidebar along with the article. I actually tried out a few different crafts before I chose one to write about.

I have worked with preschool through high school students for the past 12 years as a French teacher. As a creative outlet, I enjoy writing stories and poems. It wasn't until I took the Institute course that I discovered the fun of creative nonfiction. In addition to the article in *Faces* magazine, I have had rhyming stories and poems published in *Hopscotch: The Magazine for Girls* and *Wee Ones*, an online magazine.

—Diane Primrose Farrug

From the Editor

I chose this particular piece for our issue on Morocco because I felt the article provided a perfect opportunity to inform readers about an aspect of everyday life in Morocco, and the corresponding activity would give readers a hands-on approach to learning about a culture.

I included the activity because it was simple and straightforward. The materials list keeps in mind that most of our readers are students and these activities will be done in a classroom setting, therefore the materials must be readily available and somewhat inexpensive.

—Elizabeth Crooker Carpentiere, Editor, *Faces*

Faces
8–14 Years
500 words

Dr. David Sullivan, pediatric dentist, is just wild about teeth. So are some of his patients. Wild, that is. Really wild.

You see, Dr. David, as many people call him, has some unusual patients. They aren't the children he typically sees each day. They're, well, big . . . and hairy . . . and sometimes weigh more than four hundred pounds. They're real animals—zoo animals.

On most days, Dr. Sullivan tends to his human patients, teaching them how to brush and floss and care for their teeth. A few patients cry. Occasionally one may bite. But, all in all, there isn't much for Dr. Sullivan to be wary of in his practice.

On some days, however, the Cincinnati Zoo calls with some special work for him to do. Since 1982, Dr. Sullivan has volunteered his time performing dental surgery on many of the animals. The zoo may ask him to pull the tooth of a Bengal tiger, repair the tusk of an elephant, or give a root canal to one of their famous gorillas. Whatever they ask, it certainly wouldn't be routine work for most dentists. For most, this would be a frightening experience.

Luckily, Dr. Sullivan feels differently. "I'm not afraid of the animals," he says. "I have been around them so much that I'm used to them."

How does a children's dentist find himself caring for the teeth of a black rhino or a white gibbon? For Dr. Sullivan, it was a matter of chance.

"When I was a kid in school,

OPEN WIDE AND SAY, "ROAR!"

THIS DENTIST HAS MORE THAN JUST KIDS' TEETH TO WORRY ABOUT.

By David Richardson

the only thing I ever wanted to be was a veterinarian," says Dr. Sullivan. "I even applied to veterinary school in college."

But Dr. Sullivan soon realized that veterinary work was impossible for him. "I volunteered at a veterinarian's office to get some experience," he says. "I was miserable. I couldn't breathe. My eyes were swollen shut. I had allergy symptoms."

So Dr. Sullivan tried pediatric dentistry and found he loved it.

After he became a dentist, Dr. Sullivan worked at Children's Hospital in Cincinnati, Ohio. While there, he was asked to help with dental work on some of the animals in the hospital's research lab. It wasn't long before he began a dental program for the animals.

Word of Dr. Sullivan's work with animals spread, and soon King's Island Amusement Park and the Cincinnati Zoo were calling to ask for his help. Now he regularly gets calls from the zoo.

Once in a while, he gets calls from farther away—such as the time the owner of two leopards in Los Angeles flew them to Cincinnati so Dr. Sullivan could care for them. These animals weren't zoo animals. They were animal actors who had already been in two movies and a television show.

Dr. Sullivan has also worked on the famous white tigers belonging to performers Siegfried and Roy. It is vital for these animals to have good teeth. As everyone knows, a beautiful smile is very important in show business.

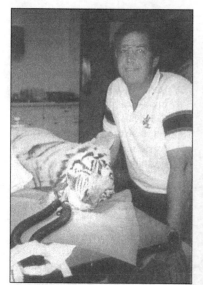

Dr. Sullivan with one of his patients.

Otter teeth may not look like human teeth, but they still need dental care.

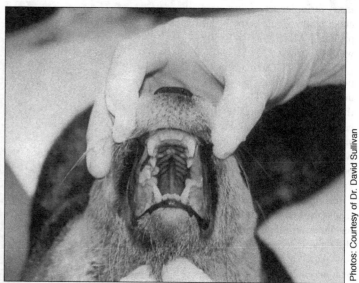

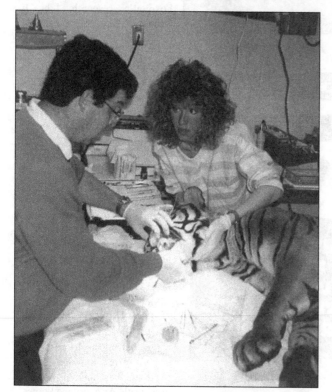

Dr. Sullivan and his assistant at work on one of their "wilder" patients.

But Dr. Sullivan is most proud of the work he did on an ailing African hornbill, an animal that doesn't even have teeth. The bird had broken its bill, which was causing its tongue to dry out. This made it difficult for the bird to eat.

"It would have died," says Dr. Sullivan. He needed something that would work and work well.

What worked was a system of metal posts that either screwed into the bill or locked onto the outside of the beak.

"I'm also proud of the work we did on the first tiger," he says. "There was no literature to go by because the field was so new, so we did it from scratch. We took X-rays and measured the teeth from tiger skulls in a museum. The treatment was one hundred percent successful."

Perhaps the most unusual work Dr. Sullivan ever did was not on a wild animal but on a pet. "I helped a vet put braces on a poodle," he remembers.

While most of Dr. Sullivan's patients have little idea that he spends some of his time working with large, dangerous animals, it's most likely good practice for him. After all, sometimes a busy dentist's office can be a real zoo.

From the Author

The idea for "Open Wide and Say 'Roar!'" originated from an old newspaper article about Dr. Sullivan's work with the tigers at the Cincinnati Zoo. I was considering ideas for an Institute writing assignment when my children had appointments with him. The minute I walked into his office and saw the article on the wall, I knew what my article subject would be.

Since I was aware that a previous article had been written about Dr. Sullivan, coming up with something different and fresh was probably the most difficult part of writing the article. I must have bounced around 10 ideas in my head and 10 more on paper before settling for the one in the article.

I searched the Internet to see if this type of work was commonplace. Then I did a newspaper/magazine article search using our local library's database and discovered yet another article. I ordered a copy, read it thoroughly, wrote down every question or thought I had on the subject, and grouped them according to topic. In my original phone conversation with Dr. Sullivan, I asked about available photographs, and he generously offered me access to his personal collection.

I wrote down additional questions that came to mind prior to my interview with Dr. Sullivan. I especially focused on the strange or unusual. Being a veteran teacher, I know that anyone who works with children or animals always has an interesting story or two, and these stories are usually the most entertaining to kids.

I listened to the interview tape a dozen times before I began writing. I wrote a first draft from the top of my head, incorporating anything that came to mind from my memory. Then I went back to the tape, made sure my facts were correct, and found the quotes that would enhance the text.

The original article was over 1,200 words long. I cut, revised, read it out loud, and put it aside for a while. The real difficulty was cutting several stories/events that I found interesting. I did six to eight drafts before I submitted it to the Institute as an assignment. My instructor's comments were positive and the suggested changes were minor.

When the article was accepted by *Highlights*, they asked for different photos, so I contacted Dr. Sullivan, and he allowed me to select more. The editor called me to get a new quote for the article, then she sent me a copy of the revisions she had made with a note telling me to contact her if there were any problems. The changes were fairly minor and, in truth, made the article flow better.

I chose to submit my article to *Highlights for Children* for two reasons. First, I was aware that they were open to working with new writers. Every piece of information I read about magazine writing for children ranked them very high in this category. Second, I was familiar with the magazine.

My advice is to look around you; we all know interesting people, chances are some of them do things that would be interesting to kids. Look for the unusual or weird for the hook or to add color to your profile. Always send a thank you note after you interview a source for an article and another when the article is published.

I work as a junior high language arts teacher, and my interests include writing for children as well as educating parents about the importance of reading and writing education. I have been published in *Spectrum*, and work as a children's book reviewer for the online e-zine *Gotta Write Network*.

—David Richardson

From the Editor

From the moment I started reading David Richardson's manuscript for "Open Wide and Say 'Roar!'" I knew it was something we'd want to publish in *Highlights*. Not only was this a story about a career many kids may not have thought of, but it also shows that if you love doing something, you can find a way to be involved with it even if you have physical or other limitations that might make it seem as if your dream is impossible. I wondered how many kids out there love animals but have allergies to them and think they could never fulfill their dream of working with them. Well, here's a guy who overcame that problem; I wanted kids to be aware of that.

I also liked that the author had gone right to the source and spent time interviewing this doctor. It gives the article a personal feel and gives the reader the chance to get to know the subject on a more intimate level. The author also did a good job of asking the questions that I felt kids would want answered.

When we originally received the manuscript, the one hesitation I had was regarding the photos. They weren't as good as I would have liked. However, the author was very helpful in securing new photos from Dr. Sullivan's collection, and the minute I saw that wide-open gorilla mouth, I knew we'd have a spread that kids would really stop and look at.

—Andra Serlin, Associate Editor,
Highlights for Children

Highlights for Children
2–12 years
700 words

The Arts at Schönbrunn

By Barbara Krasner-Khait

In 1762, six-year-old Wolfgang Amadeus Mozart and his older sister, Maria Anna (also known as Nannerl), performed a duet for Maria Theresa and her family at their summer palace, Schönbrunn. After Mozart finished, the emotional young prodigy bounded onto the lap of the empress, put his arms around her neck, and kissed her.

Mozart and his sister performed twice for the empress, and once for the children of the imperial family. The two were also given presents and invitations to concerts. On several occasions, Maria Theresa took the young boy on her knee while he played the harpsichord.

Like most Habsburgs, Maria Theresa was a well-trained musician herself. Even as a child, she was a talented singer and actress. Once, she jokingly called herself the oldest virtuosa in Europe, because her father made her sing on stage at the age of five.

In 1741, Maria Theresa had her court architect, Nicolo Pacassi, begin construction on a small theater in the northeast corner of the ceremonial courtyard at Schönbrunn. According to the empress, "We must have theatrical performances, for without them one cannot remain in such a large residence."

The theater's stage served not only as a showplace for the invited artists but for the family as well. Maria Theresa's children, including the gifted dancer Marie Antoinette, displayed their artistic talents at numerous family and public performances. Maria Theresa's court poet, Pietro Antonio Metastasio, composed words that were set to music by former music director Christoph Willibald Gluck, one of the greatest composers of the 1700s.

One attraction, in particular, set Schönbrunn apart. In the summer of 1777, a relative of Maria Theresa's son-in-law came to the palace for a visit. To honor him, Hungarian prince Miklós Esterházy brought marionettes, singers, and musicians from his estate and had them perform a *parody* of Gluck's opera, *Alceste*, a mythological story about an ancient Greek queen. With this performance, the marionette theater tradition at Schönbrunn was born.

Famous musicians and writers composed special pieces for this theater.

> **Parody** refers to a literary or musical work that imitates the characteristic style of another work or writer or composer in a satirical or humorous way.

Joseph Haydn, in charge of most of the Ezterházy family musical activities, composed several marionette operas, including *Dido*, in honor of the legendary queen of Carthage in North Africa. Mozart performed his opera, *The Impresario for the Emperor*, a one-act musical comedy. The German writers Johann Wolfgang von Goethe and Friedrich Schiller also wrote for the marionette performances.

Today, the theater is home to the Vienna Chamber Opera and to a school for aspiring young actors. Since 1992, the palace's imperial gardens have attracted many visitors to its annual outdoor Mozart Festival.

From the Author

When I attended the Highlights Foundation Writers Workshop in Chautauqua, New York, my mentor knew my interest in writing history articles for children and suggested I query *Cobblestone* and *Calliope*. When I returned from the conference, I did just that. The next themed issue for *Calliope* was about Maria Theresa, whom I had studied in high school and college. I tried to find an unusual angle and found an anecdote in a travel guide about Mozart playing for the empress as a child prodigy.

I was fortunate that because my undergraduate degree is in German, I had no trouble reading books and Web content in that language. The challenges were limiting the article's word count and keeping the content lively and engaging. I tried to put myself in the place of a 10- to 14-year-old reader when deciding which research facts to include and which to exclude.

I researched a combination of travel guides, scholarly texts from a university library, biographies of Mozart and Maria Theresa, and the Schönbrunn website, where I found Maria Theresa's quote.

I submitted a query letter, outline, and proposed bibliography according to *Calliope*'s guidelines. Editor Rosalie Baker called a few short weeks after my submission to tell me she liked the Mozart anecdote I included but wanted me to cover the arts at the palace more broadly. I later found that the more detailed I initially made the outline, the easier it was to write the article, especially with a short deadline facing me.

I felt a sense of accomplishment when this first article was published. I had set a goal and met it. I decided to write for children while lying in a hospital bed with meningitis. I wanted to do something more meaningful, impactful, and satisfying than my marketing management job in a high-tech corporation.

By the time the article was published, I had developed a practice of querying the magazine monthly. The approach paid off just a month after my first article appeared with an assignment of three articles for one issue. Since then, I've written eight articles for *Calliope* and fifteen for other Cobblestone Publishing Group magazines, which makes me feel confident in the adage, "Write what you know." The passion for the subject will come through the research and writing.

—Barbara Krasner-Khait

From the Editor

Barbara Krasner-Khait had queried several times before I called her about writing an article for *Calliope*. I liked her queries, especially as she seemed to be an author who researched her topic well, had a good grasp of the English language, and expressed her ideas in an interesting and informative manner. Her style was not flowery, nor did she feel it necessary to use short, staccato-type sentences because she was writing for 10- to 15-year-olds.

When I received her article, which arrived on time and with an excellent bibliography that included a variety of resources (especially current ones), I saw that she stayed with the assigned topic, did not include details that duplicated material assigned to other articles (I had sent her the outline for the issue), and wrote in a style that was accessible, but not condescending, to our audience.

I have since assigned Barbara several articles and will continue to consider her among my regular authors, as the characteristics that impressed me with the queries and first article continue to define her style as an author.

—Rosalie Baker, Editor, *Calliope*

Calliope
8–14 years
430 words

By Ruth Boston

Aztec Soccer

Imagine if your parents bet everything they owned on your game!

Huanco (wan-co) wiped sweat from his brow, breathing heavily. His back ached where the hard rubber ball had smacked him. He licked his dry lips, tasting dust and sweat, and passed his hand over his itchy eyes. He watched as his teammate Tlamil (tlah-meel) prepared to launch the ball again.

He tensed as the ball (about the size of a volleyball) came toward him. He got behind it and leaped to slam his knee into it. It sailed in a graceful arc over all but one of the opposing team's players, toward the wide end zone. Huanco held his breath. The last opponent butted the ball with his hip, preventing the score and pushing it back into play.

Huanco groaned and shook his head. A member of the opposing team elbowed the ball into the air, setting it up. Huanco threw his body in front of an opponent to prevent him from reaching the ball. He was shoved roughly for his trouble. His opponent kneed the ball, and it soared high over Huanco's team. Score.

The crowd around the I-shaped stone court pressed closer and cheered loudly, a few booing and throwing rocks or dirt. Their brightly colored clothing, some with feathers woven into the cloth, reminded him of jungle birds. Huanco imagined he could hear his father's proud voice telling of the honor Huanco

No matter what the score, the team that gets the ball through one of the rings wins the game.

was bringing his family by playing the game of tlachtli (t-lock-tlee). He knew that many of the crowd, like his father, had bet everything they owned on the outcome of the game. Huanco's father had seen the shaman, who had forecast good luck for Huanco's team.

Huanco grunted. The other team was winning 5-2. Usually, the shaman was more accurate.

He shifted his shoulders under the leather pads he wore. Sweat trickled from his thick black hair

into his eyes. He swiped his brow again and ground his teeth in frustration. Then he took a deep breath and released it slowly. "Only the moment matters," his tlachtli master had drilled into him. "Don't dwell on mistakes."

Tlamil launched the ball again. Huanco watched as it neared and swung his leg heartily to knee it upward, then smashed his elbow into it. The ball hurtled against the wall, bounced off and scraped through one of the iron rings mounted 20 feet up.

Huanco stopped dead, his mouth hanging open. No matter what the score, the team that gets the ball through one of the rings wins the game. The game was over! His teammates gathered around him, pumping his arms and pounding his back. The crowd, suddenly quieter, melted quickly away. Only a few disgusted spectators who had lost their bets stayed a moment longer to hurl angry words and handfuls of dirt at the players.

"Come on," Tlamil urged,

pulling at Huanco's elbow. He grinned widely. "They're getting away!"

Huanco followed his friend through the end zone and around the wall to the street. The citizens of Tenochtitlan (ten-ok-tee-tlan) were running wildly in all directions. Shopkeepers were closing their stalls. Mothers were catching their children and dragging them quickly away.

Huanco spotted a fat merchant in a tunic with red and orange trim and pointed him out to Tlamil. Tlamil's grin matched his own. They hurried through the crowds, stalking him with single-minded greed.

The merchant hadn't spotted Huanco and Tlamil yet. He was walking quickly, occasionally casting a glance over his shoulder but not running. Huanco tripped over a fruit cart, barely noticing the ripe melons scattering beneath his feet. He reached his prey just as the merchant reached the doorway of his shop. Tlamil arrived on his heels.

The shopkeeper cursed at them and tried to argue, but they laughed as they relieved him of his tunic and small purse. It was Huanco's right, having scored in the ring, to steal whatever he wanted from any spectator he and his teammates could catch. Lastly, they took his loincloth.

The poor man was so embarrassed Huanco and Tlamil turned their backs and shielded him from view until he was safely inside his shop. Then they burst out laughing and ran to see who else their team had caught.

The True Story

The story of Huanco isn't true, but it could be. The Aztecs were a real people who lived long ago in the area that is now Mexico. They rose to power in the early 1400s and ruled for almost a century before being conquered by the Spanish. The Aztec city Tenochtitlan was located where present-day Mexico City stands.

Archaeologists have learned much about Aztec culture, including the popular game of tlachtli. It was sort of like a violent mix of soccer, volleyball and the Spanish game of pelota (pay-loh-tah). There weren't any fouls in the Aztec game; players were often injured and some were even killed. Only members of the Aztec nobility played tlachtli, but anyone could (and did!) bet on it. Major decisions and whole fortunes could be influenced by the outcome of a single game. One Aztec emperor lost the marketplace of Tenochtitlan when he lost a bet on a game!

What would soccer be like if we played like the Aztecs did? And what if the winning team got to chase people and take their things? Can you imagine the chaos if the World Cup winners were allowed to raid the crowd?

You can play soccer the Aztec way. The rules are simple: only the knees, elbows and hips can be used to hit the ball. Have fun! Just one warning; your friends will probably appreciate it if you let them keep their clothes and money when you win!

For further reading:

The Mighty Aztecs, Gene S. Stuart, National Geographic Society, 1981

The Aztecs, Tim Wood, Viking, 1992

Lost Temple of the Aztecs, Shelley Tanaka, Madison Press Books, 1998

Get The Picture?

Archaeologists learned about tlachtli by studying Aztec ruins and writing. The Aztec system of writing used pictures, as well as symbols called glyphs. They decorated their buildings with glyphs, like the Egyptians, and many of these glyphs can still be seen today. Even a few Aztec books have survived, though the Spanish explorers burned the books they found. Aztec glyphs are like the symbols in a code. But archaeologists have no key. So they use clues from the past to help them figure out what each glyph means.

Has a friend ever sent you a note in code? Have you ever tried to break the code and translate the note without the key that tells you what each symbol stands for? Try this:

```
@ # % % ^ ?     * & + = ^ ? @
& < ~ ^     > #     / + – ^   +
$ + & &
```

(Look for symbols that repeat often. The most common letters in the English language are e, s, t, h and r.)

Archaeologists had many sources for clues. In the 1500s priests were sent to collect as many facts of Aztec life as they could. Much of what we know today comes from the codices, or books, the priests wrote. More clues to the past are in folklore and songs that have been handed down for generations to the descendants of the Aztecs, who live in Mexico today.

By studying the glyphs and using their knowledge of Aztec life, archaeologists have been able to figure out what many of the glyphs mean.

If you need some help breaking the code, here are a few clues: ^ = E, @ = S, > = T, / = H, and ? = R.

Glossary

Archaeologists: scientists who study people who lived long ago

Glyphs: pictures that represent ideas or words

Loincloth: a piece of cloth that usually ties around the waist and hangs down to mid-thigh

Shaman: a medicine man or priest

Tunic: a long, loose, sleeveless shirt

Answer: Soccer players like to have a ball.

From the Author

I love making up and telling stories, but it wasn't until I had four children of my own that I finally got started for real. As a mother and piano teacher, I have lots of opportunities to see and hear children's perspectives and interests. They inspire me to write about the things that catch my eye, as if I'm talking to a young person.

I like history, so when *Crayola Kids* planned an issue dealing with ancient cultures, I turned to the Internet and library for sources. I looked up everything I could find on Aztecs. I started writing about the foods they ate, when I came across a few references to the game of *tlachtli*. I was hooked. I like games. And I haven't met a kid yet who doesn't.

To me, fiction is more fun than nonfiction, and fiction based in fact is doubly interesting because it teaches and has fun at the same time.

I made up a young person to "experience" the game. I kept him middle-grade age so he would be old enough to participate in this sort of thing, yet young enough to relate to.

I wrote and rewrote for more than a month. I incorporated as many facts as I could in the fictional account but some facts refused to cooperate. They were too interesting to leave out so I put them in a sidebar, complete with a code for fellow puzzle lovers. I submitted the sidebar and bibliography with my article.

The article was rejected twice before my Institute instructor pointed out it was a sports piece as well as a history piece. She was right. *Soccer Jr.* accepted it and the rest, as they say, is history.

—Ruth Boston

From the Editor

"Aztec Soccer" was chosen because it gives our readers a nice bit of history, particularly as it relates to soccer. It is important to tell a story in a way that appeals to your audience's eye and attention, and by telling a story, the editors felt that was the way to go.

Each story in *Soccer Jr.* has a teaching element; that is, we like to give readers something to bite on, and this story fits that ideal perfectly.

—Mark Wright, Editor, *Soccer Jr.*

Soccer Jr.
8–14 years
1,300 words

Owl Prowls

By Sheri Gumina

A hush falls over the forest as darkness creeps through the trees. The creatures of the night begin to stir. One magnificent hunter swiftly and silently takes up his post on a favorite branch. His night vision is more accurate than any other creature on earth, and his hearing can pinpoint the exact location of a sound. The owl is on the prowl.

The rustling of a mouse in the woods below captures the owl's attention. He cocks his head to listen more closely. The tufted feathers on his head only look like ears. His real ears are openings on each side of his head. One opening is slightly higher than the other. He bobs his head up and down until he hears the sound equally in both ears. As soon as that happens, he knows his face is pointing right at his prey—even if it can't yet be seen. That mouse could be as far away as the other end of a football field, and the owl would still be able to hear it!

Once the owl has found the exact location of the mouse, he swoops silently into the night. The owl must fly silently for two reasons. He needs to continue to track the mouse, and he also doesn't want the mouse to hear him approaching. Most birds have a solid, crisp edge to their feathers that makes their wings beat when they fly. The flight feathers of the owl have soft fringes. This makes them silent. Wide wings let him carry his body with less noise and effort. A large owl has a wingspan as wide as your kitchen table! He glides swiftly, making adjustments along the way, as the mouse moves through the forest.

An owl has vision 100 times better than ours. You and I have special parts in our eyes called rods that help us to see when it's dark. Because the owl has so many more of these rods than we do, he can see on nights when we would feel blind! An owl's eyes are also huge so that he can take in even the smallest amount of light from the stars.

He's ready for the final attack! As the owl uses his eyes and ears to zero in on the mouse, he extends the sharp talons on his feet. They are sharper than any knife in your kitchen! The owl uses his talons to kill the mouse while it is still on the ground.

Still gripping the mouse in his talons, the owl flies back to his favorite tree. He gulps the mouse whole, swallowing it head first. There's not much time to savor the taste if you're an owl! The owl settles back on his perch. He is alert to the sounds of the forest. His incredible hearing system and keen night vision will locate his next meal. The owl is on the prowl.

From the Author

The idea for "Owl Prowls" came about through an activity at an ecology camp that I run with my husband. As we were dissecting owl pellets, the children had so many questions about owls that I went to the library to investigate. I learned so many interesting things that I decided to use the material for an article. I am also a teacher, so I enjoy making science and nature understandable to children.

To research the article, I read everything I could find at the library, and I also talked to several avid birders. This approach actually made my job harder because I had to scale back what could be included in the article. This was the hardest part of the whole process! I tried to use the facts that I thought young children could relate to the most.

I originally marketed the article at 750 words, but eventually sold it after I revised it to 500 words. It was painful to make the cuts, but I think it made it a better article in the end.

I wrote "Owl Prowls" as an assignment for my course at the Institute of Children's Literature, and it's the first article I ever sent to a publisher. I received three rejections before it was accepted by *Boys' Quest*. As an added bonus, I've now made more than 10 times my original fee through reprint requests.

—Sheri Gumina

From the Editor

"Owl Prowls" was chosen for our issue on "Night Creatures." It was well written and seemed to set the stage for the issue so I used it as the opening article. The information about the owl's sight, and how much better it is than a human's sight and why, was interesting. The author's description of the owl being on the hunt for the mouse was descriptive. I felt like I was riding on the back of the owl in the quiet of night.

—Marilyn Edwards, Editor, *Boys' Quest*

Boys' Quest
6–13 years
490 words

THE CITY OF THE DEAD

By Lisa Siegel

IN FEBRUARY 1939, *sampietrini* (artisans and workmen in permanent service to St. Peter's Basilica) digging in the grottoes of St. Peter's Basilica found traces of an ancient burial place. The grottoes are underground chambers where early popes and emperors are buried, as well as popes who have died more recently. Pope Pius XII, who was in charge at the time, gave permission in June of that year for excavations to proceed. Within a few years, archaeologists were astonished to find an entire necropolis, or city of the dead, which dated back to the first century. In that necropolis, they later discovered not only what Pope Paul VI believed was the burial place of Peter, but what could be Peter's actual bones.

The first thing that strikes a visitor to the necropolis is the two rows of tombs separated by a narrow road. The age of these small buildings seems to vary from about A.D. 130 to about 300. The tombs are made of thin brick and have decorated facades. Above their entrances are tablets indicating who is buried within.

The numerous inscriptions tell us that inhabitants of this city of the dead were people who could not claim noble origins. They were freed men, however, not slaves, who were wealthy enough to build beautiful tombs for themselves and their families.

Two types of burial rites were practiced in this cemetery: cremation, or the burning of a body; and inhumation, or the placing of the body in the earth or in a **sarcophagus**. Most of the

> A **sarcophagus** (sar-KOF-eh-gess) is a stone coffin, which is often intricately decorated.

tombs' walls contain small niches where urns for the ashes of the dead were placed. There are also sarcophagi and large empty spaces formed with tiles wherein the dead bodies were laid.

The most famous inhabitant of this necropolis is believed to be Peter. Appointed by Jesus to be the head of his disciples, Peter came to Rome, where he was killed by order of the Emperor Nero.

It is believed that Peter lies buried directly beneath the basilica's high papal altar, which belongs to the time of Clement VIII (1592 to 1605). Archaeologists began digging in that area in the middle of the Second World War, in 1942, and continued until the end of the war. They pried off marble covers and knocked down brick walls that had been untouched for centuries. Under the present altar, they found two other altars stacked one on top of the other. The top one was from the 12th century, and the bottom one was from the sixth century. Beneath those altars, they discovered a marble cube standing nine feet tall. It was quickly identified from ancient Vatican records as Emperor Constantine's monument to Peter, probably built around 315. Within the monument was a chapel, dated about 160, that stood in a little open area in the middle of various tombs. Under the chapel was a first-century grave. Several ancient coins (probably thrown by Christians as a gesture of respect) were found nearby, as well as a wall (dated to mid-third century) covered with graffiti that contains Peter's name. Near the bottom of that wall was a small, ragged opening that led to a marble-lined cavity filled with dozens of bones and a shredded piece of purple cloth with solid gold threads.

Were the bones those of Peter? A Greek inscription carved on a wall next to the chapel, just above the bone-filled cavity in the graffiti wall, was translated to read, "Peter is within." Tests done on the bones proved they were from the same individual, an elderly, robust male, of average height. The

encrusted soil on the bones matched exactly the soil found in the first-century grave. The purple cloth had been dyed with the same rare purple pigment reserved by Roman law for the emperor.

Why were these bones found in the wall and not in the shallow grave under the chapel? Scholars have proposed that perhaps during later construction that disturbed the grave area, the remains were moved to a place in the wall.

All of this evidence was so convincing that Pope Paul VI announced on June 26, 1968, that the bones of Peter had been found. But without conclusive proof, many scholars are still doubtful. They believe that it can only be said with certainty, after studying the archaeological evidence, that second- and third-century Christians believed that Peter was buried in the first-century grave.

For now, we are still uncertain about the city of the dead's most famous inhabitant. It is clear though that the Vatican's necropolis is one of the most astonishing archaeological finds of the 20th century.

From the Author

When I started researching the magazine market, I was attracted to the high quality of nonfiction writing that I found in *Faces* magazine. Writer friends also told me that *Faces* seemed to be more open to accepting new writers than most of the other historical publications.

I studied the *Faces* website and a year's worth of back issues at my local public library, and discovered that each issue of *Faces* focuses on a particular theme. (The themes for an entire year are published on its website.) One of the themes for the upcoming year was Vatican City.

I had visited Vatican City three years earlier and had been fascinated by stories of the archaeological ruins below St. Peter's Cathedral that were said to contain the actual bones of St. Peter. I was excited at the prospect of doing research regarding those ruins and thought that perhaps I could transfer that passion and excitement into a historical story that would fascinate children as well.

I started my research on the Internet where I found several good online encyclopedias with references to the underground ruins as well as other related topics. I also found several relevant books and more encyclopedias by searching my city's main public library catalogue that covers all the libraries in the city. I had the books delivered to my local library branch and then paid a visit to the main library branch to read the related reference books that I couldn't take home. While there, I also found several newspaper articles. The books that dealt specifically with the archaeological searches beneath St. Peter's Cathedral turned out to be the most helpful for my article.

In order to discover a way to present the information that would appeal to 9- to 12-year-old children (the target ages for *Faces*), I tried putting myself into their mind-set while reading everything I had collected on my topic. The facts relating to the archaeologists' searches and what they found—or at least believed they'd found—were the most fascinating to me, so I decided to take the reader on that journey and into the process of solving the mysteries that were revealed.

It was my experience that most 9- to 12-year-olds adore a good mystery. I chose the title "City of the Dead" because it sounded mysterious and a tad macabre—qualities I thought would appeal to my target age group. As I got into writing the article, I found that the 800-word limit was not as restricting as I had originally thought it would be. A lot of information can be conveyed in that limited word count.

I had learned from the *Faces* website that they wanted writers to submit query letters regarding proposed articles that contained the following information: the subject and the proposed word length, a detailed one-page outline, an extensive bibliography, and a writing sample if the writer was new to *Faces*. I sent them a description of my proposed article and a bibliography. I also sent my complete article as a writing sample! I chose to do that in the hopes of showing them that I was capable of writing a lively and original article, but I also sent a detailed outline so they wouldn't have to read my entire article if they chose not to do so.

Six months later, I received an acceptance letter from *Faces*. I was ecstatic. Writer friends had told me that the first acceptance is the most exciting and they were right.

I was pleased to discover that the *Faces* editor had only made a few minor editorial changes in my article. Other than asking me to recheck my facts carefully, she needed no other revisions. I enjoyed the whole experience so much that I submitted several other articles to *Faces*. I am happy to report that they have accepted another article of mine for publication.

In between writing for *Faces*, I am working on my picture book manuscripts. I hope my growing list of credits will help with publication in the book market.

When I graduated from high school, I wanted to write children's books. Other interests intervened as I made my way through college and life. I became an elementary school teacher, then an attorney, and then a full-time mother for my daughter. I also dabbled in adult book writing, but was told by publishers that my voice was better suited for the children's market.

—Lisa Siegel

From the Editor

It is the lucky few who actually get to travel to the world's most famous places. Vatican City, with its grand architecture and world-famous artwork, is one such place. I am not sure how many of our readers will actually make the journey, but after reading Lisa Siegel's fact-filled article in our issue on Vatican City, they may feel as if they have been there.

Ms. Siegel's article takes readers to a portion of the city that is not easily accessible—the necropolis beneath St. Peter's Basilica. In addition to a textual tour of the underground, Ms. Siegel describes the issue of Peter's bones and whether they truly are located beneath the Basilica. She does this in an objective and fair manner, and presents the facts to our readers without interjecting her own opinions or religious beliefs. She allows the readers to draw their own conclusions.

Ms. Siegel's article also helps give readers a clear understanding of the importance of Peter to the Christian faith. I was also impressed with the way she included information on ancient Roman burial rituals. Since the printing of this issue, we have used Ms. Siegel's work in other publications.

—Elizabeth Crooker Carpentiere, Editor, *Faces*

Faces
8–14 years
765 words

Soldiers of the Pope

By Karen Guest

*I*f you go to the Vatican, you will see men stationed at each of the three entrances. Normally, they wear blue doublets with matching berets, but on ceremonial occasions, they wear tunics and puffy, knee-length pants called knickerbockers that are striped red, yellow, and dark blue. At their necks are white ruffs; on their heads, plumed helmets. The men wear armor and carry their traditional halberd, a spiked ax on a seven-foot pole. This uniform belongs to the Swiss Guards, the soldiers of the pope.

From a tiny, mountainous, landlocked country, the Swiss were desperately poor in the Middle Ages and the Renaissance. Their primary export in those days was mercenaries, or soldiers for hire. Reputed to be the best, Swiss soldiers sold their services to the highest bidder, and during the Renaissance, buyers included the French, the Spanish, and the Milanese, who warred over the approaches to Rome and possession of the city of Milan itself. Many Swiss earned a great deal of money through fighting. They also died in great numbers. At the **Battle of Marignano** (mah-REE-nyah-no), 20,000 Swiss served with Milan and took 8,000 casualties—a very high price for such a small country.

The papal states, the territory controlled by the pope, covered about one-third of Italy in the Renaissance, and the pope needed an army because of frequent conflicts with neighbors such as

> The **Battle of Marignano** took place on September 13–14, 1515. A large French army defeated a powerful army of Swiss pikemen defending Milan.

Florence, Milan, Venice, and, later, France and Spain. In 1505, Pope Julius II sought to create a permanent military unit of 200 Swiss pikemen under his direct control. On January 21, 1506, the first Swiss Guards arrived at the Vatican.

They soon gained a reputation for bravery and self-sacrifice. On May 6, 1527, 147 Swiss Guards died defending Pope Clement VII from the troops of Charles V, the Holy Roman Emperor. Their spirited defense allowed the pope to escape capture by the emperor and hide in the fortress of Castel Sant'-Angelo (KAH-stel SANT'ahn-JE-lo).

The Swiss Guards renew their vows of allegiance on the anniversary of this slaughter in the Courtyard of San Damaso (SAN da-MAH-zo), located inside the Vatican. They kneel down, raise three fingers (in representation of the **Trinity**), and swear to lay down their lives for the pope. They also promise to defend the church, to guard the Apostolic Palace, and to man the portals of the Vatican.

The oath continues to define the function of the Swiss Guards. While some of their duties have disappeared and they have been reduced to 106 officers and men, they still stand guard at the Vatican entrances and keep order at papal events. The Swiss Guards

> In Christian belief, God is considered as existing as three persons—the Father, the Son, and the Holy Spirit—called the **Trinity**.

act as the bodyguards of the pope. They helped protect Pope John Paul II during an assassination attempt in 1981. Consequently, they now carry modern weaponry, usually concealed within the folds of their ceremonial uniform, and wear plain clothes and surround the pope whenever he leaves the Vatican.

To be a Swiss Guard, a young man must be a Swiss citizen, devoutly Roman Catholic, unmarried, under 30 years of age, over five-feet eight-inches tall, good-looking, and willing to learn Italian. Only officers can be married while in the Swiss Guards, and, traditionally, the commandant is a Swiss nobleman.

Being a Swiss Guard is not easy, nor does it offer many material rewards. A typical guard is on duty 60 to 70 hours per week—and that is when there are not extraordinary duties! He earns only about $1,000 per month, paid in Swiss francs. There is very little free time, and superiors conduct a bed check at midnight every night. Most young men serve only the minimum two years.

Guardsmen spend what little free time they have hanging out with their friends, and most do have girlfriends. It is common for a Swiss Guard to return to Switzerland with a wife he met in Rome.

Today, some Vatican officials are questioning the necessity of the Swiss Guards. While Pope John Paul II has full confidence in the guards, the Swiss bishops who organize the unit and select its leaders are considering changes.

Some changes have already taken place. It used to be that only Swiss from the German-speaking regions were eligible to be guards. When recruitment dropped, the doors opened to the French and Italian regions. The height requirement has also been relaxed. Two changes seem almost certain in the future: eliminating the need for a nobleman to be commandant and increasing the unattractive, low salary.

Where will these changes take the Swiss Guards? The security of the pope remains their principal function. This might mean that the Swiss Guards become a plain-clothes security service. They then would have more in common with the U.S. Secret Service than the Renaissance army of Pope Julius II.

From the Author

I was elated when *Faces* chose to publish "Soldiers of the Pope." I had selected *Faces* because it is a world history/cultures magazine, and I am a professional historian, published academically in my own field of early modern Europe. Using the guidelines *Faces* provided on the Cobblestone website, I sent a query with a detailed outline and bibliography.

Vatican City, listed as the theme of an upcoming issue, intrigued me because I have a graduate degree in the Italian Renaissance. I contemplated Michelangelo and the design for St. Peter's Basilica, but there was more good, general interest information on the Swiss Guards, who are as famous in their own right as English bobbies.

There was also the issue of the recent murder of the commandant that had been covered in the press in everything from *The Economist* to National Public Radio. I didn't need to interview any Swiss Guards; most of the press reporting covered the relevant material: structure, duties, changes.

An 800-word article has to have a focus. Fortunately, the Swiss Guards is a small, but highly interesting subject. It focused itself; the heavily political/cultural material was easy to avoid because I kept the concept of my audience—fourth and fifth graders—firmly in mind. I'd also studied several issues of the magazine at the

county library to get the tone right.

I tend to work from very detailed outlines; I frontload the outlines, so it takes me very little time to turn them into articles. I revise as I go along, and I read my article aloud. If something doesn't sound right, out it goes. Also, reading aloud forces me to see my mistakes in writing and faults of organization and logic. I spend two or three hours on the outline and another two or three hours on the article, concentrating solely on the project of the moment. For this article, I went from outline to draft in a day or two—wrote it one day, read it over the next day, then sent it out. Later, galley copies arrived, which I read through and sent back. That was it.

I addressed my audience as "you" because I had been taught that worked as a hook. If an article opens with an anecdote or an outrageous fact, then the use of "you" makes it conversational. But it isn't the only way: a direct, pithy quotation can be equally effective.

Currently, I am working on two novels—one adult, one YA. I've continued querying magazines but I have published nothing since "Soldiers of the Pope," though I continue to send out queries. And I'm planning an article on the nature reserve of Skomer Island, Pembrokeshire, Wales, which I visited during my honeymoon.

—Karen Guest Whitehurst

From the Editor

Any publication that includes material on the Vatican is sure to mention the Swiss Guards. It might comment on their colorful uniforms or the intriguing history of the men. Of the many queries I received about the Swiss Guards for the Vatican City themed issue, Karen Guest's stood out.

Ms. Guest's article goes beyond what readers might find in other sources, because she presents the guards as people, not just tourist attractions. From Ms. Guest's writing, readers learn about the lives of the Swiss Guards—from typical workweek and salary to information on curfews and training.

The article also encourages our readers to use their critical thinking skills. After describing some of the concerns surrounding the Swiss Guards, Ms. Guest asks readers to think about the future of the guards—are they necessary? Should the requirements of the Swiss Guards be changed?

This article was a great addition to the Vatican City issue, which was heavy on the history articles. It brought the city alive for readers and allowed them to see beyond the famous buildings and artwork.

—Elizabeth Crooker Carpentiere, Editor, *Faces*

Faces
8–14 years
800 words

The Summer of

By Nancy Champagne

Melissa stepped up into the train with her brother Denny behind her. "Could you move any slower, Melissa? Come on, let's go!" he barked as he pushed past her to walk down the aisle and find a seat. Then he took off his jacket and flung it at her. Melissa didn't see it coming until it hit her in the head. She heard someone near her chuckle—how embarrassing! Denny just laughed. She threw his jacket into the overhead and sat down without saying a word. First she lost the window seat, then her older brother made her look stupid in front of everyone. She raised her hands to fix her long, dark hair and flatten it down. "This is going to be one long summer," she thought.

"Your hair looks fine. Take out the game so I can beat you and get it over with already," Denny said as he ran a hand through his sandy brown hair and stared out the window. He thought he was so cool and it drove Melissa up a wall. Where did he get off bossing her around? But she listened and took out the travel-sized Clue game. She wished things could change, but then regretted the thought. She had really begun to despise change; it had been bad to her lately. Denny set up the game and turned his back to the window. "Why take the window seat if he's not going to look out the window?" Melissa asked herself.

The scenery rolled by quickly (not that she could see anything with Denny blocking her view), and in no time Melissa figured out that the murder weapon was the lead pipe. All she needed now was the room and the suspect, and victory would finally be hers. Melissa had been trying to beat her brother at this game all year long, and now she was finally about to do it! She was dying to make him eat his words. What a great way it would be to start off the summer!

Melissa couldn't wait to get to her grandparents' cottage, where she had spent most of her summers. She wondered what it would be like without Grandpa this year. He had passed away during the winter, and this was the first time in her life that he wouldn't be there.

"What's your problem?" asked Denny.

"What if the cottage isn't the same without Grandpa?"

A sad expression crossed Denny's face. Melissa was immediately sorry that she had brought it up. Grandpa's heart attack wasn't something the family liked to discuss. "I'm sure everyone will miss him this summer. I wish I could say how it's going to go, kiddo, but I can't."

Melissa felt her face turn red. "Don't call me kiddo. You know how much I hate that. I'll be a teenager in 17 days."

"Sorry, I forgot. Your move."

Melissa was squirming in her seat. "The murder took place in the hall," she said to herself. All I have to do is find the murderer and I win! She smiled and drew in a deep breath. She didn't want Denny to see how excited she was.

As she waited for her brother to make his move, her mind drifted back to the cottage. It was the only thing in her life that never changed. There was only one big bummer about the place—she had to share a room and a bunk bed with Denny. Since she was the youngest, she was always stuck on the bottom bunk. The only good thing about the bottom bunk was that there was a small window there that overlooked the screened porch. Every night after she and Denny went to bed, her grandpa would go out on the porch to sit at the table and listen to the baseball game.

Melissa stared at Denny. She wondered if he remembered the sound of the sportscasters' voices and the music, and if they served as a soothing lullaby for him when he couldn't sleep, too. "Take a picture. It'll last longer," said Denny. His voice snapped Melissa out of her daydreaming.

"I have a proposition for you. How about who- ever wins this game gets the top bunk?" Melissa asked.

"Deal," Denny replied with a smug look.

Melissa looked down at her sheet. She was so close. She had it narrowed down to two suspects: Mrs. White and Mr. Green. She moved into the lounge and flipped over a card. It was Mrs. White, which meant that Mr. Green was the murderer, and he did it in the hall with the lead pipe. Melissa had a grin from ear to ear. When it was her turn, she jumped into the air, but just then, the train slammed on its brakes, and the force threw her back into her seat. On her way down, she knocked the game onto the floor.

"Way to go!" said Denny.

"I know what they are. Mr. Green, in the hall, with the lead pipe. I guessed it! I win!"

"Of course you know what the cards say. They flipped over when you knocked them on the floor," said Denny as he bent down to pick up all of the fallen pieces.

"Look! I knew them before. I even marked them down!" Melissa showed him her paper.

"You cheated! We're here anyway, so nobody wins. The game's over."

"But I guessed it before!"

Denny started teasing her, "Liar, liar, pants . . ."

"Be quiet! You are so immature for someone who is two years older than me," she yelled as her face grew red with frustration. She had come so close! How could he think she cheated? There was no way she could have changed her paper after the cards fell. She knew the truth, she knew that she had beaten him, but that wasn't good enough.

"Why did I have to jump out of my seat?" she asked herself.

Denny handed her the game. "Put this in your bag, cheater, it's time to get off."

"I'm not a cheater!" said Melissa.

"Sure you're a cheater," said Denny.

Melissa's mood changed when she stepped off the train and saw Nana standing there waiting with open arms. "Nana!" she yelled. She started to look for Grandpa beside her, but stopped her- self when she remembered.

"My goodness, look how much the two of you have grown." Nana paused. "Let's get going—the car is waiting."

"Nana can drive," Melissa said to herself. Grandpa had always been the one behind the wheel. Nana opened the trunk and Denny threw his stuff in. "I'm in front." Not again! She would have to learn to be quicker around him.

Melissa's eyes opened wide as they entered the cottage. Everything was different! The walls had been painted a light pink and the kitchen set was different. She just stood there—afraid to enter the living room. "So, what do you think?" asked Nana with a big smile.

"It's nice," said Denny. He punched Melissa's shoulder to get her out of her trance.

"It's just so different," said Melissa.

"Wait until you see the living room," said Nana.

"No!" Melissa yelled inside. "What have you done?" Denny pushed her forward.

"Cool. You put a carpet down," said Melissa. She really did love carpets, and she had to admit to herself that the cottage did look a lot nicer— even if everything wasn't exactly the same.

"I knew you'd like it. I worked really hard all morning to finish in time. The only place left is the porch."

"The porch is fine. You don't have to change anything."

"I wrote some ideas down, Melissa. You can be in charge of the changes we make."

"Really?" Nana nodded. "Maybe it could be fun," Melissa thought.

"I'm going to start dinner. You two can put your stuff in your room."

Denny led the way to their room. Melissa put her bags down and sat on the floor. "Stop sulking," Denny reached into his pocket. "You can have the top bunk. You won fair and square, kiddo." Melissa glared at him. He raised his arms up in surrender. "Sorry! I don't mean anything by it, I'm just used to you being my baby sister."

"You really believe I beat you?" Melissa remembered how upset she had been.

He nodded. "You won. But on the way home, I want a rematch to see who really is the best."

"Fine, but if I lose, it means that this victory doesn't count."

Denny started to unpack. "Details, details."

Melissa smiled. Victory! She sighed and stared at the small window looking out onto the balcony.

Melissa could see the surface of the table and her grandpa's portable radio. The cottage was definitely different this summer—and not just because Nana had put some paint on the walls and carpet on the floors. She was going to be a teenager soon, she had finally beaten Denny at something and she was in charge of decorating the porch. She was getting some respect and her brother was actually being kind of nice. Maybe change wasn't all that bad after all. Grandpa was gone, but still, life had to go on.

Denny was staring at her. "Take a picture. It will last longer," said Melissa, using one of his favorite lines. Then she finished with, "You can have the top bunk."

"But you won."

"I know, but I don't want it. The bottom bunk is just fine." Change wasn't all that bad, but she wasn't ready to change everything. "I'm going to go help Nana."

"All right, kiddo."

Melissa turned her head sharply but for some reason, it didn't make her mad this time. "Just remember, this 'kiddo' beat you at Clue today!" Denny grabbed one of his shirts and threw it at her. Melissa dodged and it missed completely. "Yeah, this summer is definitely going to be different!" she thought as she went to the kitchen.

From the Author

"The Summer of Change" was the story I handed in as my second Institute assignment. There was a list of ten words, and I had to pick five of those words for my story.

I treated the assignment as a game and didn't take it too seriously. I think I had a few ideas end up in the garbage before I got to Denny and Melissa. Once the story was started I felt it would be more believable to write the story from Melissa's perspective than from Denny's.

I tried to limit the narrative and to give the story a nice quick pace with the dialogue. There is still quite a bit of narrative in the story, but it's in Melissa's voice, and flows naturally.

When I worked in a mall, I often heard bits and pieces of conversations from various teens.

I discovered that they're all trying to prove something to themselves and others. I think the voice in my story developed as Denny opposed Melissa's attempts at change.

I didn't work from a plan. At first I believed my story would start and finish on the train. But the story was missing something. Melissa and Denny had to reach their destination, which brought them to the cottage.

When I started writing the story I didn't have a theme. But when my rough draft was completed I noticed that change was what Melissa was trying to cope with, and what she was fighting for with Denny.

Writing the story wasn't difficult; it was the revision process that was hard. When I finished writing, my story was twice as long as it should have been.

Marketing the story was tough because it was still a little too long for most markets. *Teen* was one of the three markets my instructor had recommended. I saved *Teen* for last because I was reluctant to sell all the rights to my story. But once I sold it I realized that the rights really didn't matter that much to me.

I like to read my stories out loud, or to have someone else read them to me. I find hearing my story read by someone else helps me catch those sentences and paragraphs that don't help move the story along.

I was stunned when I learned *Teen* would publish my story! The whole process of making up a manuscript package, mailing it off, receiving a rejection, and resubmitting the manuscript had become so mechanical, that I forgot why I was doing it! My thoughts drifted from "I finally did it" to "I CAN DO IT!"

My advice is: DON'T GIVE UP! In two years I received nine rejections. Each time my story came back I read it over just to make sure I wasn't missing something. The day I got a rejection, my manuscript was back at the post office off to another destination. It takes time and I think the hardest thing is to stay motivated.

I've worked at a lot of different jobs where I've been exposed to all kinds of people. I freelance in my spare time, writing short stories for children, and poetry. I've recently started working on picture books.

My family hasn't always understood why I've stuck to writing for so long. But when I need someone to read a story back to me, there's always someone there who's willing to help. When the rejections come pouring in, someone's always there to tell me, "publication will happen again, you'll see."

—Nancy Champagne

From the Editor

Nancy Champagne's short story, "The Summer of Change," was chosen for publication in *Teen Magazine* because the story fit our readership. Our readers are young teens going through a lot of changes—physical and emotional. *Teen Magazine* helps young women through this transition with advice sections and both fiction and nonfiction articles.

In the fiction category, the editors of *Teen* look for short stories that reflect the common experiences of young women. Other short stories include topics like dating, looks, weight and body issues, family, and so on.

Nancy Champagne's story explored the topic of a young girl dealing with the death of her grandfather—perhaps the first major change in her life. The narrator of the story, Melissa, starts out by saying that she "had really begun to despise change; it had been bad to her lately." But by the end of the story, the almost 13-year-old girl has realized that not all change is bad.

Although her grandfather's death was a difficult change to deal with, Melissa is also going through another change that she's looking forward to: becoming a teenager.

Teens go through a variety of changes in adolescence, and might look on some of the changes as negative, like the narrator of Ms. Champagne's story. The editors of *Teen* selected this story in the hopes that our readers would see themselves in the narrator and also realize that change is a natural progression, and that nothing stays the same forever. Some change is good, some change is bad, but there are ways to deal with both types of change in your life.

—Cylin Busby, Former Senior Editor, *Teen Magazine*

Teen Magazine
12–19 years
1,650 words

Prayers and Other Nonsense

by
Kathleen Ahrens

"Ma, where are you?" I called. The wind grabbed the door out of my wet hand, slamming it shut. I slid my umbrella next to my mother's in the urn by the door. It made a satisfying whizzing sound before it clunked to the bottom of the porcelain.

"Wen-ling, leave your umbrella in the garage to dry." The living room was dark, save for two red candles that sputtered on the cherry-wood altar.

"Ma, the police came to my school. Everyone on Yang-Ming Mountain has to evacuate." I yanked a small wheeled suitcase out of the hall closet. "Immediately."

"Put that away," Ma said. She was hanging up strips of yellow paper covered with vermilion triangles. Buddhist spells. "Pay your

"Mother, don't be so superstitious! I'm stating a fact. There's a super-typhoon coming. There'll be landslides and flooding. Remember last time?"

respects to your father."

I put the suitcase back and lit two joss sticks at the altar. Wisps of incense twirled their way up to heaven as I stared at the black-and-white head shot of my father.

Please, Ba, make her listen to me. The wind howled through the crack at the bottom of the front door, as if in reply. I never prayed to Ma's Buddhist gods, but I talked to my father a lot. I always had.

"I went to the temple this morning and asked the priest for a spell to protect the house." Ma went to the local temple to *bai-bai* every day, usually for me to be respectful and to get good grades, whichever problem was more urgent. At least today the typhoon had taken precedence.

"Ma, listen to me."

"I'm listening. What do you want to eat?"

"If we don't leave . . . " I kneeled down and grabbed her knees. "We could die."

"Fate is fate." She pushed back my bangs. Her hand was like ice on my forehead. "And don't say 'die.' You'll bring us bad luck."

Obey. Obey. Obey. I always obey. And I'm always treated like a child.

"Mother, don't be so superstitious! I'm stating a fact. There's a super-typhoon coming. There'll be landslides and flooding. Remember last time?"

Last time was two months ago when a large chunk of our backyard slid down the mountain. One of our neighbors lost his house. A week later Ba died. Heart attack, the doctor said.

Ma finished hanging the last strip and stepped down. "A spell protected your grandfather's house when that American bomb fell and . . . "

"Didn't explode," I finished for her. "I remember that story."

"Not a story—a fact."

Ba, help! She won't listen to me.

Obey your mother. His last words.

"Give your father a bowl of rice. It's dinner time."

"He's dead," I whispered, even though I could still hear his voice.

She strode to the kitchen and scooped a bowl of rice out of the rice cooker. "Go to your room."

"Mother, I'm not a child." I snatched the rice from her and slammed it on the counter. "You've got to stop living in a fantasy world. Ba doesn't need to be fed, and strips of paper don't protect a house."

"Wen-ling Huang! You are being disrespectful and disobedient."

I swallowed hard. "Mama, please. We can both stay with Paw-Paw."

"We are not leaving this house." Ma set the rice down on the altar, lit more joss, and raised the thin sticks above her head.

I walked to the door and spun my umbrella around in the urn. Obey. Obey. Obey. I always obey. And I'm always treated like a child.

The umbrella dropped with a soft clink. I opened the door and slipped out. The rain pelted my head and battered my shoulder blades. Mud surged down the road as grass and stones swirled around my sneakers. Everything on the mountain was headed down, I thought. Everything except Ma. What if I was wrong? I stopped and peered back through the rain at the house.

"Wen-ling!" I heard the slap-slap of rubber thongs before I could see her. "Foolish child! Going out without your umbrella." Her purse got caught up with the handle as she gave it to me.

The purse meant she would come with me. I bit my lip hard so she wouldn't see me smile. *Thank you, Ba. Or Buddha. Whoever.*

We sloshed on down the hill, our umbrellas knocking together like paper lanterns.

"Let's stop," I said when we reached the temple.

"Why stop? You don't believe."

"I know." I smiled, keeping my prayers to Ba a secret. "But you do."

From the Author

After seeing news reports about how houses built on a mountainside in Taiwan had been washed away after a powerful typhoon, I wrote this story. I wondered how a child could convince a parent to evacuate if the parent was strongly against leaving his/her home. My goal was to demonstrate that two generations can compromise and show respect for each other's concerns and beliefs.

I wrote and rewrote this story over a period of several months before submitting it to my Institute instructor. She liked it and suggested submitting it to *Skipping Stones*.

My target audience was junior high school age, and my main concern was to keep the word count under 800 words. My instructor suggested some vocabulary changes such as changing "filial" to "respectful."

I know the first-person point of view has limitations, but I like being inside the character's head. Using the first-person point of view allows both the author and the reader to enter someone else's "mind" and see the world from a different perspective.

The story was revised many times—more times than I can count. One challenge was to get the story streamlined to less than 800 words because it started out at 1,000 words. My instructor pointed out some problems with the sequencing of events in the original story that I submitted to her.

As a linguist, I automatically listen and evaluate word choice and word usage in real-world conversations. My training has helped me become attuned to turn-taking and other conversational mechanics, and therefore, I feel comfortable writing dialogue. In addition, dialogue helped me to *show* the conflict between the mother and the daughter.

Advice to new writers that I heard at a SCBWI National Conference is to submit stories that are at least 25 to 50 words under the word-count requirement, because it forces an author to write tight, and it gives the editor room to add an illustration or two, which is always welcome in a children's publication.

—Kathleen Ahrens

From the Editor

"Prayers and Other Nonsense" focused on two important topics: intergenerational gaps and cultural diversity. Both themes are very dear to us. Our suggested word count is about 750 words, which allows us to publish 40 to 50 submissions per issue.

Kathleen's piece fit perfectly on all counts. The story offered a perfect example of the cultural clashes between modern and traditional ways. The pull of religious beliefs set next to modern/scientific thinking brought out important differences.

The setting of Kathleen's story was realistic. The story was succinct, and the dialogue was snappy. The ending was equally perfect—with a true-to-life yet happy resolution.

We also liked that the story did not spoon-feed all the details; it left a lot to the reader's imagination. The story did not need any revisions besides minor edits to fit our space constraints. Since we carry no advertisements in our magazine, the space constraints are very real.

Skipping Stones magazine focuses on multicultural awareness. We want children all over the world to grow up with a sense of the common threads that bind us together as people of the world—human nature and needs.

—Arun Narayan Toké,
Editor, *Skipping Stones*

Skipping Stones
8–17 years
730 words

No Way to Get Down

By Justin Stanchfield

A cold rush of wind blew across the airport ramp. Not the steady breeze Dale had felt when he left home an hour ago, but a wild and reckless gust, smelling of a storm, strong enough to rock the wings of the light airplane he was preflighting. Shivering in the chill half-light of the February dawn, Dale did a walk-around inspection, his eyes arcing skyward every minute or two. The earlier promise of clear skies rapidly dimmed as approaching snow squalls swallowed more and more of the horizon.

He paused beside the old Cessna's high wing, taking a long look at the weather. The normal vista of mountains and saw-toothed peaks was hidden by a vast slate of blue-gray clouds, white curtains of snow hanging at their faraway edges. Not the kind of weather a recently soloed student hoped for on his third flight alone. Still, the storms didn't seem to be moving any closer . . . .

"Need any fuel?"

The sound of another human voice on the deserted ramp startled Dale. He turned and saw a tall figure in grease-stained coveralls ambling past the quiet ranks of tied-down aircraft.

"No thanks, Albert," Dale told the gray-haired mechanic. "Somebody already topped off the tanks." He met Albert in front of the well-used plane and stood looking at the leaden sky. The wind cut its way underneath the glaringly new leather jacket he had received two weeks ago for his 16th birthday.

"Doesn't look too good, does it?"

Albert glanced at the clouds and shrugged. "Hard to say. I see pilots take off in this stuff all the time. Of course, I'm not the guy to ask. I don't mind fixing 'em, but you couldn't pay me enough to fly."

Dale smiled politely. He had hoped for more concrete advice than a simple shrug. "Do you know if John Richards is here? Maybe I should ask him what he thinks."

Albert looked across the icy ground toward the massive hangar. "I haven't seen any of the instructors this morning." He paused. "I suppose you could call him at home."

Dale glanced at his wristwatch. The morning was slipping away, his long-awaited hour of practice before school rapidly vanishing. "Oh, I don't think I need to. I'm only going out to the practice area. It doesn't look too bad."

"O.K.," Albert said, departing. "If I see John, I'll tell him you're looking for him."

Dale looked up. The sky actually seemed a little brighter. He made up his mind and squirmed through the narrow door into the cramped cockpit.

THE airplane rocked to another gust as Dale ran through the start-up procedures, carefully noting each item on the tattered checklist. Brakes, fuel mixture, throttle, he readied the plane for flight.

"Clear!" he yelled out the window, turning the key and reaching for the starter handle. The prop swung, slowly at first, quickly blurring as the engine sputtered to life. With the radios and beacons on, the plane now rocked to its own power as it taxied slowly toward the runway.

"Butte Radio," Dale spoke, holding the microphone close to his lips, "Cessna 4244 Lima on the ramp, request airport advisory."

For a moment there was no answer. Then, with a jarring burst of static the speaker above Dale's head replied: "Cessna Four-Four Lima. Wind is Three Four Zero at six, gusting to 12, altimeter two-nine-nine-seven. Mountain obscuration in all quadrants." There was a noticeable break in the transmission. "VFR flight is not recommended."

Visual flight not recommended! That meant there was a very real chance of becoming trapped in the clouds, something for which he definitely was not qualified.

A gnawing pit of worry opened inside Dale's stomach. He thought about taxiing back. The squall was closer but not so close as to make flight a violation of rules. Besides, as Albert said, he'd seen planes take off in worse conditions. How could he ever become a real pilot if he was afraid of a little snow? What would he tell everybody at school today when they asked him excitedly about this morning's voyage? He advanced the throttle a touch and taxied faster.

Nearing the runway, Dale coasted to a stop, making final preflight adjustments to the engine, instruments and flaps. The aircraft's howl was punctuated by the radio as a passing craft requested the current conditions. Dale tried to ignore Flight Service's reply.

"Mountain obscuration in scattered snow showers. Traffic is a Cessna ready for departure . . . I don't know why."

Doggedly he taxied onto the runway and lined up with the center, his eyes focused on the far end. Flight Service's caustic remark echoed in his mind. They didn't have the authority to stop him. Besides, the specialist on the other end of the radio was inside, not out here where he could actually see the weather. Dale's right hand closed around the faded red knob marked "throttle" and pushed it forward, his feet dancing on the rudder pedals as the plane surged ahead.

SLOWLY, steadily, the aging craft gathered speed. Engine roaring and prop whining, its stiff landing gear rumbled down the narrow asphalt strip, the three unforgiving tires relaying every crack and bump to Dale's backside. Gently, he pulled back on the steering yoke, and the tired old bird lifted skyward.

"I don't know what I was so worried about," Dale said to himself as he climbed away from the airport. He banked the wings steeply, turning toward the practice area five miles to the west. Leveling off a thousand feet above the sagebrush and snow-covered terrain, he began to feel better about the entire situation. The air was turbulent, but not uncomfortably so. As he reached the practice area, a few isolated snowflakes drifted by the wing tips.

Suddenly the plane jolted, sharp and unforgiving. The wind was picking up rapidly. So was the snow. His reverie broken, Dale watched the western horizon vanish behind a moving wall of white. Worried, he swung the nose back toward the airport. He didn't like what he saw.

Everything behind him was gone, blanked out by the squall. The mountains, the airport, even the town, all lost in the hungry whiteness. Moving against the wind, he was flying almost 100 miles an hour. The storm was moving faster.

Faster than he would have believed, the clear air became thick with uncounted flakes of wind-driven snow. Instinctively Dale hauled back on the yoke, climbing closer and closer to the bottom of the low cloud ceiling. Without warning the world went away.

THERE is a place all new pilots dread, caught off-guard inside the clouds, position unknown, visibility zero. Outside, Dale saw nothing but gray, nothing to differentiate up from down. He felt dizzy, his sense of balance insisting he was turning to the right, but when he tried to turn away, the sensation only worsened. The engine's growl became a roar as the plane nosed downward. Too late he realized he was losing control.

He tried to remember everything his instructor had taught him. "Fly the plane," John would tell him. "No matter what happens around you, keep control and fly the plane." Dale fought the panic, concentrating on the instruments, concentrating on staying calm.

Straight ahead something vague and indistinct was approaching. It took a moment to understand it was the ground he saw rushing up as he dived steeply out of the cloud deck. He pulled the aircraft up hard, G forces pushing him relentlessly into the seat. At least he could see the ground again, frighteningly less than 200 feet below. His hand shook as he clutched the mike.

"Butte Radio, Cessna Four-Four Lima, three west, returning to airport."

The reply was immediate, the reception excellent. The news was not.

"Cessna Four-Four Lima, Butte Airport is below minimums. VFR traffic is not permitted."

Dale felt the panic rise again. Impossibly, less than two minutes from the welcoming firmness of the runway, he was being told he couldn't land. Around him the storm raged on, devouring the nearby hillsides in its teeth even as the first warehouses and trailer parks of the city slid by. He had to land, or turn and fly back into the worst of the squall.

The radio crackled again. "Four-Four Lima, we could issue a special clearance," the Flight Service bluntly reminded, "but you have to request it."

That was it! That was what he couldn't remember. Relieved, he called back: "Roger, understand. Four-Four Lima requests special VFR clearance."

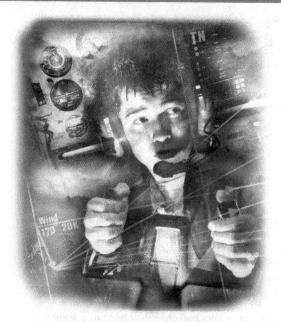

He stopped outside the hangar door for one last look at the airport. He had wanted all of this so badly, but now . . . .

H E was going to make it. Despite the snow and the turbulence and the fear, he was going to make it. He banked onto final approach just as Flight Service cleared him to land. Bouncing and skidding, the plane settled drunkenly to the pavement. The landing wasn't pretty, but he was down.

He brought the trainer back to the line and shut down. With a cough the engine died. Only the wind and the keening hum of the unwinding flight instruments broke the lonely silence. Dale unbuckled and stepped out of the plane. Ironically, the storm was beginning to die.

"What was I doing?" he said, disgusted with himself as he secured the plane. "I can't believe I was so stupid." He had broken every rule drummed into his head since his first lesson. Worse, he had ignored his own conscience and nearly piled up the plane.

"The world doesn't need a pilot like me," he muttered. He gathered his flight gear and began walking dejectedly to the hangar, his tennis shoes leaving sharp outlines in the snow left by the receding blizzard. He knew what he had to do. As soon as he found John he would tell him he was giving up his lessons. If John didn't beat him to it.

T HE door swung open. A bald man in a fluorescent orange parka stepped out, followed by a younger, sandy-haired man wearing a denim jacket. It was John Richards with another student.

"Sounds like you had some excitement this morning," the sandy-haired man said, his heavy mustache curling into a grin. "Made it out all right, I see."

Dale stared at the ground. "Just barely." He looked up at his instructor's face. "Guess that was pretty stupid, wasn't it?"

"Yep," John replied, grin fading. "But you're not the first to go brain-dead. Sooner or later everybody pushes their luck. Some just do it more successfully than others. As long as you learn from it, well, that's what counts."

Dale nodded and started through the door. He was nearly inside before John asked, "Are we still down for Saturday morning?"

"You bet," Dale was surprised to hear himself say. Of course he was going to show up. He'd made a mistake, he corrected it as best he could. It was time to move on. Danger was a part of flight. So was caution. This morning he'd had a lesson in both.

From the Author

"No Way to Get Down" was an Institute assignment, submitted to *Boys' Life* on the advice of my instructor. No one could have been more surprised than I was when I stumbled into my darkened house one evening and saw the answering machine light blinking, and heard, "Hello, this is Shannon Lowry from *Boys' Life Magazine*, and we're interested in purchasing your story . . .." A writer never forgets something like that.

This story is also, in many ways, autobiographical. Dale, the 16-year-old student pilot, puts himself in basically the same situation I had foolishly found myself in during my own flight training. Much of the action and resolution came from firsthand experience. When my instructor at the Institute suggested I write "No Way to Get Down," one of three story ideas I had submitted, I was actually relieved. It was a story I had wanted to tell for a long time.

I had submitted a brief synopsis as part of the assignment, although I didn't work from any formal outline. The theme, that the desire to do something can outweigh good judgement, developed naturally, especially since it had been part of my own real life experience.

The story isn't heavy on dialogue because so much of it takes place when Dale is alone in the airplane, but the radio communication with the Flight Service, and later Dale's conversation with his instructor, were crucial to the story's outcome.

Writing the beginning of "No Way to Get Down" was very easy, as I had a picture in my mind of the airport on a blustery spring day, a storm gathering over the nearby mountains. The character of Dale, on the other hand, was a composite of several people I knew, including one 16-year-old boy in particular who had taken flying lessons at the same time I did. He, too, had pushed his luck but also came through unscathed. I chose the name Dale in honor of a friend who worked at the airport.

Most of my fiction, especially if it's an action/adventure story, is written in the third person. It seems more natural to me, and the ability to step away from the character to describe the action can make the writing much easier when things get complicated. For this story though, it was never a conscious decision. From the very first sentence, a third-person point of view felt natural.

To keep the story moving, I wanted to include enough detail to make it seem real, but I knew from the start I couldn't include everything that would happen in a typical training flight and still describe the encounter with the storm. I compromised and wrote the action in small blocks, each leading to the section ahead. Also, I tried to use all the senses in the descriptive passages.

"No Way to Get Down" took very little revision. I wrote the first draft on the computer, edited it, and sent it to my instructor with the rest of my assignment. She found a few typos and one or two rough sentences and marked them. She also wrote across the top of the manuscript "Send this to *Boys' Life*." I don't recall making any changes to the story after it was accepted, which is unusual, as the stories I've since written for *Boys' Life* needed extensive revisions before they were published.

I had submitted at least one story to *Boys' Life* prior to "No Way to Get Down," so I was familiar with their guidelines. I used the Institute's market directories and a copy of the *Writer's Market*. It didn't hurt that I had grown up reading *Boys' Life*, either.

I write for both kids and adults, primarily science fiction and fantasy or action adventure. I've had six stories published by *Boys' Life,* as well as fiction in *Cricket, Jack And Jill,* and *Spellbound,* and I'm currently revising two novels. I'm still a full-time rancher, and I live with my wife, daughter, and son on a cattle ranch in southwest Montana, a stone's throw from the Continental Divide.

—Justin Stanchfield

From the Editor

Justin Stanchfield managed to capture a boy's fear and angst at having put himself into a very difficult situation. He succeeded by injecting real life elements into his writing. Kids are not perfect, they don't always make the right decisions, and things don't always turn out the way they planned.

Too often, first-time *Boys' Life* contributors fall into the trap of writing for too young an audience. They fail to grasp the details that make tales real; they fail to weave emotion into their writing. Mr. Stanchfield grasped the details.

—Michael Goldman, Senior Editor, *Boys' Life*

Boys' Life
6–18 years
1,800 words

Parade of Princes

By Jody Casella

My mother had a new boyfriend. Another winner, I was sure. She screeched into the driveway and practically splattered the cat against the garage door. Then she burst into the kitchen.

"He's an accountant!" she screamed. "Jennifer, he has a BMW!" She stopped for a minute and stared at the screen door blown wide open.

"That's great, Mom." But I knew this one would end up like all the others. As I watched her pace around the kitchen, I thought of Tommy for some reason. He was a guy I ate lunch with every day. Some of my friends said he was a loser, but I thought he was hilarious. He had this really strange, loud laugh. I'd say something sort of funny, and he'd burst out like a hyena, and practically the whole cafeteria would stop and stare at us.

"I know what you're thinking, but Richard is different." She reached into her purse. "Candy. He gave me candy." She waved a small box of chocolate caramel turtles at me.

I stared at her pale face, the laugh lines around her eyes. "Sure, Mom."

"Really. He's wonderful. Oh, Jennifer, I don't know, but I think maybe this time . . ." She ran over to the hall mirror and smiled widely at herself.

I turned away, wanting to shake her by the shoulders, wanting to scream: "Mom, you say this about all of them!" But it was too late. She had that look, that despicable "I'm in love" look. It meant she was losing herself in a man. It meant that our house would be filled once again with magical kingdoms, fairy godmothers, and musicals. For one minute, I almost had the urge to laugh like Tommy, one big HA, to show her how ridiculous the whole thing was.

Later that night, I pulled my bedcovers up to my ears. Mom was playing the piano, all the songs from *The Sound of Music*. I could picture her smiling face, her wide eyes on the sheet music, her head nodding in time.

When I was younger, I wished that life were like a musical. People would stroll around in color-coordinated costumes, the women holding parasols with lacy trim, the men beaming in top hats and tails. Everyone would chatter happily. Then someone would start to sing, and before you know it, everyone would be prancing around. The men would flip the ladies over their heads, and somehow everyone would know the right steps; everyone would know the words to the song.

I'd watched tons of movies like that with my mother. She really got into them, and later she'd go out and buy the soundtracks. There was a time when we'd eat dinner while *Fiddler on the Roof* blasted in the background. Mom would march the food to the table singing, "If I meet a rich man . . ."

When she first started dating, it was a big deal. She'd run around in her stockings and slip getting dinner ready, telling the babysitter about my brother's bedwetting problem, how I had to sleep with the hall light on, and how my Raggedy Ann doll had to be hidden in the highest cabinet over the refrigerator before I went to sleep.

"Why?" the baby-sitter would wonder as

she smacked her gum. "It's a long story," Mom would say while she sprayed her neck with smelly perfume. I'd stand on the top of the stairs clutching Raggedy, watching my mother go off with her date, while the babysitter stared at me as though I were a weirdo. She didn't know, of course, about the demon that possessed my doll each night.

That was Burt the Schizo's fault. He dated Mom first. She had high hopes for him and told us that he was like Prince Charming galloping in to save us after Daddy had died. He had a mustache, which she said was definitely a good sign. And he had a steady job. Sometimes he'd pick Mom up after work, and the copier machine he'd lugged around all day would be propped in the backseat. He told great stories, too. While Mom was getting ready, still running around in her robe and wet hair, Burt would tell my brother and me tales about princesses, pirates, and magic.

"You should see how good he is with children," I heard Mom tell her sister. "Mikey and Jennifer just love him to death."

One night Mikey and I curled up on my bed (his always smelled like pee) waiting for Burt to begin. "I once knew a little girl who had a Raggedy Ann doll," he said softly. "She slept with it every night. Like you probably do, huh?" He winked at me, and I squeezed Raggedy tighter. "One night, when the little girl was asleep, the Raggedy Ann doll came alive. She blinked her triangle eyes and opened her black-lined mouth. She looked at the little girl sleeping beside her."

I giggled with Mikey and wondered if *my* Raggedy came alive at night. I was sure she did.

"This doll," Burt said, "the one that belonged to the little girl I knew, it was evil. And it put its puffy hand over the little girl's neck when she was sleeping. And it pushed down hard."

Raggedy was stuffed in the kitchen cabinet after that. I watched each night as Mom shut the door, but I could imagine that doll coming

alive, blinking her eyes, stretching her mouth, and crawling into my bed to smother me.

That was the end of Burt. Mom cried for weeks when she found out about his "instability." It was like Daddy had died all over again. The musical soundtracks were put away. Mom would drag herself home after work. It was like we weren't even there. Late at night she'd watch old movies on TV and sniffle loudly.

Then she met Mario.

Mikey thought Mario looked like Elvis in his later musicals. He had slicked-back, black hair and a huge stomach. He drove a white Cadillac with a Las Vegas sticker pasted on the bumper. He talked loudly and waved his hands around when he spoke. He said things like: "Youse guys better shut your traps, or I'm gonna have to shut 'em for ya." I was in the eighth grade by then, so Mom's assurance that he once wrote a poem and knew how to make chili didn't convince me that he was the man she'd been waiting for.

"He has greasy hair," I told her. "And he talks incorrectly. Yesterday he said, 'It don't make no difference to me.' Now, isn't that wrong?" I was trying to appeal to the English major in her. But she was blind.

"Oh, honey," she had said with a smile. "I think it's cute. And anyway, he's a good person. He opens the car door for me."

Months later, after we'd almost grown used to Mom playing the theme from *Phantom of the Opera* on the piano, Mario was arrested for selling drugs. The Dark Ages descended on our house once again. This time was even worse than before. No more music. No more early dinners with Mom running around laughing in her dress and slippers. No more late-night talks about boys and invitations to parties. Mom hardly ate or slept. The circles under her eyes were so dark that sometimes I would've given anything for Mario to come back.

There were others. By the time I reached high school, I could spot the losers on the first date. Mom would have that glazed look in her eyes. "This is Bob. He had to move back in with his parents until he gets back on his feet."

"This is Don. He doesn't have a job right now, but he's looking."

"This is Ed. He's planning to get a divorce as soon as his wife comes back from Jamaica."

And now there was Richard. Richard, who gave her freaking chocolate turtles and drove a BMW. Richard, who supposedly had a steady job and treated Mom with some respect. Richard, the epitome of Prince Charming. If I, a mere junior in high school, realized that there was no such person, why couldn't Mom?

I met him before their third date. He was taking her to an outdoor concert.

"Isn't that just the most romantic idea you've ever heard, Jennifer?" Mom asked, patting her hair and smiling at herself in the hall mirror.

"Thrill," I said and rolled my eyes. I had that urge again, the feeling of Tommy's HA building up in my throat.

"It's on the park green." She dabbed some lipstick on her puckered lips. "Richard's going to bring a blanket, and I've got some cookies for us to snack on."

"Take some bug spray, too, Ma," Mikey yelled from the other room.

The doorbell rang. I had to look, in spite of it all. Mom had her glazed eyes and high-pitched voice when she opened the door. Richard had flowers and spoke grammatically correct English. He acted like the BMW was his own. He told a joke, and I could hear Mikey's laugh from the other room. Mom's face was pink when she walked out the door. She was humming. It had definitely started again.

Two months later, our house was the magical kingdom of my childhood. "Richard went to Princeton. Richard reads Wordsworth in his spare time. Richard owns a beach house. Richard speaks French. Richard said he loves me." Mom dressed up every day. At dinner she told us jokes and stories and talked about the charming things Richard had done. There were always fresh flowers in the crystal vase on the piano when she played at night.

"How are things going with you, Jennifer?" Mom asked me one night after dinner. "Wasn't there some boy you were interested in?"

HA! I covered my mouth. "Tommy, you mean?"

"He was calling for a while." She smiled.

I thought of Tommy, his raspy voice, his lopsided grin. "It's no big deal." I had told Tommy about Richard at lunch.

"Sounds like another dork," he'd said, rocking back and forth on his chair.

"Well, he hasn't slipped up yet," I told him, noticing the way his hair fell into his eyes when he rolled them.

"You fool, Jennifer. He'll mess up. You'll see."

"Tommy's O.K.," I said to my mother.

She kept smiling this really ridiculous grin. "He seems very nice to me."

That night Richard came over, and we rented *West Side Story*, Mom's favorite. She made popcorn, and even Mikey stayed to watch with us. During the sappy parts Richard squeezed Mom's hand and whispered into her ear. She'd let out this sigh, and I started thinking how really happy she was with him, like she was with Daddy. When he was alive, they used to watch movies and hold hands. I couldn't stay awake very long, so I never made it to the end. But they always let me curl up next to them, and later on, Daddy would lift me up and carry me into bed, tucking my old Raggedy Ann doll in beside me.

The best part of the movie came up, when the characters go to the dance. I loved watching them twist around, the music blaring.

Richard had this weird grin on his face. "Yeah, they *all* know how to dance."

Mom's head fell onto his shoulder. "They do," she whispered.

I could feel my face smiling, and when the movie was over, I had the urge to look in the attic for that ratty old Raggedy Ann doll. I found her in a plastic garbage bag with a bunch of other dolls. The material on her face was yellow, and a brown stain was smeared across her forehead. Was it really true that I'd once slept with her in my arms, Daddy patting her yarn hair? Could I ever have imagined her coming alive at night? Did I really beg Mom to hide her from me? I pulled her from the bag. Her black-lined smile was still the same.

A few weeks later, Mom's car squealed into the driveway. I heard the cat howl and scamper up the steps. Mom had groceries, two bags in each arm. She pushed open the door with her foot, then heaved the bags onto the counter.

"I know," she said as she walked out the door to unload the rest of the car.

I followed behind her, not even feeling like saying I told you so. Her hair had fallen into her eyes, and a glop of mascara smudged her cheek.

"Getting too serious, he said. Too much. Too fast. Too scary." She frowned. "Grab the last bag, Jennifer." She turned and walked into the house.

I leaned against the car and kicked the tire. How could I have ever thought for a minute? How could I have even considered? I thought of mom waving the box of chocolates at me, Richard squeezing her hand, and her wide smile when she played music at night. But her eyes were so bright when she talked about him!

I stomped into the kitchen. Mom was slamming cans of soup into the cabinet. "I really don't want to hear it, Jennifer." She didn't even turn around to look at me.

"Ma," I said. "Why do you do it? I mean, why does it keep happening?"

She yanked open the freezer door and plunked down a frozen chicken.

I paced around the room, watching her unload groceries like a wild woman. "Ma," I said again.

She heaved a sack of potatoes into the pantry.

"Tommy asked me to go to a movie." As soon as I said it, I almost burst out laughing.

"What?" She turned to face me. Her eyes were wet.

"Yesterday, right out of the blue, he came up and asked me." I thought of him setting his tray next to mine at lunch. Leaning over, right there, in front of everyone and asking me, like it was no big deal. He was grinning like usual, but I thought I noticed his hands shaking a little.

"What did you say to him?" My mother wiped her face with the back of her hand.

"I said yes." I shook my head. "Why *do* you do it, Mom?"

She stared right at me, and then it was like her eyes were glazed over for a minute. "Because it's good," she said.

When I went to bed that night, I heard her crying. There would be no music for a while, I knew. The CDs and piano songbooks were put away for now.

But when I closed my eyes, I saw men and women dancing in the streets. Colored skirts swaying. Shiny, black shoes tapping. Not everyone knew the steps. Not everyone knew the words to the songs. But they were dancing together.

From the Author

I was very excited when my story was accepted by *Cicada*. I had sent the same story to two other magazines, and I knew that if *Cicada* didn't accept it, there would be no other market for it. There aren't many literary-type magazines for teenage audiences.

The story is based loosely on experiences I had growing up. I write a lot of stories based on true incidents, but I never feel I have to stick strictly to what really happened. I use the real experience as a jumping-off point. The character Jennifer is probably smarter and more aware than I was.

My biggest challenge was finding the right ending. I usually have a vague idea where a story is going when I start. I wrote two-thirds of this story in one sitting, then had to stop and mull things over because I wasn't sure how it would turn out.

When I begin a story, the theme is hovering around my mind—something vague that I can't put into words. When the main character asks her mother at the end of the story why she keeps falling in love (despite always having her relationships end badly), I had to stop and ask myself, why does the mother do it? The answer, I knew, was part of the theme of the story. The mother answers, "Because it's good." I'm not sure, still, if that's the best way to phrase it, but it captured what I wanted to say. Jennifer, who has become cynical from watching her mother fall in love repeatedly, yearns for the happy ending found in fairy tales and musicals. And maybe that isn't such a bad thing!

I had a professor once who told us never to write in first person. He said that beginning writers often made the mistake of "telling instead of showing," and if you write in first person you inevitably end up telling everything. I followed his advice—until I wrote this story. I just immediately heard Jennifer's voice, and the story poured out naturally.

I do a lot of revising as I write. I continually go back to what I've written and tweak words here and there. When *Cicada* accepted the story, the editor cut a very small amount.

I taught high school English for six years before resigning to care for our two children. I try to write whenever I can—though not as much as I would like. Having "Parade of Princes" published was a big ego booster. A few months later, I received a letter from an editor at Viking, who said she loved the story and asked if I had ever considered writing a novel. This past year I finished writing a book for young adults, and I plan to send it to her after I have revised it.

—Jody Casella

From the Editor

Jody Casella's well-written story appealed to the editors of *Cicada* on several levels. First and foremost, it was witty and fun, a refreshing departure from the heavy, angst-filled fiction we often receive.

Second, we enjoyed the topsy-turvy role-playing. Usually it's the teen who is tripping through the courtship minefield, but here it's Mom. The teenager, Jennifer, gets to take on the role of the experienced parent, shaking her head sadly as Mom brings home one loser boyfriend after another. However, we gradually discover that Jennifer isn't quite as jaded as she seems, and that's another reason we liked "Parade of Princes": it's a story with humor *and* substance.

—Deborah Vetter, Executive Editor, *Cicada*

Cicada
14–21 years
2,500 words

KRK!

CRRRRUUNNCH!

POP!

POP!

POP!

CRAAACK!

KRK!

PHOTO BY MIKE CIESIELSKI

NOISY KNUCKLES AND HENRY'S LAW

By Doris R. Kimbrough

"HEY!!! STOP THAT! YOU'LL GET ARTHRITIS FROM CRACKING THOSE KNUCKLES!"

Are you someone who can't resist cracking your knuckles? Or do you cringe and shudder every time your lab partner starts the "Snap, Crackle, Pop" routine, popping the joints on every finger before moving on to the toes? Or maybe you have joints that crack and pop naturally whenever you move. What causes those sudden loud noises that come from your knuckles when you crack them?

Your noisy knuckles are governed by the same scientific principle that causes your carbonated soft drink to fizz when you open it or a scuba diver to get "the bends" when she surfaces too soon after a particularly deep dive. All three of these phenomena are explained by the relationship between the pressure of a gas and its solubility in a liquid. This relationship is described by Henry's Law:

$$P_{gas} = kHC$$

P_{gas} is the pressure of the gas that is dissolving; kH is a temperature-dependent constant (the Henry's Law constant) related to the particular gas/solvent solution; and C is the concentration of the dissolved gas in the liquid. In other words, as you increase the pressure of a gas above a solvent, more of the gas will dissolve in that solvent. As you decrease the gas pressure, less gas will dissolve.

This is how soft drinks are carbonated. At the bottling plant, the beverage is placed in the can or bottle under high pressures of carbon dioxide. These high pressures force the carbon dioxide to dissolve in the liquid. When you "pop the top," the pressure decreases and gas begins to leave the solution, forming bubbles—fizz. Eventually, most of the carbon dioxide leaves the solution, and the drink is flat.

Having bubbles leave a solution is fine for a soft drink but can be life threatening

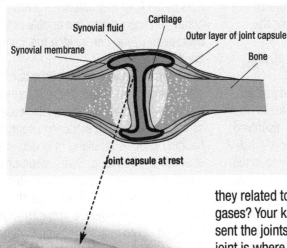

Synovial membrane
Synovial fluid
Cartilage
Outer layer of joint capsule
Bone

Joint capsule at rest

if you are scuba diving. As you go deeper into the ocean, external pressure builds, and you inhale more deeply to equalize pressure. This extra inhaling forces more and more nitrogen to dissolve in your blood. If you surface too rapidly, the gas will come out of solution, causing a painful and dangerous condition called the "bends." Gas bubbles produced in your bloodstream block capillaries, preventing the body's tissues from getting needed oxygen. The bends can be fatal if the oxygen supply to the brain is cut off.

Deep divers learn to avoid the bends by "decompressing." This means that they ascend slowly and wait for a period of time at a series of intermediate pressures. By this method, the dissolved nitrogen in their blood comes out of solution slowly and gets carried away without forming capillary-blocking bubbles. By using this technique, the divers can remove the nitrogen a little at a time before reaching the surface unharmed.

But what about those noisy knuckles? How are they related to dissolving gases? Your knuckles represent the joints in your hand. A joint is where two bones join, hence the name "joint." Joints that move around a lot—*diarthroidial joints*—are the noisiest. In diarthroidial joints, the ends of the two bones don't touch, but they are connected to each other through an enclosure called a *joint capsule.* The joint capsule allows the two bone ends to move freely in relation to each other.

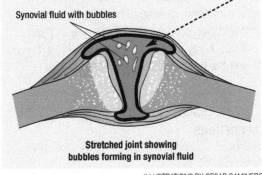

Opening a bottle of soda decreases the gas pressure of the solution. Gas leaves the solution forming bubbles—fizz!

Synovial fluid with bubbles

Stretched joint showing bubbles forming in synovial fluid

ILLUSTRATIONS BY CESAR CAMINERO

The joint capsule is a complicated structure made up of ligaments, membranes and cartilage. Think of it as a short, flexible tube that has a bone stuck in each end. Between bones, there is a cavity filled with a thick liquid. This *synovial fluid* acts as a gooey lubricant so that the two bone ends don't grind into each other. As a result, the joint moves smoothly. Doctors sometimes analyze the synovial fluid and use the results to diagnose diseases such as osteoarthritis, rheumatoid arthritis, gout, and other inflammatory diseases.

Gases dissolve in the synovial fluid just as they do in most bodily fluids. Carbon dioxide is thought to make up about 80% of this dissolved gas, with the remaining 20% a mixture of nitrogen and oxygen. The gases stay dissolved in the synovial fluid as long as the pressure in the joint capsule doesn't change. However, pulling or stretching the joint will suddenly increase the volume of the joint capsule. This increase in volume decreases the pressure on the liquid. Picture the plunger of a piston being pulled out to create a partial vacuum.

Henry's Law says that this decrease in pressure will cause some of the gas dissolved in the synovial fluid to come out of solution and form a bubble. This sudden formation of a bubble—technically, a *vapor cavity*—as a result of pressure change is called *cavitation*. Sudden cavitation disrupts the fluid, causing vibration. These vibrations, moving differently through liquid and gas, produce the loud noise or *pop*.

If you X-ray a joint right after cracking it, you can see the bubble in the joint capsule that results from cavitation. Before you can crack that same knuckle again, you must wait until the gas redissolves into the synovial fluid. This happens automatically with the increased pressure in the joint capsule when it returns to its resting position. When the bubble has completely disappeared, you can stretch the cavity again for another firing.

Is cracking your joints really harmful? Medical experts aren't sure. There is fairly substantial evidence that the habit does *not* cause arthritis as once thought. But evidence suggests that habitual knuckle cracking may decrease hand strength and function. Some researchers think that the pressure changes associated with cavitation will damage joints in much the same way cavitation wears out ship propellers. Others believe that the actual cracking isn't harmful, but the constant pulling and stretching of the joints might damage cartilage and ligaments over the long term.

So if your lifelong goal is to become a concert pianist or professional thumb wrestler, it's wise to lay off cracking those knuckles. But if all you want to do is annoy your little sister, you can probably accomplish that without any significant long-term damage. Maybe the next time your mother yells at you to stop cracking your joints, you can just smile sweetly and say, "Mom, I'm just demonstrating Henry's Law—you know—the one that relates pressure to gas solubility!" ▲

REFERENCES

Brodeur, R. *J. Manip. & Phys. Therapeutics*, 1995, *18* (3), 155.

Fox, R. W.; McDonald, A. T. *Introduction to Fluid Mechanics*, 4th ed.; Wiley & Sons: New York, 1992.

Hettinga, D. L. *Orthopaedic and Sports Physical Therapy*, Gould, J. A. ed.; Mosby: St. Louis, MO, 1990.

Kinsler, L. E.; Frey, A. R. *Fundamentals of Acoustics*, 2nd ed.; Wiley & Sons: New York, 1962.

Kimbrough, D. R. Henry's Law and Noisy Knuckles, *J. Chem. Ed.*, Nov. 1999, pp 1509–1510.

Mow, V. C.; Soslowsky, L. J. *Basic Orthopaedic Biomechanics*, Mow, V. C.; Hayes, W. C., eds. Raven Press: NY, 1991.

From the Author

As a college professor, I am asked to explain complex topics in easily understandable terms to introductory students. I wrote a more technical version of this manuscript for the *Journal of Chemical Education* that caught the attention of the *ChemMatters* staff, who suggested I try writing it up for a younger audience. It turned out to be easier than I expected. I guess I'm just in touch with my inner adolescent.

I used the original article to make an outline of the topic I wanted to cover. I took each section and expanded it into a paragraph or part of a paragraph. I went back and inserted stuff that I had either left out of the outline, or that occurred to me as I was writing the piece. I also took out or reworded/reworked the material that seemed too technical for the audience.

Deciding what facts to include and what to exclude was probably the hardest part. You can definitely lose a teenage audience if the article gets too technical. I decided to include material that was most connected to the actual cracking of knuckles, so that they could understand the phenomenon and how it related to Henry's Law. Knuckle cracking is universal, either because a student does it or hates when others do it.

I thought that the students would be more personally involved—not something that happens often in chemistry—if they felt I was speaking directly to them, so I addressed my readers as "you."

I wrote the lead after I had written the article. Sometimes you can overwork the opening, and then it loses its freshness. I reread and reworked the article (on the computer). Revision for me usually consists of rewording sentences (rather than paragraphs or major reorganization) because I work hard on the outline before I ever start writing. I remember I revised it more than I do some of the technical pieces that I have written because I wanted to make a good impression on the *ChemMatters* folks.

—Doris R. Kimbrough, Ph.D.

From the Editor

I noticed a technical paper in the *Journal of Chemical Education* by Doris Kimbrough, Ph.D., professor of chemistry at the University of Colorado-Denver, entitled "Henry's Law and Noisy Knuckles." Although the content was technical, the topic seemed a natural for our magazine. *ChemMatters* is dedicated to showing our high school readers the ways in which chemistry relates to their everyday lives.

College chemistry professors are often excited about sharing their research with high school readers, but it's rare to find one who can do so without going over the heads of even the advanced students. I wrote to Doris suggesting that she might allow us to feature her work in an article to be written by one of our staff. She wrote back with a witty reply in which she said that she thought she was still enough "in touch with her inner teenager" to try writing the piece herself. Even her first draft was a real winner. We actually had to trim some very funny lines in order to achieve the correct word count. We immediately realized that we had a found a rare writing talent—someone able to communicate a technical subject to a non-technical audience in a clear and entertaining fashion.

The "Noisy Knuckles" article reviewed well with teachers and students. Since its publication, Doris has written more articles for us, including topics on ground level ozone, body odors, caves, and her latest, urine testing.

—Helen Herlocker,
Managing Editor, *ChemMatters*

ChemMatters
14–18 years
1,035 words

ARMOR ALL

Here's how you can become a knight in shining chain-mail armor.

BY MARK P. MOOSHIAN

Two leather-clad warriors face each other, swords drawn. Suddenly one of the warriors attacks, his swinging sword clanging loudly against the defending warrior's.

Back and forth they cut and parry, the meadow ringing from impacts. Suddenly the attacker sees an opening and takes a swing he knows will surely cut his opponent in two. His sword slices through his enemy's leather clothing—but strikes metal instead of flesh! Stunned but far from dead, the attacked warrior says a silent prayer of thanks to the armorer who had saved his life by making him a coat of chain mail.

The Scouts in BSA Troop 324 at European Command Headquarters in Stuttgart, Germany, don't plan on being in any sword fights. But making their own suit of chain-mail armor can transport them to the days of shining knights, if only for one fun afternoon. Here's how you can join them.

You'll Need:

- two 500-foot rolls of 14-gauge copper wire
- electric drill with ¾-inch bit and ⅛-inch bit
- wire cutters
- hammer and nails (long enough to secure wood together)
- wood saw
- wood glue
- 3-foot-long wooden dowel, ¾-inch in diameter
- 7 feet of lumber
- adult's help and/or permission

STEP ONE: Build a Wooden Rack

A rack or frame will make it easier to produce the many rings needed in a shirt of chain mail.

1. Cut the lumber into three 1-foot-long pieces and two 2-foot-long pieces. Set one 1-foot piece aside.
2. Through the center of two 1-foot pieces, drill a ¾-inch hole. Move the drill bit around to make holes slightly larger, so the ¾-inch dowel easily slides through.
3. Build the rectangular rack with the two 2-foot pieces and two 1-foot pieces with holes.
4. Slide the dowel through both holes.

STEP TWO: Add a Crank

1. Cut 6 inches off the wooden dowel.
2. Drill two ¾-inch holes into the 1-foot piece of lumber set aside in Step One. Drill the first hole about 2 inches from one end, the other hole about 4 inches from the other end.

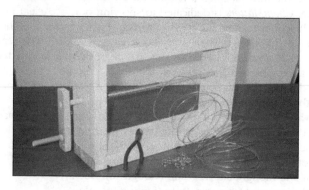

3. Take the longer dowel piece and glue into the hole drilled 2 inches from one end.

4. Take the 6-inch dowel piece and glue it into the hole drilled 4 inches from the end, on the opposite side of the lumber. This will be your crank handle.

5. Insert the crank fully into the rack. It should turn easily. About 1 inch from the inside edge of the rack, drill a ⅛-inch hole through the center of the dowel.

6. Set aside to let glue dry.

STEP THREE: Ring, Ring, Ring

1. Insert one end of the wire into the hole in the dowel and begin turning the crank. Keep turning until the entire length of the dowel has a single layer of tight wire coil. Cut the wire from the roll.

2. Cut the piece of wire that was inserted into the hole to begin the coil. Now you should be able to slide out the crank from the coil and the rack, leaving you with a coil of wire. Slightly stretch the coil.

3. Cut the rings from the coil. This should leave you a pile of rings that are just barely open. Make more coils and cut more rings.

4. Take 4 rings and twist the 2 ends together to make a closed ring. Put these 4 solid rings onto a fifth ring and close this fifth ring so you have a group of 5, four rings on one. This "fiver" is the basic building block for the chain-mail armor.

5. Make a large pile of fivers. Also keep a large group of slightly open single rings. When you have a good pile of each, it's time to begin building the armor.

STEP FOUR: Knitting the Shirt

1. Take a fiver and lay it flat, moving 2 rings to the top of the center ring and 2 rings to the bottom. Do the same with another fiver and position it below the first fiver.

2. Take a single open ring and link the bottom 2 rings of the top fiver to the bottom 2 rings of the bottom fiver. This single ring now links 4 other rings, just like the fivers you have already made. Close this open ring. Even at this early point the rings should show a pattern, tilted up and tilted down as

they rest upon each other. Add 2 more fivers to form a strip of four fivers. Make another strip of 4 fivers.

3. Lay a fiver strip flat to the right side of the first fiver strip. Take a single open ring to link the right 2 rings of the top left hand fiver in the strip to the left 2 rings of the top fiver in the right-hand strip. Continue to link the fivers as shown.

4. Hold up the linked fabric. You can "scrunch" the fabric easily in only one direction. Continue to build a large rectangular fabric. The direction of "scrunchiness" goes about the waist.

5. Once the fabric can comfortably circle your torso, with some slack, attach the 2 edges to form a cylinder.

6. Make two strips, at least 3 groups wide, that will attach to the top of the shirt. These will go over your shoulders. When you are done you should be able to put the shirt of chain mail over your head and have adequate area for your arms.

7. Small cylinders of links can be added to make sleeves. Links can also be added to lengthen the shirt, or different colored metal links can be added to decorate the bottom edge of the shirt. ❖

From the Author

I have been interested in arms and armor for many years. On a trip to Sherwood Forest in England, I met a man (armorer) at a craft fair who had a display of armor that he had made himself. When he saw me take a particular interest in a fine chain-mail shirt he had made, he said how easy it was, only very time consuming. He showed me the basics, and within 10 minutes, I had enough information to make a shirt myself. Upon returning home, I built the frame and purchased the wire I needed. Four months and about 10,000 rings later, I had my very own shirt.

Since I was interested in this kind of project, I thought it would be worthwhile to write a how-to article, taking into account the tricks I had learned in the process. I thought most folks would initially think (as I had) that building chain mail would be beyond them, but it really is an easy process once you understand it. There are many ways to make chain-mail armor. I focused on only one, the easiest and most effective. Once you make a "basic" shirt you would be ready for the more complicated styles.

I used the idea of a how-to article for my Assignment 6 in the Institute's course, and my instructor helped fine-tune it. I chose to submit the article to *Boys' Life* because it would be a perfect project for a Boy Scout troop and could also be used to earn the Boy Scout "metal working" badge.

If you're going to write an article for a teen reader, and you know in general what you want the article to say, ask some teens if they would be interested in reading such an article. In my case, I asked a couple of Boy Scouts if they thought it would be cool to make a chain-mail shirt. In most cases the answer was definitely yes.

Making chain mail can be done by young and old alike, so I did not have to gear the project to any specific age. I did not propose sidebar ideas or illustrations in the query letter; those came later after *Boys' Life* responded to the query. I had good follow-up contact with the articles editor, working out some of the finer points and answering questions and concerns by e-mail.

I provided *Boys' Life* with pictures and illustrations. However, they only used one picture and had someone else redo all the illustrations. With all the illustrations (critical for a how-to article), there was not much room for the photos. The editor also changed the title, but I forgive him.

I am a Lieutenant Colonel in the United States Air Force currently serving a tour as a communications integration officer in the Defense Information Systems Agency within the European Command. I've been writing for publications since high school when I was a reporter/writer for my high school newspaper, and have been published many times in Air Force periodicals throughout my 18-year career.

—Mark P. Mooshian

From the Editor

Mark Mooshian hit the mark on two fronts with this article: 1) he presented a unique quality how-to project, with easy-to-follow instructions and illustrator's guides, and 2) he gathered a group of Boy Scouts—in other words, a group made up of our average readers—and had them complete the project on their own.

Thanks to Lt. Col. Mooshian's due diligence in the preparation of this package, we were certain we were providing a project that an average reader would enjoy and be able to do. And thanks to his unique pitch, we were fairly certain we'd have a how-to project that would be difficult to find in any other youth publication.

—Michael Goldman, Senior Editor, *Boys' Life*

Boys' Life
6–18 years
900 words

Jackie Robinson, Baseball's Pathfinder

BY RUTH DORFMAN

How would Derek Jeter of the New York Yankees feel if he stepped back in time to the early 1940s? Very strange. The first thing he would have to do would be to change his occupation! Fifty-five years ago only white players were hired by major league baseball teams. Black men could only play on all-black minor league teams. Baseball was a segregated sport.

Grandson of a slave, son of a sharecropper, Jackie Robinson was one of five children his mother had to support when Jackie's father deserted her. Wanting the best possible future for her family, Mallie Robinson took her children and headed for Pasadena, California, where her brother lived.

As early as third grade, Jackie's outstanding athletic ability was noticed. By then, every kid in his elementary school who played sports knew the answers to the questions: Who can get the most hits? Who can score the most points? Even the youngest players in the schoolyard knew that to have Jackie on your team meant one thing: winning!

"True courage doesn't mean following the crowd. It's doing the right thing even if you have to do it alone."

Besides his mother, who taught him the importance of a close-knit family, Jackie was influenced by two other people growing up. They were Carl Anderson and the Reverend Karl Downs. Anderson was a mechanic who had a

Jackie Robinson, left, Brooklyn Dodgers' second baseman, has a wide smile that almost matches the wide eyes of Dodgers' president Branch Rickey as they get together on Jackie's 1950 contract in the Dodgers' Brooklyn offices, January 24, 1950. Jackie signed the contract, which is estimated to be for a sum between $30,000 and $35,000.

repair shop on the street where Jackie lived. The black, Japanese, and Mexican kids in Jackie's neighborhood formed street gangs to feel they were part of a group. Anderson noticed Jackie's involvement with a neighborhood gang and advised Jackie to leave them. "True courage doesn't mean following the crowd. It's doing the right thing even if you have to do it alone."

The black press, some politicians, and sportswriters were fighting to break down the Jim Crow barriers . . .

Jackie was never sorry for following that advice.

Reverend Karl Downs, pastor of the church where the Robinsons worshiped, also helped Jackie break away from the street gangs. Realizing that the church had to provide activities for young members as options to hanging out on the streets, the young minister went into action. He scheduled dances at the church and installed a badminton court. While loudly criticized for some of these changes, Reverend Downs didn't back down. His courageous attitude left a lasting impression on Jackie.

Jackie's athletic ability improved as he got older. In high school, he earned letters in football, baseball, basketball, and track. Later, playing first-string quarterback at Pasadena Junior College, Jackie helped Pasadena win all eleven football games in one season! While at Pasadena, Jackie set a new broad jump record of twenty-five feet six and a half inches, beating the record that had been set by his brother Mack. Mack was also a champion sprinter, having finished second to gold medalist Jesse

Owens in the 1936 Olympics.

Gaining publicity from his athletic feats, Jackie received many offers of athletic scholarships. He chose UCLA because it was close to home. There, he became the university's first four-letter man. A star player without a star's temperament, Jackie was always a team player first. He never risked his team's chances by grabbing the spotlight for himself. Unconvinced that a college education could help a black man get a job, Robinson left UCLA after two years. Wanting to help youngsters, he was lucky to get a job as assistant athletic director in a camp for kids from poor or broken homes. However, the job didn't last long because World War II broke out.

After serving in the army, Jackie got a job with the Kansas City Monarchs, a black professional baseball team. In those days, blacks could only play on black teams, and their living conditions were very hard. For example, in

---

"Robinson, I'm looking for a ballplayer with guts enough not to fight back!"

---

the South, even small-town coffee shops would permit blacks to only take out food, and hotel accommodations for people of color were practically nonexistent. Sometimes, they would be lucky to land in a town where black families would take in as many players as they could. Mostly, though, they had to spend their nights sleeping on the bus.

A white man could have carved out a career in baseball in 1944, but it seemed to hold no future for a black man. The black press, some politicians, and sportswriters were fighting to break down the Jim Crow barriers, but it didn't seem to Jackie that it would happen in his lifetime.

Little did he know that Branch Rickey, the

president of the Brooklyn Dodgers, was planning to challenge baseball as an all-white sport. A courageous man who felt that Jim Crow baseball was morally wrong, Rickey also felt that black players in the major leagues would bring more black fans to the games.

And so he persuaded the Brooklyn Dodgers' directors to let their club be the pioneer in bringing blacks into big-time baseball. Rickey's "noble experiment" involved finding an ideal black player who, running the gauntlet toward public acceptance, would open the

---

While it seemed an almost unbearable sacrifice that was being asked of him, Jackie knew that he had to make it.

---

doors for other black players. Such a player had to have unique qualities. He had to be able to take verbal and physical abuse and not fight back. He had to do this without bitterness in order to win acceptance. He would have to cast off his attitude of humbleness and act like a winner. But a winner without bitterness. "Mr. Rickey," Robinson asked, "are you looking for a Negro who is afraid to fight back?"

Rickey exploded. "Robinson, I'm looking for a ballplayer with guts enough not to fight back!" Thereupon, he launched into a lecture on what Jackie might have to face, including taunts about his race and his family in almost unendurable language. Rickey pointed out that some bigots might try to provoke a race riot at the game. It would be their way of proving to the public what happens when you let a black man into the major leagues.

While it seemed an almost unbearable sacrifice that was being asked of him, Jackie knew that he had to make it. He had to be the one to suffer humiliation and worse, so that black youngsters might have a future.

However, some of his Dodger teammates didn't want Robinson to have a future. A group of them secretly agreed to sign a petition stating that they would not play with him on the team.

Luckily, Rickey found out about the plot. "Anyone not willing to have a black teammate can quit!" he warned. No one left.

But Jackie's greatest test of enduring racial insults without striking back was ahead of him. Walking to the plate at the start of a three-game series against the Philadelphia Phillies, he could hardly believe the insults he heard coming from the Phillies' dugout.

"Why don't you go back to the cotton fields where you belong?"

"They're waiting for you in the jungles, black boy!"

Though the Phillies were a northern team, their manager, Ben Chapman, was a Southerner. It was Chapman who directed this stream of hatred at Jackie. Loyal to his agreement with Rickey, Jackie had to hold his tongue until he was saved by his own teammates.

Outraged by the behavior of the players from the City of Brotherly Love, Ed Stanky, a white teammate of Jackie's, yelled back, "Listen,

---

He proved that it was a person's character and ability that counted, not the color of his skin.

---

you yellow-bellied cowards. Why don't you yell at somebody who can answer back?"

In later years, Rickey said, "Chapman did more than anybody to unite the Dodgers. When he poured out that string of abuse, he unified thirty men. Chapman made Jackie a real member of the Dodgers."

In 1962, five years after he had retired from baseball, Jackie Robinson was inducted into baseball's Hall of Fame. At this ceremony, Jackie paid tribute to Branch Rickey, saying, "He was as a father to me."

While creating a path for future baseball players of color, Jackie Robinson won the respect and admiration of fans and players regardless of race. He proved that it was a person's character and ability that counted, not the color of his skin.

From the Author

When I retired as a teacher of English as a Second Language, I wanted to try writing for children. In addition to teaching children in a middle school, I had taught basic writing skills to young adults in a local community college and enjoyed it very much.

I started "Jackie Robinson, Baseball's Pathfinder" a couple of years before it was published. I wrote it for an Institute assignment and was told, while it was good, that the market was oversaturated with material about Jackie Robinson. At that time, if I had thought of looking into publications other than sports magazines—which I finally did with *AIM*—I would have marketed the article much sooner.

The actual writing of the "Jackie" article took longer than its marketing. I attributed the rejections from sports magazines to my writing instead of believing the editors' comments of "oversaturation."

My research was done using books that varied by author and age level. I researched an autobiography written by Jackie and a co-writer in addition to biographies of Jackie written by others. I also consulted children's books about Jackie to get a different voice.

Using an outline to structure the article was a great help. I followed the basic outline from the Institute's course manual, which stressed that articles, like stories, must have a beginning, middle, and an end.

I kept a folder for my drafts, and I numbered each revision. I also kept the numbered revisions on my computer as insurance against loss. I wrote four drafts before the final one was published.

I was never an enthusiastic sports fan. I was interested in Jackie Robinson as a person who made a great sacrifice. With that focus, I decided to submit my manuscript to *AIM*, which describes its goal as erasing prejudice, especially that of racism.

When I wrote my query to *AIM*, it was easy for me to talk about breaking the color barrier because, as a young adult in the 1940s, I had witnessed Jackie's historic breakthrough in baseball. The editor responded to the query with a note saying she'd like to see the article.

I advise new writers to find out the style of writing that the editor requires. My latest submission had to be rewritten six times because, although it was a nonfiction article, the editor wanted it written as a fictional drama! It was a difficult project, but I feel that those revisions taught me a lot about writing.

—Ruth Dorfman

From the Editor

With wholesome parental guidance and assistance from successful individuals outside, underprivileged youngsters do succeed. Racism will diminish when it is an established fact that all youngsters, regardless of their racial/ethnic backgrounds, achieve. Thousands of youngsters have proven the above. Jackie Robinson is one of them.

—Ruth Apilado, Associate Editor, *AIM Magazine*

AIM
Teens
1,300 words

MÖBIUS MAGIC

By Diana Thistle Tremblay

How many sides does a strip of paper have? Two, right? Unless it's a Möbius strip—then it has only one.

To prove this to yourself, cut a strip of paper 28 centimetres long and 2.5 centimetres wide. Give one end a half twist (turn it 180 degrees) and tape the two ends together. Then start drawing a line down the centre of the strip. You'll find yourself back where you started! How is this possible?

The Möbius strip is named after mathematician and astronomer August Ferdinand Möbius, who invented the idea in 1858 and presented the Möbius strip to the world in 1865.

The world has since found many uses for the Möbius strip. It's used to make a filmstrip that records sound on both sides. Conveyor belts were designed with the twist so that they would wear equally on both sides. It's used in sculpture and in knitting patterns. It's even seen as an acrobatic skiing maneuver.

Since you could go round the Möbius strip forever without getting anywhere, the model is used by some to illustrate the idea of infinity. You've also probably seen it as a recycling symbol.

MIND-BENDING MÖBIUS

The first group to put the Möbius strip to work were magicians. They started using it as early as 1882. Today, the trick is referred to by some as "Afghan bands" and it's easy to do.

Prepare your loops ahead of time. For the first loop, just tape the ends straight together. Make a second loop with a 180 degree twist to make a Möbius strip. For the third loop, make a 360 degree twist.

Now present your audience with the three loops of paper. After you have invited predictions about the outcomes, have audience members cut straight down the middle of the loops, or do it yourself. The first loop, which is just taped straight together, will end up as two loops. The second loop, taped with a 180 degree twist to make a Möbius strip, will form one loop twice as long as the original. The third loop, taped with a 360 degree twist, will form two interlocking loops.

To present this as a magic trick, you may want to use longer loops so that your audience won't notice the twists. For example, you could cut a long strip from a newspaper. To avoid boring the audience, think up some jokes or a story to tell during the cutting, or ask for predictions.

Try it—and make some Möbius magic!

Art by Paula Stuckey

ROPE TRICK

Ask your friend to help you with this trick. Take two lengths of string or rope and tie the ends of one to your friend's wrists.

Take the other rope and tie one end to your left wrist. Take the other free end and pass it under the rope between your friend's wrists, tying it to your right wrist.

You should be able to unlink your rope from the one on your friend's wrists, without untying the end from your wrists.

Can you do it?

Answer: Hold your rope in the middle and make a small loop. Pass the loop under the rope on your friend's right wrist, pushing it toward her fingers. Pass the loop over her hand, and work it back under the rope on her wrist. You should now be free, although each of you will still have your wrists tied.

From the Author

My childhood fascination with the Möbius strip resurfaced while I was brainstorming ideas for *YES Mag*'s Math Mayhem issue. I've had success in the past when I select a magazine, request their theme list, and then propose articles that fit the themes. I also study several issues of the magazine at the library before I write the article.

I targeted this article for 8- to 14-year-olds, according to the magazine's writers' guidelines. For this age group, I figured I needed a "cool" factor, so I presented it as a magic trick to amaze friends.

The Internet was the most helpful source for research. There's so much information there. You do need to ensure that any facts you use are backed up by a reliable source, since not everything on the Net is reliable. There was lots of historical information that I didn't include about the invention of the Möbius strip. I kept it simple and concentrated on describing how to do the trick. Performing the magic trick before writing the article and again during revisions helped me to explain how to do the trick.

I revised the article perhaps five or six times. I found some interesting facts to add to the introduction, made it longer than it needed to be, and then trimmed it back.

I'm presently writing my first children's book, a nonfiction science book about hippos. I live in Ottawa, Canada, with my husband and my 13-year-old daughter, Ali, who has been a great help with my children's writing. She gives me feedback and encouragement, and she lets me know what's cool and what's not!

—Diana Thistle Tremblay

From the Editor

We chose "Möbius Magic" because it fit so well into our theme for that issue—math!

We do our own research before deciding what to cover in the theme. The Möbius strip was on our own list of topics to cover and Diana just happened to query us with the idea. (Her original query for Fibonacci numbers had already been suggested by someone else, so she e-mailed back right away with "Möbius Magic.") Yes, Diana's choices were obvious. But we sometimes have to cover the obvious to do justice to a theme, especially something as diverse as math.

This was the first time we worked with Diana, and we rarely use a new (to us) writer for the theme section or features. In her query, Diana's explanation of the Möbius strip was so simple and accurate, it convinced us that she could write the article. She had a concise explanation, a bit of history, and a fun example of how magicians used Möbius strips. It also helped that her curriculum vitae was available online. From her past experience we could tell she was a professional. And it showed—her article was hardly revised.

—Jude Isabella, Managing Editor, *YES Mag*

YES Mag
8–14 years
400 words

AMERICAN MORSE CODE

By Hamor Gardner

If you had been sightseeing around Washington, D.C., on 25 May 1844, you could have witnessed an important event in the history of communications. In a small building away from the downtown area, a serious looking group watched a man tapping out the world's first telegraph message. It was being sent to Baltimore and consisted of four words: "What hath God wrought."

Seven years earlier, Samuel Morse had developed a crude type of code which he hoped to use with a new gizmo—electricity. Before that could happen, Mr. Morse and his partners had to figure out how to get coded letters into an electrical circuit. With the help of $30,000 from the United States government, Morse's company solved the puzzle. They built an electromagnetic device to "make and break" the electrical circuit in sequence with the code signals. The coded letters were sent on their electrical way.

In 1849 Morse and his partners sold their telegraph patents. In 1851, a more practical code was developed and named the American Morse code. The clicks, clacks, and spaces sent on a telegraph key were read mentally by a receiving operator from the sound reproduced on a receiving instrument called a sounder (box). Telegraphy swept around the world. It was the 19th century version of the Internet!

Around 1900, inventors were working on another new gizmo called wireless, later known as radio. Guglielmo Marconi's name jumped into headlines on 22 December 1902, when he sent a message from Newfoundland to England using radiotelegraphy.

International Morse code was born when American Morse code proved to be unsuitable for radiotelegraph use. A number of American Morse letters use spaces along with dots and dashes. These spaces were easily missed when copying code during electrical storms.

Governments and shipping companies quickly accepted radiotelegraphy as a new means of keeping in touch with their ships. Radiotelegraph operators became known as "sparks," a nickname referring to their old spark-gap radio transmitters.

Remember that unfortunate ship, the *Titanic*? The use of radiotelegraphy saved many of the *Titanic*'s passengers. "Sparks" on sinking ships have helped save thousands of lives.

The original distress signal, and the one used by the *Titanic*'s radio operator, consisted of three letters, CQD. Later, S ... O --- S ... was adopted because it was easier to transmit and recognize. What does SOS mean? "Save our ship." During World War II, different distress signals were used when ships were under attack. For example, if torpedoed by a submarine, you sent the signal SSSS. If attacked by aircraft, you sent AAAA.

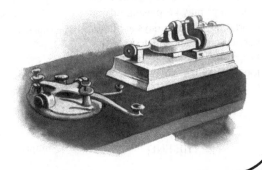

"Sparks" use a Q code to ask and answer routine questions. An example is QRU? (Do you have any messages for me?) There are more than 70 Q codes.

The use of International Morse code began to decline after World War II as marine radio telephone equipment became popular. This equipment allows ship personnel to speak directly with anyone ashore via a marine radio coast station and the telephone system. The use of American Morse code on land disappeared as teletype equipment came into service. A teletype is a machine that is part automatic telegraph and part typewriter. A message is whizzed away to its destination while being typed.

Then along came satellites. Today, the captain on a ship anywhere on the ocean can dial a few numbers and speak with you on your home telephone. That wizardry is done through a series of satellites whirling around in the sky. This new form of communication has replaced radiotelegraphy. Effective January 1999, a ship equipped with the appropriate satellite radio communication gear is not required to employ a radiotelegraph operator.

Morse code is disappearing from the radio waves. "Sparks" on older ships may keep using it for a short time, but their days are numbered. Some radio amateurs will keep using Morse code until they too tap out their end of work signal (...- .-).

- .... .   . -. -..

THE END

International Morse Code Alphabet		American Morse Code Alphabet	
A	.-	A	.-
B	-...	B	-...
C	-.-.	C	.. .
D	-..	D	-..
E	.	E	.
F	..-.	F	..-.
G	--.	G	--.
H	....	H	....
I	..	I	..
J	.---	J	-.-.
K	-.-	K	-.-
L	.-..	L	—
M	--	M	- -
N	-.	N	-.
O	---	O	..
P	.--.	P	.....
Q	--.-	Q	..-.
R	.-.	R	. ..
S	...	S	...
T	-	T	-
U	..-	U	..-
V	...-	V	...-
W	.--	W	.--
X	-..-	X	.-..
Y	-.--	Y	.. ..
Z	--..	Z	.... .

Numerals		Numerals	
1	.----	1	.--.
2	..---	2	..-..
3	...--	3	...-.
4	....-	4	....-
5	.....	5	---
6	-....	6	......
7	--...	7	--..
8	---..	8	-....
9	----.	9	-..-
10	-----	0	—

Punctuation
Period	.-.-.-	Period	..--..
Comma	--..--	Comma	-.-.
Question	..--..	Question	-..-.
Colon	---...	Colon	-.-. .
Semicolon	-.-.-.	Semicolon	... ..
Hyphen	-....-	Hyphen	-.... .-..
Quotation Marks	.-..-.	Quotation Marks	
Brackets	-.--.-	(on) ..-.. (off) .-. -.-.

Punctuation (American) continues:

Brackets
(on) .....-. (off)..... ... ..

If you live near a railroad crossing, you can hear one Morse code letter many times each day. When a train is approaching a crossing, the locomotive engineer is required to blow two long toots, one short toot, followed by a single long one. An engineer may not know he is blowing a Morse code letter—he is simply following railroad rules. See if you can find two long, one short, one long (--.-) in the list of Morse code signals.

From the Author

For an assignment during my Institute writing course, I wrote a piece about how I thought communications had evolved from caveman days to the present time. It was entitled "Shout, Wave, Run." My patient instructor suggested that an article about communications should be more focused, and the piece on Morse code came to life. Due to new regulations, and the growing use of satellites, I knew that shipboard radio operators would soon be akin to the dodo bird, so I wanted to inform young people about the important part Morse code played in the evolution of communications.

Radio communication is a topic close to my heart. Semaphore signaling in high school led me to radio college and service as a radiotelegraph operator in the Canadian Merchant Marine during and after World War II. Later, I worked at radio coast stations and in the administration of marine radio communications.

My background made research easier. Marconi's name is remembered, yet many other men did a lot of the early work.

I found interesting facts in a set of reference books, *The Book of Popular Science* (1924). These go back to my boyhood when I would while away stormbound days thumbing my way through the fifteen volumes. My research record keeping wasn't too scientific. I simply jotted down names, dates, and pertinent details in a rough notebook.

I went back to the early 1800s when electricity was in its infancy. Samuel Morse knew something about this new phenomenon, yet he still had many technical and financial problems to resolve. The article took shape as more stand-out dates appeared.

I wrote about five drafts before I was happy with the article. My first attempt was 1,200 words. Knowing articles for children's magazines should not be too wordy, I cut little bits of information. One such deletion concerned personal information about Samuel Morse.

I selected *High Adventure* along with other publications through an exercise during my writing course, when I had to study the magazine market and select publishers I thought might be interested in an article about Morse code. I tended to restrict my research to magazines featuring out-of-the-way stories, or articles, aimed at more adventuresome youth. I obtained sample copies of magazines including *High Adventure*. In my query to *High Adventure* I mentioned the American Morse code signals sidebar.

Over the past few years I have written about my two voyages to India during the war. A true story entitled "Quarantined with Smallpox" appeared in the *Kingston Whig-Standard*. It was about my second radio operator succumbing to smallpox at Colombo (Sri Lanka) in January 1945.

—Hamor Gardner

From the Editor

The decision to purchase "American Morse Code" was based on our target audience. Our publication reaches boys ages 5 to 17. It's our desire to not only minister to them on a spiritual basis, but to also provide educational value through historical events. Mr. Gardner's story met the need. The only revisions were trimming the story to our maximum word count and standard proofreading. Otherwise, it was an interesting account of historical significance that was well written.

Reading has almost become a lost art, and we typically choose manuscripts that will encourage the boys to read. This is just one part of our overall program that will help turn curious and awkward boys into creative and mature adults.

—Gerald Parks, Editor-in-Chief, *High Adventure*

High Adventure
5–17 years
950 words

Artist Workshop

Oil Painting for Beginners

By Rita D'Alessio

Believe it or not, oil painting is not just for the masters. Almost anybody can work in oils. Start with a very simple subject and surprise yourself. It could be a delicious red apple, a vase full of lovely flowers, a green tree or a single yellow leaf.

Why has oil painting been so popular since oils were first used in the early 15th century? One reason is that oil paint stays wet longer and can be changed and fixed while the paint is wet. Oils allow you to work with a variety of brush strokes to create texture and other visual effects. The colors are rich and easy to mix. And let's not forget that there's something about oil paint that just smells like, well, *art*.

What You Need to Start

A concern for many beginners is cost. You can pick up a set of cheap water colors at the grocery store for $1.99, but aren't oil paints a little more expensive? Well, a little, but you can get started for under thirty bucks, no problem. If you don't have thirty dollars lying around, well, honey, somebody needs a babysitter tonight, now don't they?

You can find everything you need in an art supply store or an arts and crafts store. Check out the yellow pages for discount art stores in your area (or see what you can find online). Be sure to shop around at garage sales. Sometimes people sell canvases and tubes of paint they don't need anymore. You can also find frames; some bargains are as cheap as a quarter.

A Few Tips

1. Don't worry if you make a mistake. Just wipe off and start over. That's why oil painting is a beautiful thing—you can change any mistake while the paint is still wet.

2. You can paint from a photo, a still life setting, or your imagination. Try a few sketches before you start a painting. You might also consider copying one of your favorite paintings. By attempting to imitate, you can learn the techniques master painters use.

Wherever you shop, here's what to look for:

- **Water-soluble oil paint**—It cleans easily and is great for beginners. Be sure to invest in a large tube of titanium white and a tube of ochre, too. Get your hands on a studio set of basic colors: yellow, green, blue, red, alizarin crimson, umber, black.
- **Brushes**—Flats #2, #6 and #10; Rounds #1 and #4 (synthetic or bristle)
- **Canvas** (12 x 16 to start)
- **Palette**—a plate, usually plastic, sometimes wood, on which you mix your paints
- **Odorless turpentine**
- **Rags**
- **Easel**—A temporary easel can be made from a cardboard box. All you need here is something to lean your canvas against while you paint.

Painting Exercise: Landscape Painting

1. Copy the picture above, drawing lightly with charcoal or pencil. Think in terms of general shapes—trees, hills, road, sky. In other words, simplify.

2. Mix your colors. You need to think in terms of three values (in other words, three shades of the same color). So . . .
   Put three dabs of green paint on your palette and
   - Add black for shadow—the darkest value.
   - Add white for lightest value.
   - Add ochre for half tone (medium) value.
   Mix your other colors the same way.

3. Next, lay in your underpainting. Underpainting is a sketch in paint. It helps you compose your painting before you begin to do any detailed work. So block out those mountains in green (or blue or purple, whatever color you intend to make them) and make a few brown strokes for your trees, some more green for the grassy areas.

4. Get the details down. Experiment with different textures (how can you make tree bark look rough? the sky smooth? the road rocky?) by playing with your brush strokes. What part of the mountains are in the shadows (use your darkest value of green) and what part is in the light (use your lightest value)?

A Few Tips (cont.)

3. Try painting a single object—a piece of fruit, for instance, or a red ball. Consider: color and shape, light and shade. Can you make a lemon appear three-dimensional? Where does the light hit it? What parts of it are shaded?

4. When you've experimented with painting a single object, compose a still life. Arrange a group of three or four objects on a table—a bowl filled with three lemons, a wedge of cheese, a knife and a cluster of grapes. This is a good way to experiment with shape, colors and contrasts.

From the Author

One of the things I learned when I took the Institute's course is to write what you know. I drew on my experience as a painter to write "Oil Painting for Beginners."

Although I had always wanted to write, I had no time while working and raising children. After I retired, I signed up for a weekly painting workshop and enrolled at the Institute. I submitted "Oil Painting for Beginners" as a course assignment, then incorporated my instructor's comments into my revisions.

Because I was targeting the 11 to 15 age group, I tried to keep the article as simple as I could. "Oil Painting for Beginners" went through five rewrites before I felt ready to submit it to a publisher.

Dream Girl's description in the *Children's Magazine Market* caught my attention because it is listed as a magazine about the creative arts for readers of my target age group. But before mailing my article to the editor, I studied a sample issue and sent for the writers' guidelines.

Frances Dowell responded with a request for more revisions—she wanted me to add instructions, so I created the numbered steps. At her suggestion, I also included the sidebar.

—Rita D'Alessio

From the Editor

We get a lot of material that just isn't right for our magazine, so any query or article that meets our needs is taken seriously. "Oil Painting for Beginners" was right up our alley. We're always looking for how-to articles for young artists. We're also interested in articles we can build around or that work with a particular theme. In this case, in addition to "Oil Painting for Beginners," we ran a short piece on the painter Elaine DeKooning and photos of North Carolina painter Judy Crane in her studio.

The trick for writing how-to articles for our audience, girls ages 9 to 14, is presenting easy-to-follow instructions in a funny, light tone. We thought Ms. D'Alessio did a fine job of writing to the *D/G* audience, and her instructions were clear and concise, not at all overwhelming.

As editor, I added a few bits here and there (" . . . well, honey, somebody needs a babysitter tonight, now don't they?" is a bit of typical *D/G* business I threw in), and added the sidebar with painting tips, re-routing some points from the body of the article. Rita gave me a lot to work with, and editing her piece wasn't hard to do.

—Frances Dowell, Editor,
Dream Girl: The Arts Magazine for Girls

Dream Girl
9–14 years
750 words

By Joanne Winetzki

It's Never too Early to Get Financially FIT

Everyone is into physical fitness these days. Some people enjoy it and reap the reward of a healthy body. Others procrastinate and never get started on a fitness program. It's the same way with financial fitness. Smart investors, like savvy physical fitness buffs, use the same methods to achieve success. The two means of becoming financially fit are to start saving now, and keep it up.

Sounds easy, doesn't it? Most people, however, make the mistake of not taking now literally. Now means today, when you finish reading this article. Start by making a decision to save a certain amount each week. Certainly your future is worth the price of a movie and a large popcorn, a pizza, or a smoothie and snack at the local juice bar. With physical fitness nothing happens unless you get onto the court or into the pool. It's the same way with saving money. You can't just talk about it. You have to do it.

Occasional exercise isn't sufficient to keep in shape and occasional saving really doesn't work either. You need a plan you are comfortable with and the ability to stick with it. Make it fun. People who truly enjoy exercise stick with it. They can feel the results of their efforts. You will see your savings grow if you stick with your savings plan.

Why is it essential to start saving now? I asked a local stockbroker to describe his most financially successful client. His reply was startling. The client was a U.S. postal service employee with a family. The secret of his success, according to the broker, was the fact that he started saving as soon as he started earning money. And, he'd kept it up over the years.

The broker worked up an example of how money grows. He used an interest rate of five percent. If you put away $50.00 each month for a period of ten years your account will grow to $8,678.00. But look what happens in twenty years if you keep it up. Your account will total $22,019.00! That's a pretty nice reward for being consistent and patient.

Investors not only set money aside, they put it to work. If you had not invested the money, only hid it away in your jewelry box, the results would be quite different. In ten years you would only have $6,550.00 and in twenty, only $12,550.00. The above illustration should give you a good idea of the difference between just saving money and investing it.

The best investment for you is one you understand. If you have a checking account at a local bank or savings and loan association, ask about their interest rate on savings accounts. Shop around for the best rate. It's important to set your savings aside from the money you spend. Otherwise, it's just too easy to "borrow" a little from yourself with the best intention of paying it back. Once you have accumulated a reasonable balance, ask the bank representative if you are eligible for a money market account that pays even more interest.

Are you employed? Does your employer have a credit union? These "mini banks," designed to help employees, are available for you to use. Ask about an automatic savings withdrawal program. After all, the easiest money to save is money deposited directly into your account from your paycheck before it gets into your wallet.

You can ask your employer to deduct more withholding than you will pay in income taxes. This amount will be returned to you as a tax rebate. The government doesn't pay you interest, but you can't withdraw the money on impulse either. You can use it to qualify for a savings account with a better rate of interest. Although your goal is to keep your money working for you, i.e., earning interest, this is the one way to accumulate savings.

Do you have what it takes to be a successful investor? Sure. Just start today and keep it up. Think long term. No one expects to be physically fit overnight. Financial fitness takes time and effort too. But you are on your way today. Just keep it up.

From the Author

"Since one of your goals is to reach out to young women, and one of your areas of knowledge is investing, you might consider a light piece aimed at high school-aged girls," suggested my instructor for Assignment 2 of my Institute course.

My biggest challenge was to come up with a strong and appealing lead. Fitness is a hot topic in California, and I personally love doing hatha yoga and tai chi. As a writer, I like to compare and contrast unrelated topics to encourage people to look beyond the obvious. Playing around with this idea, I realized that I used the same methods to achieve success in both physical and financial fitness.

The basic idea for this article came from personal experience. I wrote down all my thoughts about the subject. Then I made a rough outline to determine what additional material I needed. I worked up a few questions for my broker along with a request for some hard facts. By preparing myself beforehand, I obtained the answers from him in one telephone interview and the fact sheet followed shortly in the mail.

I revise and rewrite my work until I'm satisfied that it's the best I can do. First, I focus on content and the flow of ideas. Next comes culling every line for awkward or vague phrasing, weedy words, grammar, spelling, and punctuation errors. I read my work aloud constantly to make sure that I've chosen the most appropriate words and that the piece moves smoothly. Finally, I give it the Eleanor Roosevelt speech test: "Have something to say, say it, and sit down."

Blue Jean Magazine accepted my article based on the query letter, but the magazine ceased publication before my article appeared in print. I revised my query to appeal to magazines for college-bound women and men. *First Opportunity* responded to my query and forwarded the manuscript to *CP College PreView*. I later received a check and notification that the article had appeared in a recent issue.

If you want to write for teens, become one again. Instead of writing about popular teen topics, find new ones that will appeal to them. Open up their world and they will open up to your writing. I find it helpful to think about a personal friend in the age bracket I'm trying to reach, and then write as though I'm speaking directly to that person. I submit only my best work. Then I can look upon a rejection as merely a notice that a submission didn't fit a publication's current needs and not as a put-down of that work.

Being a new writer, I constantly experiment with all types of writing. *The News Times*, Seattle, WA, publishes my short creative nonfiction pieces from time to time. *Young and Alive* recently published my profile about children's author Beverly Cleary. I never thought about becoming a writer; I knew that I was one. Now that I don't work full-time, I can fulfill my dream. Hang on to *your* dreams, write, rewrite continually, and study the teen market every minute you can spare.

—Joanne Winetzki

College PreView
Teens
745 words

it pays to *think* **twice**

about a Telecom Career

Ken Borison

Eugene Whitlock

■ CLAIRE MCKIERNAN

You may not think twice before putting your friend on hold while you answer another incoming call or looking at your caller ID before picking up a ringing phone, but quite a bit of work went into these technological developments. Telecommunications is the industry responsible for making telephone communication available.

A team of **hardware designers** and **software programmers** develop these phone capabilities at companies such as Nortel Networks and Lucent. **Technical writers** work with the designers and programmers to document the installation procedures. **Instructors** use training materials to show technicians how to install and maintain the phone options.

In the background, internal **technical support workers** make sure all the processes are running so the telecom workers can communicate with each other to get their jobs done. **Sales and marketing professionals** contact phone companies like Sprint and MCI to

a **crafty** way
TO ENTER A TECH CAREER

Information cabling – the electrical wiring that brings voice, data and video connections through a building to the desktop – is one of the hottest "techno-trade" career paths today, according to the National Electronic Contractors Association (NECA) and the International Brotherhood of Electrical Workers.

The industry predicts that 50,000 telecom installer-technicians will need to be recruited and trained over the next 10 years just to meet the wiring demand for the country's commercial buildings.

Unlike most instructional programs, apprenticeships offer regular paychecks, health and pension benefits and the chance to earn college credits during training. The training period is three years for installer-technicians and five years for journeyman wiremen.

Interested? For a free brochure, write to Electrical Construction Careers, P.O. Box 2532, North Babylon, NY 11703.

drum up business for these new phone designs and options. **Field technicians**, trained by telecom instructors and using documents written by technical writers, help the phone companies set up the new equipment. External technical support is made available to the phone companies in case any questions or problems arise.

These are just a few of the jobs available in the telecom field. Whether you obtain an apprenticeship as an electrical technician, or get a college degree in computer science, English, journalism, business, education, or communications, a career in telecommunications may be a viable option for you.

Eugene Whitlock started out as a co-op student at Nortel Networks and has since transferred to Computer Sciences Corporation.

According to Eugene, a DOTS (documentation ordering and tracking system) programmer, "When I applied for this job as a co-op student, I was looking for any type of job that would give me some work experience in the computer science field. I provide technical support to the DOTS database users who are clients of Nortel Networks."

If chance landed Eugene a job in telecom, does he intend to stay there?

"Currently, I am happy with what I'm doing; the experience in programming is great. I think I would stay in the field of telecommunications because of the number of different jobs available and because of the number of opportunities present. That is the biggest attraction to the telecom field."

Ken Borison works as a senior technical writer at Nortel Networks and creates customer documentation to support the company product line. To establish a career in telecom, Ken says, "Almost every technical writer I've met in the telecom industry started from a different background. I've been a technical writer in the telecom industry for 15 years and although I started from a technical background, I've found that technical knowledge is not always a requirement."

Although telecom workers have varied backgrounds, they all contribute to technological advances.

"New technologies are constantly being introduced in order to meet market demands. In today's market, the networking and telecom industries have merged. In addition, authoring tools and platforms used by writers constantly change and it becomes necessary for writers to become proficient in the latest technologies specific to their profession," says Ken.

Related to the telecom industry are technology providers, such as Sun Microsystems, that enable wireless devices to handle data as well as voice

look twice

Engineering, science, computer information systems manager: $57,610-94,450; M preferred
Computer programmer: $36,020-70,612; B, A
Computer systems analyst, engineer, scientist: $40,570-74,180; B
Services sales representative, computer and data processing: $41,200; B or some college, ST
Marketing manager: $64,100; M, B
Telecommunications analyst I: $39,668; A, exp.
Telecommunications technician I: $36,801; A or equivalent
Training manager: $67,423, B, exp.
Technical trainer: $47,504; B, exp.
Documentation specialist: $44,496; A
Technical writer I: $42,681; B, related exp. preferred
Line installer and repairer: $19.09/hour; HS, OJT, mechanical aptitude, physical agility
Telephone maintenance mechanic: $40,202; post-secondary training in electronics, ST

SOURCE: 2000-01 Occupational Outlook Handbook (*http://stats.bls.gov/ocohome.htm*); Salary Wizard™ on Salary.com site (*http://www.salary.com*). ABBREVIATIONS: A=two-year associate's degree, B=four-year college degree, exp.=experience, HS=high school diploma, M=master's degree, OJT=on-the-job training, ST=special training.

communications. Sun Microsystems develops software that allows phones to have text messaging, games and online access. As we move ahead in the 21st century, jobs within telecom companies and their technology partners will only increase. Whether you enjoy working with computers, writing, electrical work, or salesmanship, the field of telecommunications can provide you with a high-tech and often well-paid career. ■

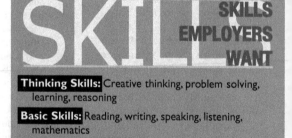

SKILLS EMPLOYERS WANT

Thinking Skills: Creative thinking, problem solving, learning, reasoning

Basic Skills: Reading, writing, speaking, listening, mathematics

Interpersonal Skills: Teamwork, customer service, negotiating, works well with culturally diverse people

Personal Qualities: Responsibility, self-management, respect for others, integrity and honesty, sociability

From the Author

I decided to try article writing while continuing to work on my novels. I submitted numerous children's stories, but the market is saturated, and I sometimes wondered if my stories were even read. Nonfiction was an avenue I had not tried. I wrote what I knew and submitted a query letter to *American Careers* magazine with several ideas for articles. A few months later the editor, Mary Pitchford, called me for an article about the telecom field.

The word "telecommunications" can make your eyes gloss over. How do I demystify the word, but also spark a teenager's interest? Luckily, telecom is directly related to many a teen's favorite pastime: talking on the phone. My lead makes the teen reader visualize talking on the phone and then wonder how all those phone features work. An introduction to telecom easily follows.

Having worked for three years as a technical writer in the telecom field, I was able to contact people for interviews. Some people were too shy to be interviewed, but Ken and Eugene were eager to help.

I put together a list of questions so that I had plenty to work with, yet didn't overload them with unnecessary questions. When they had some free time, they sent me e-mails with their responses. This process gave them a chance to think through their answers, and I didn't have to rely on memory or notes when I wanted to quote them!

An outline helped determine what I wanted to get across. Then, I decided which quotes would fit into my article. The decision to address the reader as "you" came from looking at past articles from the magazine, as well as an attempt to keep the reader involved. This article required one or two revisions to keep within the word count requirement and have the article read "smoothly."

I sent a query to *American Careers* with several article ideas. When I worked for my college newspaper, there was no room for "extras," so it did not occur to me to include more than what I was asked. When I saw my article in print with all new sidebars, I realized I had missed a chance to recommend those sidebars myself. Everything is a learning experience, and I'm glad that *American Careers* gave me the opportunity to witness my first publication!

Know your market, write what you know (or what interests you enough to research), and remember what you were like as a teenager.

—Claire McKiernan

From the Editor

The *American Careers* high school edition carries stories on each of 16 career clusters established by the U.S. Department of Education Office of Vocational and Adult education. Claire McKiernan's article proposal on telecommunications careers and her experience in the field met our need for a story related to the information technology career cluster.

As with all of our writers, we sent Claire a list of content-related questions to ask her interviewees. She did a very good job of developing the article from an interest-grabbing lead, to a behind-the-scenes look at occupations in the telecommunications industry, to comments from interviewees, to photos. She gave us what we needed the first time, met our requirements, and no revisions were necessary. A very professional job!

—Mary Pitchford, Editor,
American Careers

American Careers
12–18 years
440 words

Chemical Foams in the Line of Fire

By Myrna Zelaya-Quesada

"I could see the big fireball rolling across the sky from treetop to treetop, and the winds it created just roared like a tornado." Retired Deputy Chief Jim Tuma was describing his unforgettable first-hand experience fighting the wildfire that burned 450 acres of the dense ponderosa pine forest near Los Alamos, NM, in May 2000.

Most of us who watched the scene on TV saw acres of trees blazing like candles on a cake. And many lamented the loss of a forest of pines, once stretching 60–80 ft into the sky with trunks that could not be contained in a hug.

While most forest fires begin accidentally, this fire began with a routine "controlled burn" that shortly became anything but that. Starting a fire intentionally sounds foolhardy, but burning is actually a commonly used forest management technique for clearing underbrush. In some locations, burning requires more careful control than in others. Los Alamos, where 60-mph winds can blow among the trees in topsy-turvy directions, is an area where burning is particularly risky.

Feeding a fire

"To exist, a fire needs three things—heat, oxygen, and fuel," states Tuma. Once ignition occurs, the rapid winds wick the flames from treetop to treetop. Errant sparks fly through the air landing on lower branches and underbrush for rapid ignition. As more and more of the forest burns, the increase in temperature agitates the air into convection currents of almost 100 mph, the Deputy Chief explained. When the whole forest becomes inflamed, temperatures may reach several thousand degrees Fahrenheit. If water boils at a mere 212 degrees, how can a forest fire be stopped?

Understanding how fires thrive helps firefighters to design strategies for controlling them. To put out a fire, they need to remove at least one of the elements that feed it. Imagine going on a camping trip and building a fire. As a responsible camper, you extinguish the fire upon leaving, generally by applying water and shovels of dirt to the flames. Why is this effective? The rapidly evaporating water cools the area, dropping the temperature— no heat, no fire. Water soaks the wood, making it less flammable to the next spark. Before wet wood can burn, heat energy must first supply enough energy to vaporize the water. And with your shovelful of dirt, you create a barrier that prevents oxygen from reaching any potentially burnable material remaining in the campfire area.

In fact, until recently, water and dirt remained the predominant means of controlling a blaze. But many blazes prove to be too great for this simple strategy. Forest fires, like those in Los Alamos, are particularly difficult to control because their main source of fuel is pine. "Pine needles catch on fire so easily it's like miniature explosions," said Deputy Chief Frank Geigler of the Bethesda–Chevy Chase Rescue Squad in Maryland. "You ever see a Christmas tree catch on fire? It goes like that," he said, snapping his fingers. Pine needles greatly increase the flammable surface area of these trees, making ideal tinder for rapid ignition.

When the whole forest becomes inflamed, temperatures may reach several thousand degrees Fahrenheit. Traditional firefighting weapons like water and soil just can't do the job.

The foam solution

Additives can be combined with water to make it more effective for extinguishing flames. Some of these additives are foam solutions, first used by firefighters in 1928. Some ingredients in foams raise the boiling point of water, making it more effective in combating large blazes. Firefighting foams penetrate flames, spreading over them like a shield. They extinguish fires by removing the heat from the fuel source and blocking its access to oxygen.

Appearing frothy and fairly solid, foams are actually *aerated liquids*— liquids combined with air. As liquids, they cool the area they cover. As millions of frothy bubbles, they act like a blanket, preventing fuel vapors from escaping into the air while preventing oxygen in the air from feeding remaining flames.

Over the past 72 years, hundreds of fire-fighting foams have been developed from a wide variety of sources. There are even protein foams made from hooves and fish and meal—effective but smelly.

Fire fighting goes green

The newest members of the fire-fighting foam team are "green foams," so-called because they are more biodegradable than all the rest. Why is this important? Many of the substances that cause the most hard-to-combat fires are not only flammable, but also poisonous in the environment. They destroy the microorganisms in the soil, preventing the decomposition of organic matter, a crucial step in maintaining a balanced ecosystem.

The responsibility of fire stations is not only to put out a fire, but also to make sure that the fuels that started it do not reignite or contaminate the groundwater. But of equal importance is making sure that the chemicals used to fight the fires do no environmental harm of their own. Nature can eventually break down the components in fire-fighting foams. However, if their concentration is too high, soil organisms may not be up to the task.

"Is it bad?" asked Kenny Plunkett, a senior firefighter with a Hazmat station in Chevy Chase, MD, when I asked if fuel and foam could be dangerous to the environment. "We got called in to investigate a creek up in Rockville where the fish were belly up. The neighbors were complaining of a smell of gasoline. We found out that a car had caught on fire and an aqueous film-forming foam (AFFF) had been used. Somehow, runoff ended up in the creek. You tell me."

"If foam is being used, we need to be there." He showed me large drums for storing vacuumed debris to be used in combination with huge bags of different absorbents. Some looked like mixes of kitty litter and dust bunnies from under the bed.

I learned that paper absorbents can be laid over water to pick up floating fuel and foam. The "kitty litter" is used on the ground or on roads. Everything is shoveled, scooped, or suctioned into drums for disposal.

Green foams are classified as the most biofriendly foams on the market. Currently, the National Fire Protection Association is working on developing standards or guidelines to be met for fire-fighting foams used across the country. Many standards are already in effect.

Last year, *ChemMatters* reported on Pyrocool fire-fighting foam as a winner of the President's Green Chemistry Award (See "Green Chemistry— Benign by Design" in December 1999 *ChemMatters*). In the spring of 2000, Pyrocool Technologies, Inc., donated supplies of the foam for use against the fires threatening a Pueblo Indian Reservation near Los Alamos. Micro-Blaze Out, a biofriendly foam manufactured by Verde Environmental, Inc., was also donated to fight the fires in Los Alamos. This unique foam is the only one on the market partially composed of live organisms. Wayne Fellers of Micro-Blaze Out explains that the foam is filled with bacterial spores— bacteria in an inactive state encased within resistant cell walls. The bacteria need only water and nutrients to become active. When the foam concentrate is combined with water, the bacterial spores break open, and growth begins. The foam partially protects the bacteria from the heat of the fire while depositing them onto the fuel. The foam acts to cool the fuel and stop the flames from reforming. With the flames gone, surviving bacteria go to work, eating up the remaining fuel.

Firefighters nationwide are working at teaching the public how to protect themselves and the areas in which they live from fires. Just as new fire-fighting foams are constantly being developed for this purpose, perhaps the future will also see foams that help reestablish life in areas left sterile by natural and human-made fires. ▲

Pyrocool Fire Extinguishing Foam smothers flames and leaves residues that soil bacteria can digest.

Myrna Zelaya-Quesada is a science writer who lives in Washington, DC. She is a volunteer firefighter with the Bethesda–Chevy Chase, MD, Rescue Squad.

REFERENCE

Duggan, P.; Pincus, W. Fire Ravages Los Alamos. *The Washington Post*, Friday, May 12, 2000.

From the Author

When I wrote the article, I had been a volunteer with the Bethesda Chevy Chase Rescue Squad for about four years and had just begun the arduous training required to respond as a rescue technician to nonmedical emergency situations. Rescue technicians work with firefighters on many critical calls and receive much of the same training, including how to fight fires.

At the university, one of my majors was biology, and I focused my study on the evolution of animals, plants, and their different environments. I am concerned about the damage that we humans cause our environment. Although fires destroy forests, the ash they leave behind can initiate the process of re-growth. Many of the most effective foams for fighting fires, because of their toxicity, retard an ecosystem's regeneration. I wanted my readers to have more than the image provided during a television news report. I wanted them to understand the science of flames, the "whys" and "becauses."

My research began with general questions. Then I split my questions into those that would provide a large picture and those that would focus on the minutia. Books are always reliable, particularly if they are texts. Pamphlets, brochures, and articles can provide information but may contain the spin of the author or the group that sponsored the publication. I read a great deal about fire science, and I jotted down questions that I would have wanted answered for myself. I took these to the experts. Many questions developed during our conversations and during the review of my notes. Was what I was told correct? Was it an opinion? Did I understand it as it was intended?

Deciding which quotes to include can be difficult. Some people are born storytellers and spin a yarn easily. I had to tug on others just to confirm what someone else had said. In my opinion, quotes should bring the story to the present for the reader. They should give it life and evoke images. I never write a lead first. The lead of all my pieces develops as I'm writing the other sections.

I felt elated, tickled, and thrilled to see my first piece in print! I stood in my living room staring at it and could not stop smiling.

My advice to new writers is to select a subject that feeds your inner curiosity, get excited about it, and tell the story as if you are speaking with your best friend who knows nothing about your subject. Stay excited—it's contagious.

—Myrna Zelaya-Quesada

From the Editor

When Myrna Zelaya-Quesada expressed interest in writing a piece on the chemistry of the new fire-fighting foams, I hesitated. We had already mentioned these products in an article the previous year. But when Myrna said that she had received training in using foams during her orientation as a volunteer firefighter, I became very interested. Here was someone who had some personal, exciting stories for connecting the chemistry of the products to the real world.

Myrna's writing style was appropriate for our young readers. Quotations and scenarios carried the story. We needed to do some moderate editing on some of the technical details of the foams and their underlying chemistry. The availability of a cover photo showing Myrna in her fire-fighting gear was a huge plus for conveying to our readers that chemistry involves young, interesting, and even courageous role models like Myrna.

—Helen Herlocker,
Managing Editor, *ChemMatters*

ChemMatters
14–18 years
1,265 words

Structural Engineers Respond to WTC

By Jae O. Haroldsen

George Tamaro was worried. Like most Americans, he was upset over the toppling of New York's tallest towers. But Tamaro—an engineer who had helped build the World Trade Center's foundation years earlier—had other concerns on September 11. The towers had already fallen, but Tamaro knew there was still another structure under them that might collapse and endanger hundreds more lives: the slurry wall, a 21-meter-deep, 90-centimeter-thick underground concrete wall that held back the Hudson River, which ran next to the World Trade Center.

Up Against a Wall

Tamaro was anxious about damage to the wall. It was still standing. But what if parts of it were supported only by debris? What would happen if that debris fell down—or worse, if excavators accidentally moved it? Inside the slurry wall was a dry 4.4-hectare "bathtub" with seven stories of occupied space, including a major subway stop on the bottom level. Without the wall to dam the river, gravity would send many thousands of liters of water rushing into the "bathtub" and through the subway tubes across the river toward the Jersey City subway stop, which was 6 meters deeper underground. The station would be completely submerged. With that worry weighing heavily on his mind, Tamaro went to the ruins of the World Trade Center.

Firefighters and policemen were the heroes of September 11, but structural engineers like Tamaro saved the day on September 12, helping as only they could. Their job: To evaluate the safety of a new kind of structure, a five-story-tall mound of shattered steel and concrete. Rescue workers needed information that could mean life or death to trapped victims and to themselves, and they needed it fast. Only structural engineers could provide

that information—and with 6 hectares of rubble, they had their work cut out for them.

Are Surrounding Buildings Safe?

Maintaining the soundness of the slurry wall was a top priority, but there were other things to think about, too, like the surrounding buildings. Were they stable, or had the rush of air and debris during the collapse of the World Trade Center made them wobbly? To answer this question, the Structural Engineers Association of New York (SEAoNY) asked 50 volunteers to inspect 400 buildings in just two days, using standards that engineers usually apply to cities hit by earthquakes.

Vicki Arbitrio, a member of SEAoNY, was one of the volunteers. She inspected buildings for partial collapse and falling rubble as well as to see if they were still standing straight, or if floors that might have moved in opposite sideways directions during the collapse had made them unstable. To assess the buildings, she needed both education and intuition. "Engineering judgment and experience are vital in these situations," she said later. "A crack in the surface of a building may hide a bigger problem in the structural support, depending on the construction of the building and size and location of the cracks."

Arbitrio examined several buildings. Fortunately, she found that most of them were safe—the air and debris spewed around the buildings had mainly just left dust and broken glass, not larger flaws and cracks.

Technology and Know-how to the Rescue

Back at the wreckage, rescue workers could barely tell where the two towers had been before they collapsed. Again, it was a problem that only a structural engineer could solve. Eugenia Roman, president of the American Society of Civil Engineers' North Jersey branch, organized a task force to find architectural plans for the buildings and the plaza between them. The group also pinpointed the utilities—such as water and gas pipes—under the site. With help from computer-aided design and development (CADD) specialists, they created an aerial photograph of the site with a diagram of where the buildings used to be, and delivered it to rescue workers at 2 a.m. on September 16. "Our work proved to be critical to the rescue efforts," says Roman. "I met some of the firemen and rescuers. They came to shake my hand, to thank us for the work we did. They said we saved their lives."

When the rescue teams called for more, the engineers responded. One company flew a plane over the WTC site daily, capturing three different images: black-and-white digital photos, thermal images to track underground fires that might ignite gas and electric lines, and images generated by millions of laser pulses that helped engineers direct debris removal and look for air pockets in the wreckage. Meanwhile, Roman's team turned to more intricate building plans. The team added to their earlier diagram possible entrances that rescue workers should look for, like old elevator shafts and stairwells.

And they added something else, too: the slurry wall.

Mission Accomplished

By this time, Tamaro had already come up with a solution to the problem of the unstable wall. While he kept a constant eye on the excavation, his colleagues strategically placed heavy equipment around the slurry wall and subway tubes to ensure that any debris supporting the wall would stay firmly in place. It's lucky they did: When rescue workers finally dug deep enough to check out parts of the slurry wall, they discovered that the collapse of WTC 2 (a smaller tower near the main towers) had slashed the south wall of the "bathtub," creating a hole 60 meters long and 9 meters wide at a depth of 12

Photo: New Jersey Task Force 1

Experience aided by technology enabled structural engineers to do their own kind of heroic work at Ground Zero.

to 21 meters underground. Miraculously, though, the wall had stayed standing.

On October 17, workers began burying huge anchors at a 45-degree angle into bedrock located 1.5 meters below the wall. The extra support ensured that the wall would stay standing and hold back the Hudson River. One more disaster had been averted, thanks to the quick thinking and hard work of structural engineers. Finally, George Tamaro—and hundreds of rescue workers—could stop worrying.

From the Author

Like the rest of America, the events of September 11 shocked me. I read every article appearing in *ASCE News* and *Civil Engineering Magazine* related to that day. I read about New York City's appeal to engineers for help. In George Tamaro's diligence to maintain the integrity of the slurry wall, and Eugenia Roman's team superimposing the original location of the towers over a photo of the rubble, I saw a story worth telling, and a means of helping children understand the engineering profession.

In my market research, I looked for magazines taking hard science articles. *Odyssey* fit, so I looked up their web page. The theme list showed a future issue would be devoted to engineering. I checked out a number of back issues from the library and got a feel for their style and content. Most of the articles were written by someone with a professional background. I felt like I had an edge with my professional training and experience. I have a BS degree in civil engineering with emphasis in environmental engineering, and I worked for three years in environmental compliance.

After further research on the Internet, I drew up an outline for a proposed article and took it to my writing critique group. They helped me split the outline into three different articles.

I followed *Odyssey*'s submission requirements. I sent an article on concrete canoes as a writing sample to accompany four different proposals, including three on the events surrounding September 11.

The editor, Beth Lindstrom, contacted me a couple of weeks later. She wanted to use the concrete canoe article with a few minor changes and asked me to write my proposal on structural engineers' response at the WTC. I had a week to write the article.

Luckily, I'd already done the majority of my research. I used search engines on the Internet to locate George Tamaro and Eugenia Roman. I interviewed Mr. Tamaro via phone.

While using the Internet to find information on evaluating the surrounding buildings for safety, I found Vicki Arbitrio listed as a contact person and conducted an interview via e-mail. After I'd written the article, Vicki graciously checked it for technical content.

I felt Ms. Roman's statement in the civil engineering magazine concisely relayed the human emotion of the situation. I obtained her permission to use it and conducted a brief interview with her via e-mail.

I gathered an inch-high stack of information. Weeding it all down to a 950-word limit required me to stick to four main points: the slurry wall, surrounding structures, stability, and the superimposed photos. I used the quotes that helped move the article forward to the next point and worked to use precise language that teenagers could understand.

In writing the article, I wanted to convey the tenseness, the split-second decisions, and the midnight hours pouring over maps, all to preserve as many lives as possible. I needed a lead-in, a focus point. The slurry wall posed the most danger and Mr. Tamaro was a unique character. This starting point also provided a good closing point since chronologically it was the last emergency item stabilized. After the lead-in, I followed events as they unfolded chronologically for the engineers.

I sent the article to Ms. Lindstrom. She liked its content, but not its form. She said it was too technical and didn't contain enough drama. I was fortunate to have an editor willing to work with me. She reworked the article into its current form and helped me see the story in a chain of events.

A couple of years ago, I began toying with writing for children. It was a way for me to stay home with my children while expanding my mind. With my technical background, writing nonfiction science articles comes naturally. The market appears hungry for nonfiction, especially science topics.

—Jae O. Haroldsen

From the Editor

Although this article contains technical information about structural engineering, it also has a human element—people doing their jobs and helping others in the process. The story tells the little-known side of the World Trade Center disaster, one of the biggest news events in history. In doing so, it shows that people in careers that seldom are considered glamorous can be heroes.

Haroldsen is an engineer and submitted a query that showed she understood the subject matter and had the right contacts. However, she submitted an article that was extremely "well reported," but written with too much technical jargon. It also lacked the sense of story and adventure that the final piece has. Because it contained the necessary information, it was easy to revise the piece and make it a worthy article.

I think our readers will get a better understanding of what a structural engineering career is about and enjoy the sense of excitement in the way this story is told.

—Elizabeth Lindstrom,
Senior Editor, *Odyssey*

Odyssey
10–16 years
960 words

Title Index

Author Index

Magazine Index

This index lists stories and articles under the magazines in which they were published, along with the magazine's designated readership. The following key identifies reader age level:

> **YF= Youngest Readers' Fiction**
> **YNF = Youngest Readers' Nonfiction**
> **IF= Intermediate Fiction**
> **INF= Intermediate Nonfiction**
> **TF = Teen Fiction**
> **TNF= Teen Nonfiction**

Magazine Index *(continued)*

Magazine Index *(continued)*

Acknowledgments

The editors wish to thank the following authors, artists, and publishers who graciously gave permission for use of the articles, stories, and art appearing in this anthology.

"Gabriella's Whisper" by Janice Graham. Reprinted from *Turtle Magazine for Preschoolers*, Copyright © 1999 by Children's Better Health Institute, Benjamin Franklin Literary & Medical Society, Inc., Indianapolis, Indiana. Used by permission. Art by Dominic Catalano.

"Runaway Rosie" by Shellie Ripple. Reprinted by permission of CLICK Magazine, November 2001, Copyright © 2001 by Shellie Ripple. Art by Deborah Garber.

"Squeaks in the Floorboard" by Cynthia Bryning Johnson. Used by permission of Highlights for Children, Inc., Columbus, Ohio. Copyright © 2001. Art by Valeri Gorbachev.

"Broccoli Berkeley" by Paula K. Obering. Originally published in the April 2001 issue of *Pockets*. Reprinted by permission of the author. Art by Kathryn Mitter.

"No Play for Andrew" by Eileen Rosenbloom, originally appeared in *Wee Ones E-Magazine*, June 2001. Reprinted by permission of the author.

"My Best Friend Is a Juniper Tree" by Judith Lee Nilsson. Reprinted by permission of LADYBUG magazine, August 2002, Copyright © 2002 by Judith Lee Nilsson. Art by Yoshi Miyake.

"Jamila Did Not Want a Bat in Her House" by Phyllis Ring. Originally published in the June 2001 issue of *Pockets*. Reprinted by permission of the author. Art by Kathryn Mitter.

"Just a Little Whistle" by Katy Doran. Originally published in the February 2002 issue of *Story Friends*. Used by permission of the author. Magazine cover art by Lavonne Dyck.

"A Lemon Friendship" by Maureen Webster. Originally published in the February 2001 issue of *Story Friends*. Reprinted by permission of the author. Magazine cover art by Joanna Borrero.

"Marissa's Berries" by Ann E. Wagner. Originally appeared as the Contemporary Fiction Contest Grand-Prize Winner in the June 1993 issue of the Institute of Children's Literature *Children's Writer Newsletter*. Used by permission of the author.

"Where Does the Water Go?" by Jacqueline J. Christensen. Reprinted by *Turtle Magazine for Preschoolers*, Copyright © 1999 by Children's Better Health Institute, Benjamin Franklin Literary & Medical Society, Inc., Indianapolis, Indiana. Used by permission. Art by Michael Palan.

"How Is Your Horse Talk?" by John L. Sperry. Reprinted from August 2001 issue of *Hopscotch*. Used by permission of the author. Illustrated by Pam Harden. Magazine cover art by Joan C. Waites.

"Raindrops" by Nancy Roskam. Used by permission of Highlights for Children, Inc., Columbus, Ohio. Copyright © 2001. Illustrated by Len Ebert.

"Snapping Snack" by Beth Edwards. From *U*S* Kids*, Copyright © 2002 by Children's Better Health Institute, Benjamin Franklin Literary & Medical Society, Inc., Indianapolis, Indiana. Used by permission.

"Andrea's Unusual Pet" by Phyllis S. Dixon. Appeared in the June 2001 issue of *Lighthouse*. Used by permission of the author.

"Feeling Lucky?" by Beverly Patt. Originally published in the September 1996 issue of *Guideposts for Kids*. Used by permission of the author. Art by John Aardema.

"Fantastic Fishes" by Brenda Lee Marshall. From the January 2002 issue of *Nature Friend*. Used by permission of the author. Art by Tim Davis. Magazine cover photo by Jim Roetzel.

"Bug Net" by Linda Coleman. Originally published in the January 2002 issue of *Fun for Kidz*. Used by permission of the author. Magazine cover art by Chris Sabatino.

"Alligators Are Really Shy" by Pringle Pipkin. Used by permission of Highlights for Children, Inc., Columbus, Ohio. Copyright © 2001. Photos by Thomas E. McCarver.